# AS/400 Architecture and Application: The Database Machine

# AS/400 Architecture and Application: The Database Machine

Jill T. Lawrence

**A Wiley–QED Publication**

**John Wiley & Sons, Inc.**

New York • Chichester • Brisbane • Toronto • Singapore

Designations used by companies to distinguish their products are often claimed as trademarks. In all instances where John Wiley & Sons, Inc. is aware of a claim, the product names appear in initial capital or all capital letters. Readers, however, should contact the appropriate companies for more complete information regarding trademarks and registration.

This text is printed on acid-free paper.

© 1993 by John Wiley & Sons, Inc.

All rights reserved.

This publication is designed to provide accurate and authoritative information in regard to the subject matter covered. It is sold with the understanding that the publisher is not engaged in rendering legal, accounting, or other professional services. If legal advice or other expert assistance is required, the services of a competent professional person should be sought. FROM A DECLARATION OF PRINCIPLES JOINTLY ADOPTED BY A COMMITTEE OF THE AMERICAN BAR ASSOCIATION AND A COMMITTEE OF PUBLISHERS.

Reproduction or translation of any part of this work beyond that permitted by section 107 or 108 of the 1976 United States Copyright Act without the permission of the copyright owner is unlawful. Requests for permission or further information should be addressed to the Permissions Department, John Wiley & Sons, Inc.

**Library of Congress Cataloging-in-Publication Data**

Lawrence, Jill T.
AS/400 architecture and application: the database machine / Jill T. Lawrence.
p. cm.
Includes index.
ISBN 0-471-58141-0
1. IBM AS/400 (Computer) I. Title.
QA76.8.I25919L39 1992
004.1'45—dc20 92-23767
CIP

Printed in the United States of America

10 9 8 7 6 5 4 3 2 1

*For Ross, who pushed me.*

# Contents

# Preface

The AS/400 was developed in the late 1980's by IBM to be a departmental computer and a computer for small- to medium-sized companies to handle their total information processing needs. It was designed to handle interactive applications that are emerging with the migration to client/server environments.

My purpose in writing this book is to describe the machine and what it can do for you. I show how the design makes the AS/400 more efficient, functionally richer, more reliable, more stable, and in my view, more productive than other systems in its category. My "working" title for the book was *AS / 400: The Database Machine* because of the built-in functionality for data handling. The AS/400 is a database machine par excellence as you will see. Its integrated database design makes data access fast and easy for programmers and users alike.

There is not a lot of literature about the AS/400, so many people are not aware of its capabilities. It's:

1. easy to install and make operational,
2. easy to use and build applications,
3. fail safe,
4. data-flexible
5. fault tolerant, user friendly, easy to repair,

6. operational in all physical environments (normal electric currents, normal temperatures world wide, and in normal office locations), and
7. self-educational for novice and experienced users.

Because it's easy to build applications, third-party vendors have developed thousands of applications for it. These "solutions" have made the system very attractive for end users in hundreds of different businesses. As those of you who have an AS/400 already know, there is a love affair going on between this machine and its users. It is being used in ways never dreamed of by the designers. This book will provide you with a fuller understanding of the capabilities of this machine and why it is so successful.

PART 1

# The AS/400 Design Overview

The AS/400 is an entirely new design concept for computer systems. It provides a much higher level of function and much easier access for the user than any prior system. In 1990 the IBM laboratory in Rochester, Minnesota, that designed and built the AS/400 system was awarded the U.S. Government's prestigious Malcolm Baldridge Quality Award for the design and usability of this computer system. The U.S. Department of Commerce began awarding these kudos in 1988 in order to enhance U.S. worldwide competitiveness on the basis of quality.

The AS/400 is one of those projects that develop from the bottom up—from the people in the lab, not from specifications laid on them from above. In fact, little or no marketing support was given this system until customers aggressively bought it, and demanded attention from IBM. Typically for such breakthroughs, the advanced ideas and invention came from a small lab, out of the mainstream and far from corporate staffs and political power. There was always an *attitude* of hard work and pride in product in the Rochester lab, perhaps stemming from the distant natural Minnesota setting and old-world work ethic.

## VERY HIGH-LEVEL USER INTERFACES

The AS/400 has advanced hardware and new programming technology architected into a self-contained database management system, with all the concomitant data and usage protection, security, backup, recovery, sharing, and lock control. All of this function is encapsulated in microcode such that the user never sees or touches it. Services are handed to the user at a very high level, so there is a richness of data function and variety of user interface, both input and output, not seen before in the industry. The "programmer" (end user) is relieved of the intricacies of data manipulation required on other systems to insure data integrity, consistency, security, freshness, universality, and availability. He is catapulted into a world where his concerns are with data meaning, not form and placement, which gives both a broader interpretation of data and a productivity gain in data presentation and use of anywhere from 10 to 20 times that of other currently available systems.

How is this achieved? The AS/400 is designed as an entire system, taking into account all the layers that were added to systems over the last 30 years as we discovered one need after another while the computer industry matured. Current mature operating systems were originally batch processors, many times patched to accommodate interactive and database use with many faster, roomier disk drives. The user sees these systems today through various and complicated interfaces and paths, which handicap what can be done and how and when it can be done.

With the advantage of hindsight, AS/400 design engineers created the layers of the onion from the outside in—the opposite of the design of older machines. First they acknowledged the function we all wanted, then they designed user-level interfaces that would make that function easy and accessible. Then they built the layers below those interfaces that would shield us from the intricacies of getting the function; and finally they built a layered and queued system beneath the software, in "hardware" (putting much software function of today into microcode). Paths among the layers were made standard and therefore movable and changeable. This means faster, cheaper hardware can be slipped underneath as soon as it comes off the shelves, enabling the AS/400 to grow with usage and time and taking advantage of the progress of invention while amortizing the investment in system microcode and system and user software over many machine sizes and over a long time. Advances in software design, too, can be slipped into the system without interruption to the user level of code—a new accessing technology, for instance.

## OBJECT ORIENTATION

AS/400 instructions handle objects. The system's addressing structure and operations are oriented more toward objects than toward byte strings. All data structures in the instruction interface are called objects. Some are similar to programs and datasets or files on other systems; many others are unique to the AS/400. There are many types of objects, but they all have the same basic characteristics: Their internal detail cannot be seen by the user. The machine itself manages all space and the use of it by all objects in the system.

Specific functionally oriented machine instructions operate on objects. Users request services of the machine; it does the actual work, asynchronous to the user request, and in its own priority and place (space). Once a data space object has been created the user can request that records be inserted into it, but he does not know exactly where or how the system will do this. The records' internal format may be different from what he sees and manipulates, and the space used to store the object does not concern the data user. Machine resource usage is not in the programmer's domain. He is left to do real work with real data, not to manage the machine or its pathways. (See Appendix A for a list of system object types.)

## MACHINE INSTRUCTIONS

Machine instructions create, delete, and modify objects. They are at that generic a level. Many instructions really are generic in that they apply to any object type; some, for reasons of system integrity, are only usable on a specific object type.

An object is self-contained. Within itself it has identifiers that indicate who can use it, how it can be used, what its priorities are, what queues it is in, etc. Objects have implicit security authorization, lock enforcement, and shared or exclusive operation capabilities. To insure safe operation within these functions, objects are not externally visible; they must be "encapsulated" into the hardware before they are actually addressed, and they are addressed only by the machine itself, not by any caller or user. An object's internal structure is never available to the user. The user's wishes are interpreted by the machine. In this way object integrity is built into the system. If some years later the machine instruction interface were to be implemented differently, the system user would not be affected. (More about objects in Chapter 3.)

## MECHANICS OF ADDRESSING

Addressing on the AS/400 is object-oriented rather than byte-oriented. Addresses are not data and cannot be acted upon by data manipulation instructions. They are a different kind of object. Actually, there are no addresses, just pointers. There are no registers. Pointers address all objects (and can find specific bytes within space objects). A special "program operand" addressing mechanism handles program references to the "values" within a space object.

Any number of pointers can be defined by a program. They are only used for addressing and are embedded in space objects, identified by special tag bits in the machine hardware that enable the machine to protect them from misuse, accidental or otherwise. Tag bits are not accessible through the normal instruction interface; instead, there are specific machine-protected instructions to set and manipulate pointers in a controlled environment.

Pointers contain status information about objects, as well as location information. Here is where security authorization information and other attributes of object usage are kept. A pointer is more than an address on the AS/400; it defines object usage: who, what, where.

How is a user request translated into a functional request to the system and an address of the item to be manipulated? Users, both external and within the system's function control, invoke symbolic names when requesting that work be done within the system. The hardware uses a special addressing object, called a Context, to resolve symbolic requests to machine pointers. A Context object is logically a catalog of object names and their machine addresses. The object you are working on may be found via a different Context, in which case the work you do on it will be done in a different environment. For instance, you can execute a program with or without live database data depending on whether you invoke the program in a run-mode Context or in a test-mode Context. In the latter case, no real data modification will be made; updates will be simulated. There can thus be more than one Context to "materialize" your object within, causing quite different operation of the machine.

An AS/400 user program can be thought of much like programs on other systems. Traditional "high-level" language programs (COBOL, FORTRAN, PL/I, PASCAL, BASIC) on the AS/400 operate sequentially, executing a series of statements that have a couple of operands: "from" addresses and "to" addresses. However, on the AS/400, unlike any current system, operands of program statements are defined in a special program dictionary, separate from the program instruction itself. The operand that is physically in the program statement is actually an index reference to the dictionary entries that define such operand characteristics as the type of data to be manipulated, the length of the fields to be worked on, and whether the data type is character, binary, decimal, signed, or unsigned. It is this level of indirection that allows the late binding of data attributes to program, which in turn gives you the ability to format data differently on different runs of your program, or to define data output formats today that are different from yesterday's, without rewriting your program. (See Appendix B for system bind times.)

## LIMITATIONS

Few limits are built into the design of the AS/400 system. There is no limit on the number of objects that can be created or how large a set of code (a program) can be, other than the amount of auxiliary storage you have. All objects are addressed virtually, including both system and user code. Virtual addresses are converted into real object pointers at run time, and if need be the object required is brought into main storage for work to be done. The timing of when and how this object actually appears in main memory is not always synchronous with your requests (speaking in nanoseconds, that is). Since the system owns both your code and your data (you are not running the system, it is running your program in its own way and in its own time), your requests are known ahead of time. Block reads from auxiliary storage are done so that the system will be ready for your requests with good performance.

Program size and other hardware-oriented constraints are not designed into the system as they are on other systems. Some objects have a 16-megabyte size limitation, but many, such as data spaces, don't even have that limit. See Appendix C for explicit system limits.

## SPACE MANAGEMENT

The addressing capability of the AS/400 machine is 64 bits; that of PCs today is 16 bits. This means that because PCs are binary machines, you can run software that uses up to $2^{16}$ (64K) bytes (there are unnatural acts used to manipulate addressing to get more out of the machine than this, but with great architectural inhibitions). Adding one more bit, in binary math, allows you to double the count to 128K. The 32nd bit, in a 32-bit "mini," gives you the ability to run 4096 MB (4 billion bytes) worth of programming in the machine. One more bit would double the address space again, to 8 billion bytes, the next bit to 16BB, and if you went up to 48 bits, as the current models of the AS/400 allow you to, you could address up to 281 trillion bytes (281,474,976,600,000). The machine actually is a 64-bit machine, so one day when further addressability is needed, it will reach $2^{64}$, or 18,446,744,060,000,000,000, somewhere over 18 quintillion bytes of memory.

Since the AS/400 is a "single-level store" machine, its memory space encompasses one large virtual memory scratch pad, which you can envision as starting in the upper left-hand corner of the CPU (byte 0) and extending through the CPU down to the lower right-hand corner (main memory), then jumping out to the first outside cylinder of the first disk drive and traveling cylinder by cylinder to the inside tracks, then jumping over to the next drive's outside cylinder of tracks, traversing this drive, then on to the next drive until the last attached drive is counted . . . and way beyond into virtual space.

Virtual addresses not in main memory are swapped back and forth continually as the machine needs more of your program or data to work on, in long strings of 4K blocks chained together because of usage grouping or other efficiency criteria. These use-related clusters of information (control blocks, data, code) are placed on disk in the manner in which the machine will work on them, usually in a single chained write that may, for maximum efficiency, contain megabytes of information for one disk access.

Do not think in the old-fashioned way of collecting all data, code, etc., of a single type (say all COBOL programming) in one set of tracks or cylinders on a disk drive. Do not try to "optimize disk" by telling the system where to put your most popular programs or data. If you do, you will interfere with the efficiency of the system, which takes into consideration all the priorities you have stated for work and data types and, of course, knows its own workings and which system code and control information is going to be needed to satisfy a certain type of user request.

There are better ways to increase your system performance: add more main memory to the CPU; add another control unit string to the disk configuration and split your drives across multiple controllers (the system manager automatically takes advantage of this by spreading single-operation writes to disk across multiple available controller paths and multiple disks); exchange your disk for faster-accessing ones as they become available; and, eventually, change to array type or bubble memories when they are cost-effective. One of the great luxuries of the AS/400 is that hardware can be changed freely without old-fashioned system "migration" headaches. That is what data, code, and device independence means (which does not truly exist on any other machine).

A large address space and the circuitry to address it are required to implement the concept of single-level store. But once implemented, this single-level store concept enables the system designers to take over management and control of the entire system—all control programming, including data and device management, plus all data and programs sometimes housed on "external" disk devices. The user *never* has to know where anything actually is; he only has to know the name of the thing he wants to manipulate. Ask for it by name; the system control will point you to it (indirectly of course—you never really get to touch anything yourself).

About one third of all current user program code is devoted to the job of getting you the data you want to work on. All AS/400 programs are at least that much smaller and easier to write because the system does all the data finding and getting for you, feeding the data to you in the sequence you specify. Data specifications are outside your program. (See Chapter 7 on Logical Files). The access path to all objects is machine controlled. Pointers that address objects cannot be counterfeited. They are protected by hardware access control bits in the circuitry, preventing unauthorized addressing of objects (and the virtual storage addresses used by the microcode). This is a big step forward in data integrity and system security.

Each user of the system is allocated a personal, protected 16MB virtual address space, unreachable by other users. No imperfect or test program can reach across your boundary and bring your program down due to an addressing bug or a mistaken instruction execution. You can run tests on new programs right alongside your important interactive terminal control accounting programs.

To share with other users, explicit authorization to particular data can be granted by the user. Interprocess communication (me to you or system to me or me to system) uses queues and event signals and is managed by the system (microcode). If you want to share objects among several processes, you can request that locks be applied to the objects to control and serialize concurrent access to them. The system uses these same tools for its own multithread control should one event or data manipulation be dependent upon another. You request such locks by stating (when you define your data) what kind of processing you are going to do, not by actually doing the locking and unlocking. The work will be done for you by the system. Your part is only to know what you want to do with the data.

For better performance, programs are converted into microcode along with their data. Work storage is allocated by the system manager. Your program variables were defined with attributes, *which the system keeps* (Why in past systems did we compile them and then throw them away, causing many a run-time bug due to mismatch of attributes?). This allows the machine to perform data "type" conversions during program execution, for efficiency of instruction execution and for compatibility of data type. (For instance, it is perfectly all right to add a binary field to a signed decimal field—the machine uses those attributes for your external presentation, not for actual instruction execution!)

## I/O INDEPENDENCE

This level of independence from the data type is carried one step further to I/O devices as well. The intricacies of the devices, control units, channels, and networks are all handled by the machine. Your program is not burdened with miles of communication access method interface code, for instance. Nor do you need to know how the printer prints or what codes cause the display to blink. These device-dependent attributes are described once, for all users, in separate objects called Device Files, stored and managed separately from your program by the system and modifiable at run time. Merging and matching with your program requests for input and output operations is a specialty of the system manager, in microcode and hardware. This is true regardless of machine size or model. All the AS/400 systems have this very highly architected user/system interface, which allows you to get on with the work of managing your company's data rather than having to deal with the quirks of the computer system.

# 1

# The Data Machine

## 1.1. THE MACHINE INTERFACE (MI)

The MI is the top of the machine, what in other computer systems you thought of as the hardware/software line. In the sense that you cannot touch anything below this level, the comparison is valid. However, because of new concepts—for example, "encapsulation," wherein the "machine" takes into its bosom control blocks and tables the user caused to be created and exercises its own functions with user input—the MI interface has a new meaning. Some of the new concepts are very important. One is that below the Machine Interface are microcoded all the functions of current systems' Operating Systems software. Everything below this MI line is the same on all AS/400 systems. You get a complete system; therefore there is no concept of "system generation," of the user having to build up a system from component parts, as in past systems.

Included in every AS/400 machine are the following:

1. System Storage management—the CPU's memory as well as auxiliary disk storage.
2. Virtual System management—paging control of the one contiguous memory system spanning all system memory modules and all auxiliary disk storage, incorporating automatically,

with no system regeneration, all newly added memory and disk added at later dates.

3. System management of Job Queues, Libraries, Program Invocation, Data Flow, Data Editing and Presentation:
   - Based on user-defined tables.
   - All data management: user, system, program.
   - All data security, including data and functional authorization.
   - All communication with terminals and other systems, including PCs on LANs, other AS/400s, and mainframes that follow the IBM Standard System Architecture interface rules.
   - All communication with I/O devices, including user-defined menus on local and remote displays.

Since all of this control is integrated into one system—the same system on every AS/400; *not* layered and managed by the user or software packages as on other systems, it is no longer up to the user to ensure that a component, say the DB/DC layer, agrees with the operating system. The AS/400 is a *data management system machine*. Its assumptions are that everyone needs concomitant integrity and security control plus a fully interactive, multithreaded, fully shared, but user definable, system.

## 1.2. THE SYSTEM AS SHIPPED

The AS/400 is shipped as a working system, with a predefined set of objects. It contains the necessary object definitions to allow you to go right to work, as follows:

| Subsystem Description | Jobs and Descriptions |
|---|---|
| One Batch environment | The Batch queue manager |
| One Interactive terminal environment | The Interactive terminal manager |
| One Interactive Programming environment | Interactive Programming managers for all HLL |
| A Command Language environment | System work control |
| The Spooling environment | The Spool reader |

The system comes with Interactive Menus and the programs to manage them for: User Programming (all HLL languages); the Operator; Automatic Start-up (calling a particular program to run); and for the use of the Command Language to define or issue a command to the system. A complete duplicate set of objects is supplied so that you can modify the system provided environments with the interactive Command Language (CL) without stopping the machine. (Modify one set of objects while running with the other. It's a good idea to keep the original duplicate set so that you can copy a later system from it or ship down line to another system should you ever have the need.)

Subsystem descriptions are shipped with operational rights given to all users of the system. This means that any user profile can execute a job within any of the subsystems. To change a description so that only authorized users can use it requires so-called Object Management rights, which are identified in a user's profile. The system as shipped gives these rights to the programmer through his or her profile "QPGMR." Further rights over security authorization are given to the profile (as shipped) called QSYSOPR, the operator.

When you sign on interactively to the new system, you sign on through one of the available profiles. Depending on which one you specify when the system prompts you, a particular program is invoked automatically. The profile QUSER invokes QCALLMENU, a menu-driven interactive program that provides a simplified way to select basic functions to be performed.

To use the menu you do not need to know the system Command Language. Every step of the way will be prompted, with underlying assumptions for the end user. If ever in doubt, you can ask for help by mashing the F1 function key on your terminal keyboard at any time. Wherever you are in the system, you will be given help and new lower-level prompts. You can continue asking for help to any level, help upon help, and get right back where you came from, or to the prior help level, by pressing another function key. This rather spectacular help system is part of the microcode/OS. It is available all the time, when the system is in full use, by anyone, at any level. No error codes need ever be remembered or looked up; when one arrives on your screen, just mash F1 to find out what it means.

## 1.3. SYSTEM SYMMETRY

Everything in the system is an object. An object is self-contained: it has a specified NAME, which is how you reach it, a specific TYPE, identified by a code within the object, permissible users, and attributes that allow it to be used for specific purposes by specific user types. Associated with an object is a SPACE, which is a place where attributes are defined and is the part of the object a user can affect by using specific CL (system Command Language) statements for that purpose. For instance, a user cannot reach the instructions in a compiled program but he or she can change the associated space object wherein reside the attributes that describe what data is to be worked on, and can modify these attributes using certain CL commands from a terminal.

The objects in this system are independent of one another and of hardware and software. Likewise, programs are independent of the data they are to operate upon. Terminals and other hardware are independent of user-defined actual formats; and data is independent from user-defined actual formats at the user interface levels. Interactive users are independent of program interfaces—that is, interactive control commands can be issued by an operator at a terminal, any terminal, or out of a running program, using the same command format. Also, the exact same SEND and RECEIVE (SND, RCV) commands are used to talk to local stations on-site or to remote terminals or computers, or to a different program in this same system. In addition, a screen format, whether for the entire screen or only a portion of it, is just a record format like a record format in a database member; it is not something married to the physical characteristics of the terminal (as it is in most systems), so it can alternatively be sent to a printer or to another medium. The presentation of the format will be managed by the system, depending upon which medium it is to be used with, not what the programmer coded.

Run-time rather than compile-time binding is required for all these interfaces (which on other systems are bound forever at program compile time, never to run differently from the way the programmer planned for today). The general rule is to use your system in this "late binding" manner to save reprogramming when system conditions change or when data to be presented or manipulated should be changed, or for that ad hoc quick report on everyday run-data. There is always the ability to nail your program down to the data or input–output device at compile time by "qualifying" the objects you are working on. This means you can specify absolutely that a particular object in a particular library is always to be used with this program. It is more flexible, however, to use generic names for the library (LIBL* is the system's generic library list) at compile time and allow binding to occur depending upon which object is first encountered in the list and has the object's name that you refer to at run time. This latter method allows you to compile programs that refer to non-existent data or devices, to be made ready by run time.

Items are found at run time by their logical *names* (not by compiled physical addresses as on current systems). This is an important difference from existing computers, and it has repercussions on just about everything you do on this system. The use of logical names allows for a great deal of flexibility in job flow and in what a program can be used for. One program can serve more than one purpose. (For example, an inventory "detail"-listing program can also be used to print summary data at the end of a cycle by redefining what data it should print via a CL command from a terminal at run time.) One day the program may be run in batch mode, printing a detail-list of all the collected invoices for a month; another time the program may be invoked interactively, to print out a single item as defined at run time.

The one caution for experienced programmers is that the NAME of the object your program is to manipulate must be in your LIBL (library list) or your qualified (particular) library at run time. The address resolution from the name is done (again) at run time even if it was done earlier at compile time. For example, a program your program CALLs from within does not have to exist when you compile your calling program; nor must it exist at test time. But at run time, when your program hits the CALL statement, the called program must exist in either LIBL or the library you particularly qualified for this run. (You may, however, create that called program from within your calling program as late as immediately before the CALL statement.)

Here is an example for the interested:

```
.
.   CRTCLPGM PGM(LIBL*/Jillsprog2)
```

*(Create a Command Language program. Call it Jillsprog2, using the statements in LIBL general purpose library list)*

```
CALL PGM(LIBL*/Jillsprog2)
```

*(Now after creating the program, call it and branch to it for execution)*. .

For this example to create an object at run time that your live program is going to access, the *source* for the CRT creation command must be available for compilation in your LIBL library (or another library that you identify in the command)—for what is, in essence, a live compile within a run-time environment (you may think of it as a live interactive command from within a batch program). You may even have changed the command definition or perhaps its defaults.

## 1.4. SOURCE FILES

Source files for objects you use in a program must be available at compile time. This sounds obvious, but because of the flexibility of the AS/400 you do not assume, as in more rigid systems, that the compilers and source statements for HLL programs (COBOL, PL/I, etc.) are within reach of the system just because they are in the library. There are as many libraries as you want to have, one for every type of user if you wish, so the system is not the owner and only user of the libraries, as in past systems.

If you are compiling a COBOL program, you must identify to the system what library it is to use for this compilation, and that library must contain the COBOL source statements. The same is true for CL programs or command invocations. The system has to construct the commands from source. Because this is true, you can change the source or add source of your own. In fact, the CL language contains commands that allow you to create new commands of your own, if you can think of something new to do with the objects of the system. One thing you might do is invent a command to do all the things you want the operator to do first thing in the morning. You could create a small CL program to be invoked by one interactive statement or automatically invoked by the system. One thing I would do is OPEN all the files to be used for the next few hours, in case some updating of Logical File indexes must be done before the next usage of the data. (There is more on this concept in Chapter 7—the section on Logical Files (Data Views)).

For the CL language, source statements need to be available at compile time (if you do compile statements into a program instead of running them interactively) *and* at run time. Source files for data (DDS statements) record formats that you want to use must also be in your library or LIBL when you compile a program that refers to this data. How you put these items into libraries is explained in the chapter on DDS.

# 2

# Objects and Libraries

## 2.1. OBJECTS

What is an object to the AS/400? All things: programs, control blocks, data format descriptions, system control block descriptions, space objects to house all of these objects, attribute tables, data, system commands (each one is an object), system grouping and classification control mechanisms (queues, chains of pointers, and so forth) to name a few (see Appendix A for more).

Libraries are objects that are collections of objects—or at least collections of pointers to find the objects said to be *in* the library. Nothing is really *in* a library except pointers and normal object description information.

## 2.2. NORMAL OBJECT DESCRIPTION INFORMATION

Each object type has a unique purpose. There is a unique set of hardware instructions (which translate into high-level commands in a special language called CL) that operate on specific object types. Every object in the system has a common structure that causes it to be self-contained—that is, allows it to float freely through the system bound to no specific address or liaison. All the system needs to know about any object can be found out by observing the object. (Figure 2.1 illustrates the general attributes of all objects.)

The library reference enables the machine to find the real object in question, this object control block merely being a descriptor. The objects are self-contained to the point that if the system were struck by lightning and parts of its memory or disk were destroyed, it would automatically scan its interior to verify and rebuild whatever chains, object lists, and datasets for those object descriptors it could find, notifying you of what it was able to recover and in what condition other items in the system were found. You would be given a chance to input reconstructive data into the system in an attempt to finish recovery.

Any portions of the system that are runnable can be run even without complete system recovery. All this recovery happens automatically at normal system IPL with warm start.

The system verifies objects each time they are processed. It checks the type and the function to be performed for correctness and checks the user's authority to do this function on this object. No one can ADD into a piece of nonnumeric data, for instance or CALL a display device instead of a program. You cannot do the wrong thing to an object. The *system* will stop you and tell on you

| | |
|---|---|
| OBJECT TYPE CODE | OBJECT NAME |
| OBJECT SIZE | LIBRARY NAME |
| Text DESCRIPTION of object (you supply) | |
| STATUS (in use, free, etc.) | SECURITY AUTHORIZATION INFORMATION |
| More attributes if needed . . . | |

**Figure 2.1.** Common self-contained attributes found in all objects.

with messages to appropriate parties at run time, not just at compile time. Fully half of the world's common programming bugs, both careless and logical errors, are eliminated by these system checks. Every action on every object by every user, be it system, programmer, or end user, is checked every time against the following questions:

1. Is this the correct type of object for this activity?
2. Is the command being executed allowed at this time on this object?
3. Is anybody else using this object now? If so, the machine, in hardware, ensures that one use of the object does not impair another use in process (auto-lockout at the object level, if needed, to ensure object integrity). Since the system manages all the processes and all the objects, it knows what is in use throughout the system.

On the other hand, you are perfectly free to ADD to, or do any other math on or among fields that are stored as decimal numbers, from fields of binary, floating point, packed, or other types of numeric data. Math is math. In any case, the AS/400 doesn't do the actual work using the formats you are working with, since those are just presentation formats for your convenience. It does the actual math inside the bowels of the machine in its own space and then presents the answer to you formatted and edited as you request. You are not tied to, nor do you program to, the hardware format. Machine instructions like ADD are at a generic level, one instruction applying to all kinds of numeric data. Since attributes are housed with the data or object, the machine instruction does not need to be tailored to each mathematical data type as it is in other systems. You will not make a mistake if you do not know exactly what precision your mathematical function will end up with. The machine, not your program, finds the work space. If it needs more work space it can get more.

System-controlled object sharing (among users) works as follows: You can read objects that are currently being used by someone else and being displayed, dumped, or saved, but you cannot access an object that is currently being changed, deleted, renamed, moved, or restored.

Objects are allocated by the system as called for, as the job step needs them. They are deallocated after each single usage. If you need to ensure object availability to your job step with no waiting, you can preallocate objects with the CL command ALOBJ before running this job step. To do this you will need Existence, Management, and Operational authority. (See Chapter 8 on security.)

As you read about objects, remember that *everything* is an object. The system repercussions from this fact take some thought.

## 2.3. THINGS YOU CAN DO WITH OBJECTS

Here are the things you can do from your display station or from your program with objects:

1. Search for objects in libraries or among libraries.
2. Look at objects (descriptions) on your screen or in your program.
3. Put objects into libraries.
4. Move objects among libraries.
5. Describe objects—inserting "Text" into the attribute box of the object.
6. Give security authority rules to your own objects, reassign the current authority, or broadcast it further.
7. Duplicate objects.
8. Rename objects.
9. Delete your own objects.
10. Allocate and deallocate your objects for special purposes.
11. Find out the lock status of objects.
12. Find out if an object exists and its conditions of existence.

The list that follows presents some object attributes you can look at using the DSP (Display) command from your terminal (you answer a prompt that asks if you want to see just the Basic Attributes set, a Full set, or, additionally, the Service set):

- Basic set: Object Name, Library Name, Object Type, and Size (see Appendix A); the Text Description for this Object (up to 50 characters of description); Status information (in use, free, and so forth); and whether there are extended attributes.

- Full Attribute set: the Basic set, plus the Object's Creation Date and Time, Creator, Domain (where usable), Last Date of Change, is Use data collected on it, when last used, count of days used, when count was last reset, how much storage is needed for it, how much auxiliary storage is needed to save it, last Save Date, last Restored Date, what Save command was used, and File label ID if the Object is a data Object.
- If you ask for Service Attributes, you will receive the SOURCE file from which this object was created, Date and Time the Source File was last updated, System level at the time, which compiler was used, control level of the object, whether or not it was ever changed by the user, APAR information, and so forth.

I have gone into some detail about looking at an object. I have done so to indicate that the AS/400 has built into it a deep level of helpful prompting, with good screen menu prompts for each CL command that allow you to browse through the entire system at your programming level, at the system programming level, and actually at the machine level itself, without needing manuals of instruction.

## 2.4. LIBRARIES

What is a library on the AS/400? A library is an object. A library object is a directory of other objects that have unique names within this library. You use the library concept to group together a set of objects for an individual user, for a type of user (that is, an application), or for a department of users. We talk about libraries as if they contain programs, data, and things, but they actually contain only pointers and those attributes common to all objects.

A library is an object full of objects that can be of mixed types; in other words, in just one library you can put programs, data the programs work on, and user profiles of the people who use these programs and data. AS/400 libraries are not like libraries on other systems, where, for instance, only COBOL programs go in one library, only Assembler programs go in another, compilers go in a dedicated library, and there is no library at all for data. Here libraries are use-oriented; you divide up your material however you want to control it.

Perhaps you want a library for a certain department of your company containing all the items used by that department, and secured against other users' access, which can be saved as a unit when that set of users has finished their work. The entire library could then be shipped around the network with a single command, dumped to auxiliary tape for historical backup periodically, given departmental security access protection, and level-checked as a whole for data and program currency compatibility. Or you may want to separate libraries according to work flow, putting all data manipulation programs for one type of data in one library and housing casual search and inquiry type programs in another; then keeping user types and run times separate for saving and recovering according to user type. Some users prefer to separate their libraries by logical function because it is easy to think about—for example, all data definition statements for one data type together, all interactive programs together, all batch programs together, and all high-performance mathematical routines together. I prefer to see library material based upon recovery considerations: everything needed for certain types of work in one package for quick (one-command) saving and recovery and for shipping around the network, which can be a recovery method.*

## 2.5. GETTING TO A LIBRARY—AUTHORITY

To get to an object the user must first have the authority to use:

- The library
- The object
- The command by which you access the library

In the command (let's say from an interactive terminal, but it could be from a running program) you give the name of the object,

---

*The fact that items of data, programs, etc., are adjacent to one another within a library has no bearing on the actual location of these items in virtual address space or on auxiliary storage. Remember, the library is merely a list of pointers used to find the objects. Placing items in a certain library or library list will not control performance. This note is for systems programmers from other systems who are used to designing storage layouts on disk with an eye to enhancing a specific program's performance. On the AS/400, the system Data Manager does the layout and all other optimizing based upon user-specified data and work priorities.

its type, and the library name. Using the library name is called qualifying the object. If you do not specify a specific library name, you may specify a list of library names, which the system will search for your object in the order from the list.

Here is an example of a display command to display a description of an object named Rabbit, which is in a library called Jillslib:

```
DSPOBJD OBJ(Jillslib/Rabbit) OBJTYPE(PROG)
```

With this command you will get back on your screen the following: object name "Rabbit," library name, object type, status (in use, free), size, text description, creation date and time, who created it, domain (where usable), when it was changed, usage counts, date of last use, number of days used, storage size it uses, save/restore size needed on file, which pool of auxiliary storage it is in, last saved date, last restored date, the SAVE command used (the file label ID if it was a data object), date and time this member of the SOURCE file was last updated, system level when last updated, compiler used, object control level, APARs applied, and so on.

## 2.6. SYSTEM-SUPPLIED LIBRARIES

This is the sequence the system would use to find your item if you did not name a specific library but rather a library list:

1. QSYSLIBL, the system's own portion of your LIBrary list, which houses objects needed by the system itself. There can be up to 15 libraries in the QSYSLIBL.
2. Software PRODUCT Libraries, up to two per library list. These libraries house the language compilers such as SQL, COBOL, PL/I, FORTRAN, PASCAL, BASIC, RPG, etc. If you were using the interactive programming tool SOURCE ENTRY UTILITY (SEU), it would be housed in Product Library one, and the language compiler itself would be in Product Library two.
3. *CURLIB, the Current Library that is the working library you specified, used for the running job you are working within.
4. QGPL, the system's General Purpose Library, if you did not specify a current library for this job.
5. QUSRLIBL, which means all the other libraries you have put in this library list for use by the system's users and applications which name this LIBLST when invoked.

Of course, if you specify a particular library in an object manipulation command, the system looks only in that particular library for your object.

You can change the library contents around (see "commands," below). You create a library list for a job, or for a group of jobs, using commands from your terminal that are interactively prompted. The prompts have several levels of help, so you can hardly do anything incorrectly unless you doze off or forget the logic of what you are doing. Even then, there are commands at hand to recover such mistakes, and you cannot interfere with anyone else's live work because the system won't permit it.

When a job is started, there is a job description that determines the contents of the user's portion of the library list used (QUSRLIBL). These contents can also be determined by a command used to start a job, the Submit Job command (SBMJOB). In cases of doubt (you have specified library list names in two or more places) the latest action taken presides; if you override a system definition by putting something else in a command at run time, the run-time option is the one the system uses.

In general, this rule applies throughout the system: Almost everything is changeable live, and the latest change is the option that will be used. If a series of changes to the same object or library is specified before actual job execution, only the last change will be assigned (not one, then the other, then the other). If changes are made during a job run (you can invoke a CL command in the middle of a COBOL job if you like), those changes will occur live at run time.

Shorter library lists usually give better performance, but they should be designed for ease of use.

You may ask the system to list the objects over which you have control (user authority to see and handle them) by name, type, or some combination of name and type. If it is a long list, you may want to print it. Output from a command is normal output, so it can be redirected anywhere in the system.

Some system-supplied libraries are as follows:

- QSYS—System objects kept here
- QGPL—General Purpose Library for system and user default objects
- QHLPSYS—System Help messages and information
- QSSP—System Operating System objects

## 2.7. FOREIGN LANGUAGES FOR MENUS, MESSAGES, AND HELP

If your primary language has been specified as English, all the Q libraries will give help and messages in English. If you position another preferred language library first in the SYSLIB list, you will get your messages in that language. Since all messages come from a library no matter what programming you are running, they can all be issued in the language of your choice. All screens, messages, command prompts, and help information for all IBM-supplied programs can be in one of 28 languages, which any user can request by issuing the command CHGSYSLIBL LIB(QSYS2928) before running a job. For example, "...2928" gives French messages. This change can be made automatically via your sign-on profile if you are the only one on the system who wants messages in, say, French.

The table that follows contains codes to change screen menu prompts, Help text, and messages to languages other than English.

**Language Code Numbers**

| | | | |
|---|---|---|---|
| French (Parisian) | 2928 | English DBCS* | 2984 |
| French (Belgian) | 2966 | Dutch (Netherlands) | 2923 |
| French (Canadian) | 2981 | Dutch (Belgian) | 2963 |
| French (Multinational) | 2940 | Danish | 2926 |
| German | 2929 | Icelandic | 2958 |
| German (Multinational) | 2939 | Finnish | 2925 |
| Italian | 2932 | Norwegian | 2933 |
| Italian (Multinational) | 2942 | Swedish | 2937 |
| Spanish | 2931 | Greek | 2957 |
| Portuguese | 2922 | Turkish | 2956 |
| Portuguese (Multinational) | 2991 | Chinese Kanji* | 2987 |
| English (Uppercase only) | 2950 | Simplified Chinese* | 2989 |
| Korean* | 2986 | Japanese* | 2962 |

*These are 16-bit letters, *D*ouble *B*yte *C*haracter *S*ets. The special English goes with the oriental DBCS languages.

I have shown you the language codes to indicate how user-friendly the AS/400 is. On no other system will you find system support, including multiple levels of Help information, in various languages.

## 2.8. SUMMARY

At this point you should be starting to get a picture of the AS/400. The onion skin unwraps as follows:

1. The user comes in via CL commands that affect an object (the CL language part of the system).
2. The system automatically performs system security checks (who is trying to do what to whom).
3. The user's request is placed on a system queue in priority position (based on request priority and operation type).
4. When all required resources, both program and data, are available and no higher-priority operation is in queue, the system will execute this action. All required work space, data, and so forth, will be organized and run by the system. The user will be told what is going on through output queues or messages.

Another way to come into the system (not using CL) is to write or use an application program. You prepare this object with a compiler, and when you issue the command to "create" the object, it will go into the temporary job library, CURRENT LIBRARY (CURLIB*), or, if none exists, into QGPL, the system's General Purpose Library. The application can then be run in one of the following ways:

1. By expressly starting it through the Command Language program prompt menu.
2. Via a CL program CALL or similar invocation.
3. As part of a batch job stream CL definition.

To sum up, the system has queues of requests and libraries (directories) of objects. Objects include programs to be run and data, including control block information. You create some programs by making statements in source languages, then using CL to "create" them and put them into some library. (You get data into the machine using a different language, a data definition language called DDS, which is described in later chapters. You invoke programs in batch mode or interactively. Batch mode implies a string of programs, one following another, being called through CL in a way similar to other computer types' job control statements, either precataloged on the system or submitted live. Interactive implies that you call the program from a system menu at your terminal or that it is invoked automatically when a certain type of data hits the system or a certain user signs on (as predefined in his or her Profile). Programs use resources pulled out of libraries, meaning you alter what data a program works on by changing the sequence of datasets defined as being in this library or by changing the sequence of libraries defined within a library list. All objects are found by the system for you by name, not by address, so the first encounter of the name your program asks for is the one the system will give you. Your placement of test data ahead of live data in the library list will relegate this run to a test run. The selection of a different device type for output, or a different output spool to write to, can change your program's output from yesterday's run. Once you understand the variety of run-time options you have, the AS/400 becomes extremely flexible and programs can be used for more than one purpose, saving coding.

# 3

# The Data Management Structure

## 3.1. COMPONENTS OF THE DATA STRUCTURE

### 3.1.1. Device and Data Files

The following questions will be answered in this chapter:

1. How does the AS/400 Database Machine really work?
2. How is that different from current computer systems?
3. What are the advantages of this very different system architecture for the data owner?

We have already seen that *everything* on the AS/400 is an object and that objects are capable of reconstruction, should pointers and liaison with other objects be broken. The AS/400 talks to data, devices, and other remote systems in the same way: They are all simply objects to be referred to by name. The style of address will be determined from attribute tables, which are attached to the objects' descriptions.

Datasets are objects, too. The database(s) on the AS/400 are divided into so-called physical FILES, for want of a better word. Data FILES can be broken into MEMBERS for management purposes, but this is not necessary. Typically, if you have more than one type of record in a dataset, you put one type in one file member and another in the other file member in order to keep track of them. But the structure of the data is relational, that is, rectangular tables (fixed-length records), so it is rare that you have two or more record types in one physical file.

"Physical" here means real, live data. This definition is important, because in the AS/400 literature the word FILE is used for many different things. It is a generic word meaning format: The description of the fields of data in a record is called a record format, but the congregation of these records—not the data, but the type of format for it—is called a PHYSICAL FILE. Then there is the LOGICAL FILE, which takes an entire chapter to describe. Here let us say that a Logical File is just a view of data—the format I would like to see it in, nicely edited and sequenced, with certain records selected and others deleted from my view based upon my individual selection criteria. (The Logical View is much more than this because the selection of records is done for me ahead of time, preselected, by the data management system, before I ever ask for them. Thus, the Logical View is a path table as well.)

The AS/400 describes database formats as files. It also calls the device tables that define how data should be input or output as DEVICE FILES. The editing, sequencing, data checking, and so forth, that needs to be done, say to display output to make it presentable to the terminal operator, is called a DEVICE FILE (presentation management). DEVICE DESCRIPTION is the AS/400 term used to define the fixed, hardware-oriented information the system will use to physically control the device. The DEVICE FILE uses the DEVICE DESCRIPTION to get the data to and from the hardware device.

Another file is the remote system file, called the Distributed Data File (DDM). For this type of file, which is across a communication line at a distance, there will be three kinds of Device Descriptions: one for the teleprocessing control unit, one for the telephone line, and one for the "device" at the end of the line, which can be a program in the remote CPU, a device attached to it, or a remote database.

In summary, the AS/400 thinks of databases, devices, and other systems as FILES. You define to your system FILES that become the doorways to whatever resources you need to talk to or see. You define these files to your *system*, not to your program, using DDS, a special data definition language. These definitions then go into your system library, to be used by running programs that need to talk to these resources in the manner you prescribe in the DDS.

Here is an illustration of the relationships among Data Manger, data, programs, and Access Paths.

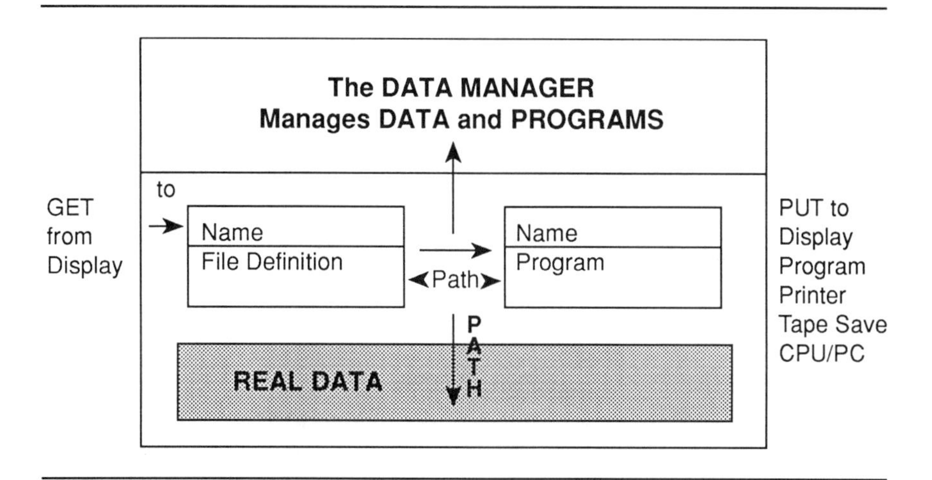


**Figure 3.1.** The system Data Manager.

A File object and a Program object being managed by data management. The program has issued a GET from a display. Input data feeds through an editing file definition to a system queue. The program sees the data in its edited form. The program PUTS the data to the database or to another output destination, local or remote, intelligent or not, without having to think about the hardware characteristics of the path or of the devices.

You may create more than one set of DDS for any resource (data type, device type). The data presentation definition is called a LOGICAL FILE; the device presentation definition is called a DEVICE FILE. These "files" are objects, managed by the system Data Manager. Your program talks to these files, not directly to the data or devices. In programming jargon these are "externally described files," meaning the definitions are outside your program. For instance, a COBOL, PL/I, PASCAL, FORTRAN, or RPG program on the AS/400 needs no data division (file definitions) or device configuration section. You merely name the system-defined

FILE through which you plan to manipulate your data. The Data Manager will connect your program to the file at run time, feeding data to the program when the data and the program are ready for each other, taking into consideration the priorities of both, the priorities of other system users of the same resources, and other resources necessary to make the transaction work.

Programs talk to DEVICE FILES and/or DATA FILES. Device Files control the sequence and form of data input and output from and to devices. They use DEVICE DESCRIPTION information to figure out how to actually get the physical data to and from the hardware devices. DEVICE DESCRIPTIONs give Device Files the fixed information to define how a hardware device is actually to be used. You create both the files and the descriptions using the DDS language before you ever run your program. You can see that a program may put out its output to a printer on one run and, down the line, to another system on another run, because where and how the output goes is not a function of the program but rather of the tables ("files") invoked at run time. These are merely CL assignments. "File" and "program" are merely objects managed by the Data Manager, independent of one another; they are named and stored in libraries when not in use, dynamically alterable, securable, and sharable.

If you need more files than are supplied by IBM, you can define, create, use, and delete them through the system's DDS language combined with the Command Language, CL. To simplify things there is an interactive menu-driven utility called IDDU (Interactive Data Definition Utility), which you can allow your novice programmers to use for this purpose. IDDU is a fill-in-the-blanks menu-driven utility that protects the user from mistakes.

## 3.2. DEVICE DESCRIPTIONS

You need to set up one DEVICE DESCRIPTION per hardware device attached to the CPU. For remote teleprocessing lines this translates into three: for controller, line, and end data receiver. You may define as many DEVICE FILES as you wish—one for every format method you will regularly use for input and output. Device Files have attributes, such as "spooling," invisible to the program, that you may want to use. If the Data Manager uses such a file with your program, it will hide the data in a special interim file until the device is ready for input or output or both, depending upon your program needs.

## 3.3. CREATING FILES

The CL command to create a FILE is CRT . . , where " . . " is filled in by the file type abbreviation. This rather high level "assembler" type language expands into the real machine level language, which on the AS/400 bears no resemblance to other systems' machine languages. The AS/400 machine language is a higher level language than many compiler languages on current systems. For example, the CL command CRTPF (Create Physical File), explodes into a series of machine instructions on the AS/400, as shown below:

| CL Command | AS/400 Machine instructions |
| --- | --- |
| CRTPF | Create Data Space<br>Create Cursor<br>Activate Cursor<br>Create Data Space Index<br>Ensure Data Space Entries<br>Set Cursor<br>Copy Data Space Entries<br>Insert Data Space Entry<br>Materialize Data Space Attributes<br>Materialize Data Space Index Attributes<br>. . . and more |

I list these hardware instructions just to give you a feel for the architecture of the system. Most present-day computers have instructions such as "Move binary bits left one bit," hundreds of which the compiler programmer must manipulate with brute-force logic to create for himself the function he will use to manage data. On this system the instruction set was raised to the logical level needed to manage data and built into the hardware. Instead of the current RISC concept of providing minimal instructions for so-called machine instruction execution performance reasons (which was always a mirage), the AS/400 uses the concept of maximal instructions at the highest level useful to the system programmers for people performance reasons. After all, I am interested in how fast my job gets done, not in how fast a bit moves from left to right inside the machine.

Besides providing easy logic for systems programmers, the high level instruction set on the AS/400 eliminates hundreds of hours of debugging time because what used to be whole sequences of instructions on prior systems, on the AS/400 becomes one already debugged hardware instruction. In addition, these instructions cannot work in a deleterious fashion with one another. They are like meshed gears that will not work if one is missing and will always fit together when all are in place. One of the pleasant results of this is that "high level" language compilers (COBOL, PL/I, PASCAL, and the like) are cheap and easy to add to the system. Whole routines underneath the language statements in former systems are single AS/400 instructions or, at best, a few. Witness the number of languages you have to choose from.

## 3.4. SPECIFICATIONS FOR DATA FORMAT, DEVICE DESCRIPTIONS, AND LOGICAL DATA

The CREATE A FILE CL command, applied via the IDDU utility or DDS (data description specifications), creates a File Description Table and defines a path to the data, be it in-house or remote (by DDM—Distributed Data Management). It delimits what you will be able to do on this file from your program. The operating system will deny you data access that is not explicitly defined here. Thus, you will design into your system specific access to data for specific users. This kind of data control exists in no other system and is very difficult to program into older architected systems (and therefore is almost never done). It seems an obvious need today, but it is a major weakness in most database systems.

The fulfillment of user needs on a system level is the great advantage of a system being designed from the ground up for data management. You say what you want to do with this particular physical file (disk, tape, printer, line, display, and so forth). You create the FILE DESCRIPTION (FD) in a separate operation (from your programs) using CL, before ever attempting to use the device or data. Now many different programs/people can use the interface you have created.

This is different from most other systems. They hand you one or two predefined user interfaces, which you can only use the way a systems programmer designed them (most likely 20 years ago) because they are totally inflexible and ungrowable. Then you must send your users to school to learn how to use them. This, again, is a reflection of the architecture of past machines—they have to be heavily programmed to handle data interfaces from various device types because the instruction set is at such a low level and not data-oriented. Since on the AS/400 it requires at best three or four CL commands to create an interface to data or a device (each command, being so high level, doing such a vast amount of work), not only can you formulate a system to the needs of each user type, but you can add new interfaces at will as the years go by. There is none of the "design for eternity" concept of older systems.

After you create the physical file space and descriptions with CRTPF and define the physical devices attached to your system with the CRT Device File command, then you say precisely what you want to do with the data from this file using a Logical File command, CRTLF. By defining Logical Files you set up Access Paths and reference tables that data management will use to bring you precisely the data you need in your program or on your display screen.

In your device definition you actually design your screen layout, as well as what data checking on input and data editing on output you require, and what particular device control you want when you invoke this Device File in your program. For a screen this could be highlighting, blinking, or blanking out of certain fields for certain viewers; it could also mean editing monetary fields for different currencies or dates for U.S. or European sequences, or range checking for numeric entries and validity checking for data entry.

As you can see, much of the work formerly done in your user program is now done by data management per your instructions in the file definition's DDS statements. This makes these definitions both bug-free and reusable, a decided productivity advantage for your programmers. In fact, by careful use of file definitions and Logical Views of data (LOGICAL FILES), many data manipulation programs of today can be eliminated altogether. If you only need to see the data, not physically change it, you can probably get it onto your screen or printer formatted, edited, sorted, sequenced, and preselected simply by using a CL browsing command on predefined file types (or by using the system's Query interface).

## 3.5. FIELDS, RECORDS, AND FILES

A *field* on the AS/400 is the smallest unit of data, as you define it to the system, that data management will handle for you as an individual entity. A *record* is a set of fields that belong more with each other than with any other fields you define to the system. A record on the AS/400 is a relational "tuple," for those of you who speak relational. A *file* is a formal set (as in set theory) of like records. When you define fields you define data shapes; when you define records and files you define structures to house the fields of data.

# 4

# The Data Manager

## 4.1. OS/400—THE OPERATING SYSTEM

OS/400, the software operating system for the AS/400 machine, together with the hardware, does all data management. This comprises creating, storing, and accessing data for applications, and means data for or from:

- Database
- Diskette
- Tape
- Another computer system's database
- Another computer system's devices
- Spool queues when needed
- Printers

The Command Language, CL, and the Data Definition Language, DDS, are used to create the object definitions (blocks) data management uses to run the system for you. Your program or display does *not* run the system—it only makes requests of the system to do work for it. You use the SEU (Source Entry Utility) to enter the statements to create these objects. The CL commands have parameters from which you choose to define the attributes of the objects (for example, how much space the system should allocate for a data file when first created and how much additional space to grab when a user tries to expand the file beyond the original definition by adding one too many records to it). All of this is prompted by the system; you do not have to memorize DDS or CL in order to use either language to create your working environment.

In addition to the menus and prompts you use to create the objects of your system, there are many levels of help at every step to explain the prompts themselves or any and all parameters of the commands. You do not need manuals or documentation to define the commands.

## 4.2. SYSTEM SETUP

Although the Data Manager is built in, you must tell it how you plan to use the system. You define the database in enough detail to get started. Using CL, you "create" the device "files" as well as the database "files" according to your own specifications. You do this once for the system rather than once per program as in other systems. You give a name to every object you create; it is this name a program will use to find the object, be it a printer, another system, or a database item. Later on, when your program is using these files of data, the Data Manager will do all the queuing and answering of data requests, the invoking of application programs when input has arrived from devices or database, the device control itself, all the spooling of input and output to synchronize the use of system devices, and work storage allocation and management. In other words, the Data Manager does all the navigation through the system that used to be within a user program, in a way that shares resources and thus allows more than one data user to access a pathway to and from a data type.

No one user monopolizes a data path or an interface or a set of data. All users are controlled by the system rather than the other way around. This is a significant change from other systems you may know. Not only does it open up the database to concurrent applications without the risk of bottlenecks, but it also opens the system up over time to changes in environment and use. There is never the need to redesign the database in order to add a new application because the database is not designed for or by an application but by the system itself, and program access is optimized as a function of system load, not programmer ingenuity. The word is *shared*, and it applies over space and over time. No new use or interface to data will disable an older use or interface because each path or interface is an object, self-contained and independent, managed as one of many system objects according to the system's and object's priorities. Refer to Figure 4.1 for a layered view of how the Data Manager sees data.

## 4.3. FIELD, RECORD, AND FILE DEFINITIONS

A record is the unit of transfer from file to system to program. At a minimum, you define to the system, using DDS (separately from any programs), the length of the record in bytes. If that is all you do, the system will hand you the entire record on a data request, without breaking it down or doing specific field editing or verification. With added field definition the system will, with your request for data:

- Rearrange fields as specified in your data request.
- Edit fields differently for different data requests or output devices.
- Check input data field by field, according to prespecified field definition parameters.
- Sequence input to programs or output to screens by fields selected at run time.
- Hide certain fields from a program's or certain user's view.
- Map data fields into your program or onto your screen differently from the actual record format.

A record type is defined within a FILE, which is an unordered set of like records that is sequenced only if you so specify. Sequencing of records occurs at usage time (when you are looking at the records) and according to the path control you use to access the data. Retrieval sequence can be through a run-time choice of "logical view," the so-called LOGICAL FILE of the AS/400, or through SQL or AS/QUERY or other inquiry-type programming language requests, or by time-of-arrival of the record into the database. Unlike in systems left over from the era of batch pro-

**APPLICATION PROGRAMS, 4GLS, PACKAGES, SQL, QUERY**

| Application CL commands: | Data management programs: |
|---|---|
| CREATE<br>Read, Write, Change, Refer to, Override, Delete: BY NAME | |

| data | from<br>via | datasets<br>queue requests |
|---|---|---|

Data management uses device and file definitions created by CL earlier to get data to and from the applications.

Data File

| Physical File used by DM to find data |
|---|

Defines size
and format
of Records,
Fields
Input/Output Size

Other "file" types:

| Device File Definitions:<br>Displays-access and format<br>Printers-output format<br>tapes<br>diskettes<br>other computer systems |
|---|

Defines attributes of:
Devices, some constant data Editing

Editing

| Logical File definition |
|---|

User-selected Logical File defines how data is to be sequenced, on what criteria it should be selected for passing to the application, which records should be included or omitted, which fields should be shown to the user, what kind of checking and editing should be done on the data before it is input to the application or output to the device or other system, etc.

**Figure 4.1.** Interaction of programmer and data management on the AS/400.

gramming, you should never read every record into your program and personally sift out the records you want to see, discarding the ones you don't want. This would be a terrible tax on the system and on the programmer.

Notice that with the system presorting and sifting records for you, your program becomes very much shorter and easier to write, and many programs from today's systems can be replaced with a query language like SQL. This language is a much more powerful tool because 98 percent of the work languages used to do is now done naturally by the AS/400 as a system before it engages your programs or inquiry.

## 4.4. FILES

You use FILE definitions to define to the system the sets of data it will house and to define each device on which the data will be presented. It is in these file definitions that the method of data presentation and retrieval is determined. For displays, for instance, you define as many FILES as you have output or input formats for each data type: What are the valid record formats, device types, graphics, character sets, number of lines, wait-time for input, etc.; whether or not a field should be displayed to a certain profiled user; what kind of highlighting each field is to get; when fields need to be erased, or compared to some constant stored in the FILE definition, and selected accordingly. Etc. etc.

So much work is done by the Screen FILE definition object that many programs of today that manipulate data for display screens can be eliminated and replaced by simple FILE definition statements.

As you know, these screen control programs are some of the most complicated on any system. Being able to do without them enables much faster production of interactive and on-line "programs," much less debugging to go through, and much quicker response to clients who need interactive information tailored almost daily to their needs. The system provides all the required interactive system and device control, the Data Manager provides all the data security and locking/sharing, and the FILE definitions provide the presentation sifting and editing and layouts for each new application. You never have to be concerned with wha is already running on the system (Will you disturb the currently running system?) or with entanglements with other users' data requests (gridlocks, deadly embraces, and the like). These are major stumbling blocks to fast application growth on older systems.

## 4.5. OPEN A FILE

On earlier systems a program had to "Open" a file before requesting data. The OPEN statement in a COBOL or other program was the place of connection: Execution of OPEN in my program caused the program to lock to a data file—"file" meaning both hardware medium and data type. In order to connect, my program had to house the exact file specifications, down to exact record and field definitions, which had to match exactly the physical format of the data and its storage medium. To err here in the program was to cause a bug, meaning the program wouldn't work. This is called early binding.

The AS system binds later. The system does not have to know the exact length of fields or records until it actually does a read for you. This means you can supply such information outside your program, using FILE objects that reside outside your program, which you select for your program's use some time before an actual record is needed. OPENs are still used in COBOL programs, but they serve a different purpose now. They signal the system to prepare the paths for data retrieval based on the logical and physical views (also called files) that you have invoked this run time. In this way OPEN speeds up performance on random retrieval by having the path ready when the program makes the singular request for data. It sees to it that the FILE object is ready to use, the data is available, and the sifting out of chosen records for program viewing is already done. The OPEN of a DDM (Distributed Data Management) FILE also verifies that the path to another system, including modems, controllers, and lines, is ready to use and that the data there is available. It also does a large part of security clearance.

Figure 4.2 shows how the system gets data to the display screen when your application asks it to.

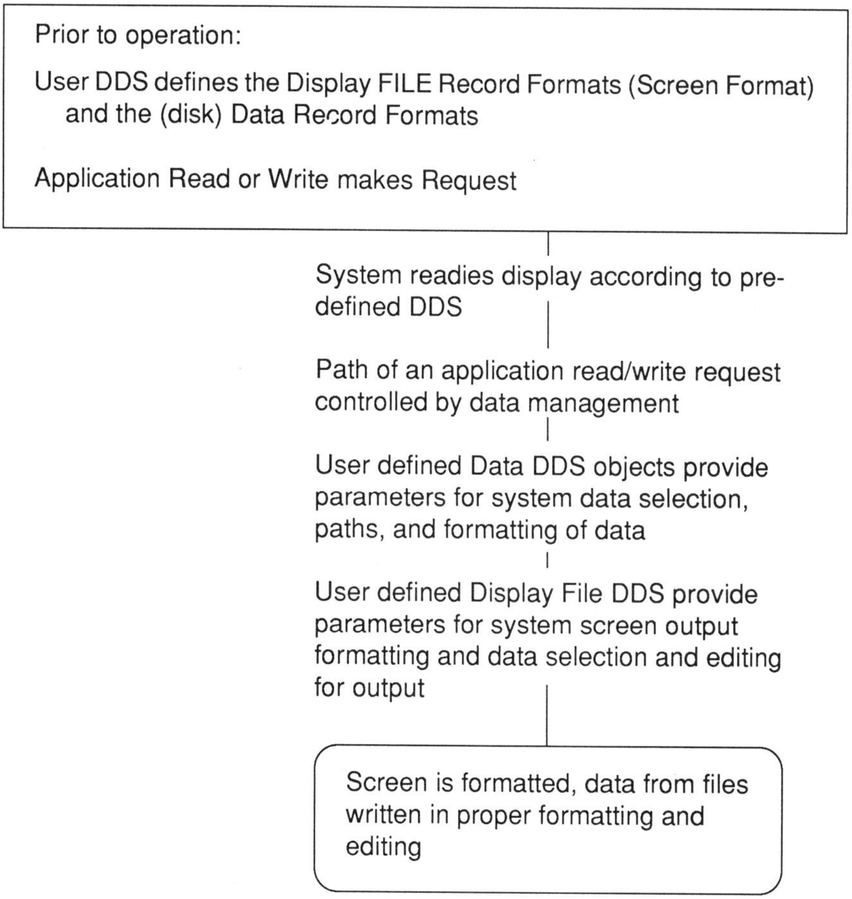

Prior to operation:

User DDS defines the Display FILE Record Formats (Screen Format) and the (disk) Data Record Formats

Application Read or Write makes Request

System readies display according to pre-defined DDS

Path of an application read/write request controlled by data management

User defined Data DDS objects provide parameters for system data selection, paths, and formatting of data

User defined Display File DDS provide parameters for system screen output formatting and data selection and editing for output

Screen is formatted, data from files written in proper formatting and editing

**Figure 4.2.** Getting data to the display screen.

## 4.6. READ AND WRITE FLOW

The Read and Write commands cause an entire chain of events. On a Write To Display operation:

1. The screen is cleared.
2. The data from buffer is formatted according to Record formats in the display FILE object.

3. The formatted data is written to display.
4. The input-capable fields on display are readied as defined in the display FILE object; the keyboard is unlocked.

On a Read operation:

1. The keyboard is unlocked.
2. Input fields are validated per DDS for the display file.
3. Response attributes and data pass to the application.
4. The screen clears per DDS (some parts may be left on, for example, input format fields, if you choose).
5. The keyboard locks, awaiting application okay to data (may be nullified per DDS).

On Write/Read the system does the above two requests, locking the display between the Write and Read operations.

INVITE is a special display command that talks to groups of terminals as a unit, waiting for a response from any terminal. It allows the application program to continue until any screen signals that data has been entered for processing by this application (an "invited" terminal hits the Enter key), at which point the application is switched to its Read sequence. The user's input area will show the device name and the results of the operation as well as the data.

This kind of operation requires multithreaded and reentrant application and system code, but you have probably guessed by now that this is the only code that the AS/400 creates, since it could not efficiently handle all the locking and sharing required by database usage otherwise. This means that all work areas are provided by the Data Manager and that your program requests are all queued, prioritized, and scheduled by the system, as is all work on the system, including work by and for the system itself. The system is a user just as you are, but of a higher priority most times.

SCROLLING is an interesting attribute for display operations. You can define a display file as a SUBFILE, in which case each Write to the display file adds a record to a list of records on queue, called a subfile. You may write to the end of this subfile or to somewhere in the middle. Then a Write, to a "control record" format, scrolls the entire list of records onto the terminal user's screen, page by page. By using a Scroll key at the terminal, the user can browse back and forth through the data, updating at will or adding records to the list. When done, the user hits Enter to pass the entire list back to the system, and the program can then add whole records to the list, change fields in records permitted by DDS, or read terminal-user–changed fields or records back into the application-assigned work area for review or change or writing to disk.

Using subfiles with displays can save a great deal of programming and operator time. It is well worth reading Chapter 4 of the *IBM AS/400 Programmer's Guide* for complete information about this function.

# 5

# Job Flow

## 5.1. COMPONENTS OF CONTROL

The flow of work parcels on the AS/400 is prescribed by Job Step, Routing Step, Job, and Program object definitions within Subsystems. The system uses Job Queues and Job-related objects full of run-time parameter definitions to decide which jobs to run when and how (in what environment) to run them. The system comes with two running subsystems: one for interactive jobs and one for batch. Essentially, these are the queues and boxes (objects) of parameters that define how a job should be run.

You can modify or change all of these parameters with CL commands, but you may just want to run the system as is. There are CL commands to create and change entire subsystems. You can have as many interactive subsystems as you choose, each with its own private, invulnerable space for operation. With virtual address space ranging in the hundreds of trillions of bytes, each subsystem will be assigned unique, private addressing areas. Storage pools will be dedicated to each subsystem and to each job within a subsystem.

Think of a subsystem as if it were a distinct computer for a certain class of users, which is really what it is. The machine is virtually divided up among the subsystems, floating over hardware that is lit upon, quickly used, and released as needed. You can define, modify, or completely change subsystem attributes. To facilitate this, the system delivered to you comes with duplicate subsystems, one of which you can modify while using the other.

## 5.2. SUBSYSTEMS

Subsystem attributes include the following:

1. From where jobs will be invoked (a certain piece of input, a certain user sign-on, a certain queue of work to be done, and so on).
2. Whether jobs are to be scheduled in batch mode, interactively, or both, within a subsystem.
3. How much storage and other object sharing there will be within the subsystem.
4. Whether or not the subsystem is to be continuously ready to activate a job to process certain (live) data arrivals.
5. Which terminals are to be activated when this subsystem is started, or which jobs.
6. Which jobs should start automatically, and when.
7. Job entries for work that is to be done *before* a job starts, that is, Logical FILE openings to reduce transaction turnaround time ("Prestart" entries).
8. Job queue entries for this subsystem.

Subsystems also own so-called Work Entries, definitions of which jobs should be invoked and which user profiles are allowable when input from specific terminals arrives. A sequenced list of job steps to be followed is defined in an object called a Routing Entry. You can change all of these items anytime before job execution: For instance, you may want to cut out a set of terminals coming from a certain time zone one morning, and reactivate them the next morning, without stopping the other terminal users from using the subsystem in a normal manner. Or you may want to eliminate certain user profiles or even certain queues of work or output spoolers. (See the *IBM AS/400 Work Management Guide* for more information.)

## 5.3. HOW A JOB WORKS

A user at a terminal who signs on and requests that the system invoke a program is assigned 16MB of private, protected address space to work within, and gets a logical copy of the program. Users at other terminals who request the use of the same program get attached to other logical copies of the program, in other private space. Each user has his own copy of display FILES for use with this program on this device. Each user is now running a separate JOB. The system manager ensures that the terminals' workings do not interfere with each other.*

## 5.4. SPOOLING

Spooling equals queuing for input or output. Because the CPU instruction execution is magnitudes faster than mechanical I/O device speeds, spooling is required to balance system flow, allowing the Data Manager to continue processing data even when a printer putting out the results of a process is falling behind or not available. The same is true for input: You do not want a stream of input from another system forced to be retransmitted just because a processing program is not able to keep up with the data input flow.

The AS/400 spools all input and output (most systems have one output spool queue, designed for printers and not good for much else). There is a whole set of CL commands to manage spool queues. They include browsing through the queues from your terminal and editing the output before you externalize it, getting yourself duplicate copies, copying parts of a job's output only, and sending some of the spooled output back into another job or across a telecommunications line.

---

*If for some reason you would like to write your own terminal control program, the facilities are there in CL, together with all the inherent wait control and multithreading demands. However, these things are built into this system with system performance you will not be able to beat.

## 5.5. USER CONTROL OF PRINT SPOOL QUEUES

Here are some things you may want to do with your printer output queue using CL:

1. Look at the spool queues, the records, and their attributes and change them.
2. Change output priority for printing.
3. Add some new user data to the output.
4. Change the actual spool queue.
5. Change the number of copies to be printed.
6. Change to output format for a new form (no other current system can do this).
7. Schedule a new time for printing.
8. Change the maximum amount of output for this run.
9. Keep or not keep the output source.
10. Change the number of blank pages between job output.
11. Put this output onto a database.
12. Send the output to another job on another system, or to another spool queue on this or another system.
13. Display, delete, or alter some of these records (providing you have the security clearance to do so).
14. Interrupt this spool output for an emergency job, then save the remainder or resume later.

And here are some CL commands you can use from a terminal to peruse your spooled output (or input):

- WRKSPLF—to see all of your spooled files.
- WRKOUTQ—to see the particular spool you need.
- CHGSPLFA—to move the file you want to an active writer (printer).
- WRKWTR—to find a vacant printer.
- STRPRTWTR—to activate an unused printer.
- CHGWTR—to start a writer from a different queue.
- RESTART CHGSPLFA PAGE=n—to restart an incomplete printout.
- CHGSPLFA + PRTSEQ=*NEXT + HLDSPLF—to interrupt one printer's output with an emergency print job, holding the remainder to be printed later.

- WRKSPLF SELECT (*ALL)—to clean up leftover spoolers from the system and free up storage tied to them (you would be surprised at how many users view the output and then leave it as trash).

Such a variety of user options is the rule on the AS/400. The simple default of just printing a normal copy of each output once on the standard device is also the rule. Recognize, however, that the complex functions derive from a basically simple system: All transactions are handled alike, always through queues, be they spoolers or job entries or data files. The CL commands such as COPY, used in a thinking manner, can save a lot of work. For example, spool queues could be used as temporary storage vehicles for work or data to go down line, or for very long query output. COPY could be used to transfer the work or data to another system or a batch device, or to take sections of it to your terminal (after you browse it).

# 6

# Using the Database Manager

## 6.1. READING AND WRITING DATA RECORDS

The database management system "GETS" and "PUTS" (or the equivalent) completely manage all your data as well as the system's own objects. This means that a program that needs to update a customer master record with a new transaction no longer has to read both files of data—old master record and new transaction update file—then match them, make the changes, merge them in proper sequence, and then, after completing all the housekeeping, go on to the next transaction to repeat the process. Such a program in the AS/400 DMS (Data Management System) merely makes a statement to the effect that this particular set of transactions is to be used (by the DMS) to update that master file under certain conditions. The DMS will do all the selection, matching, updating, merging, and housekeeping. In other words, a program now thinks *logically* about the *data problem*, the updating of data, rather than about the computer flow and control of getting the two types of data (old master and new transaction) together, as in other systems. An analogy might be the way we drive cars today: We think about the traffic around us, red lights, and where we are trying to go, rather than worrying about the choke and the alternator and the mechanical gear in the engine. We are able to do a lot more driving because the management of the motor has been automated for us and we no longer have to think about how it actually works as we drive.

The AS/400 manages your data on three levels:

1. The physical layout of data on disk.
2. The "Logical View" of data, which is the shape and a sequence of that portion of the data to be delivered to a program on a GET.
3. Delivery, or presentation, that is, the way you would actually see the data in your program or on a screen or a printer.

The management comprises:

1. Placement and retrieval of actual physical (real) data to and from its disk home (or from input devices).
2. Protection of data from improper purposes or illegal usage (the wrong person or program asking for it).
3. Sharing of data among concurrent users with concomitant time and usage control.
4. Criteria selection of discrete data records for presentation to a program or output device.
5. Resequencing of records for presentation to the user or program.
6. Editing of the selected and sequenced data records and final presentation to the requester (user).

These steps provide the much touted but virtually nonexistent buzz-word functions, listed below, that users had hoped to get from management information systems (MIS):

- Data independence from program and system code and structure
- Data sharing and consistency
- Field-, record-, and file-level security
- Data integrity
- Data recovery according to usage, not system, criteria

The benefits you derive from the separation of user program requests from actual system data manipulation are these:

1. Programs that are one-tenth the size of those on prior systems.

2. Removal of housekeeping complexities from user programs or fourth generation language applications.
3. Correlated or merged and matched data that is delivered directly to the user.

All this means in this era of data overload is that the automation process can keep up with the data buildup and that the data analyzers (users) can predefine to the system the particular selection of data they are interested in and, quite literally, can turn on the system and have their selected data delivered to them in the form and quantity they can handle.

## 6.2. DATA SETUP

The setup to make this all happen involves data design at the three levels mentioned earlier. First, using DMS (a fill-in-the-boxes RPG-like effort, prompted via the interactive utility IDDU), a data person defines the physical data layout you expect your system to handle. One benefit of a full DMS is that you do not have to preplan for all time. You simply have to define today's actual data needs and shapes so that the system can collect the data as it is sent in. Once this physical layout has been defined you can use special system interfaces (IDDU, SEU, and others) to generate data key-entry programs with which to input the live data into the physical files housed on your disks. You can also use traditional GET/PUT routines in any language to get your data into the system.

Next, also using DDS, you define the "Logical Views" (Logical FILES in AS/400 parlance) that will index and tailor your real data and sift and sort it out for each type of user need you now foresee. Later you will add other Logical Views for new data uses. In these Views you specify which field of which records a user wishes to see on a GET (any request); how these fields are to be matched to other records to pair them if need be; what sequence based on which field of data they should be delivered in; how the system should edit them using monetary symbols, credit signs, zeroes, commas, and dots; what constant additional data you want to be appended to this data as it is delivered; simple math to be applied to certain fields; what security level to apply to which data fields, records, and files; what sharing options to apply if other users are present; what error messages to send in case users violate the "rules"; and where to send the messages. These selection, sequencing, and control rules *live with* the data, in the sense that whenever a user or program requests this data via this Logical View, these rules apply. If the user wants different rules to apply, he must come in through a different Logical View or create a new one for his own use.

## 6.3. THE DATA MANAGEMENT SYSTEM (DMS) AND YOUR DATA

The DMS will organize, prioritize, separate, share, correlate, and control all users of the data, all the time. Even when no user program is running, DMS *is* running.

There is some flexibility in how you use the system. You can get and put data directly into the physical, real data level, bypassing the editing/sequencing control levels. Some users of older systems may think they can achieve better performance (read: "speed") this way; but they will be incorrect because the DMS decides about the real disk access—where data should be put (physically) and exactly when updates really do occur on disk. So the user, even when getting/putting at the "physical" level, is still only making requests of the system, he is *not* controlling real disk access as he might have done on prior systems. In a shared DBMS system, it would not make sense to allow one user to come in at a level of control beneath everyone else, as if he owned the system, and possibly bottleneck or lock out other system users, no matter how efficient the one user was. The way to expedite certain "users" is to give high-priority levels to their data-handling function and let the DMS push their requests ahead of other lower priority items in the shared environment. Be data driven, not user driven.

## 6.4. DATABASE STRUCTURE: INSIDE, LOOKING OUT

The smallest item the DMS can access and manage is the FIELD. To define a field of data using the DDS language, you name it and then describe it: how long it is, what kind of data should be in it (alphabetic, double-byte Kanji or other double-byte language data, numeric—decimal, packed or not, signed or unsigned, binary, hexadecimal, floating point). You specify these data types with one of 15 data type symbols on your RPG-like DDS screen. You will be prompted to fill in the correct item in the correct place in the correct way. There is plenty of help. Whatever you specify here will be used by the system to check incoming data for correctness or type and size, and to edit outgoing data from these fields to some output device. You can also specify authority checks to be made for specific users to see this data (through the view usage parameters, by selecting out certain fields for certain users' views of this data). And you can specify data padding, translations, editing, and so forth, as the data is accessed for viewing.

## 6.5. DEFINING FIELDS OF DATA

The next unit size of manageable data is the RECORD, or in relational terminology, the *tuple*: a *set* of uniquely defined *fields* that relate to one another primarily one to one and are used more with each other than they ever are used with fields from other record field sets. With DDS you give the set a record name and define some rules for its usage, such as which are the retrieval keys and sequencing data-fields (any and/or all are allowed), who may use the data, how it may be used, what checking should be done by DMS on input to these datasets, what editing is to be done on output, what calculations can be done on fields, and so forth.

A conglomeration of records or tuples is grouped by DMS into a string called a FILE. This FILE has no beginning or end, but is just a set of like records to be sent to the user/requester in a sequence based on some field in the record, or in original data input arrival sequence, as specified in the window (view) invoked by the user to get or see the data (the so-called Access Path). Remembering how objects were defined, it will be no surprise that a string of extra data description can accompany each field definition, each record definition, and each file type definition. You, the user, can use these descriptor words for prompting a key-entry person who should fill in this field, say, or to explain the field when it is used for output. These words can show up on your screen designs just by your so designating them at screen definition time (the screen FILE definition).

Following are a few of the optional selection criteria parameters you can have the system apply to your data records when you define user views of data for specific user types. Simply use these parameters when you define the fields in the Logical View (FILE). Since you can define as many Logical Views (AS/400 terminology: LOGICAL FILES) as you wish, you can thus instruct the system to sort, sequence, and select a type of data in as many different ways as can benefit your data usage or analysis. The "paths" to these various views of your data are built by the system at "create view" time and *kept up to date for each instance of data added to this dataset, all day long, every day,* whether or not any of your programs that use this data type are running. DMS is always running, so your private data selection is always ready for you to browse or manipulate.

ABSVAL. You could say, for instance, that a field (or more than one) in your record type is to be taken as an absolute value when used as a sequencing field. If the field had a positive or negative sign, this would then be disregarded every time the DMS used this field to arrange records sequentially for you.

ALIAS. You can give an extra name to the field, say for use by a program written on a different system that happens to use different names for the same fields.

ALTSEQ. You can specify an alternative collating sequence, using this field in a different way from the primary way.

CHECK. This field will be tested for validity at key-entry time at the display station for whatever parameters you specify here: AB allows blank input; ME indicates that this field input is mandatory—without it this record will not be added to the file; M10 and M11 are arithmetic modulus checks on numeric input data; and VN means the name must be correctly matched against a list of 100 or fewer names you supply or against valid existing object, file, or record names you indicate here.

CHKMSGID. This parameter allows you to specify the message a key-entry operator will receive when he tries to enter incorrect data for this field (see CHECK above).

COMP. You can ask for, or omit (Select/Omit option), the

records from this dataset that agree with a constant you supply here, or that match a field name specification based on the following logical operators:

LT—field is less than constant
EQ—equal to
GT—greater than
LE—equal to or less than
GE—equal to or greater than
NL—not less than
NE—not equal to
NG—not greater than

CONCAT. You can string together (concatenate) two or more fields from the physical file structure definition into one field definition for this particular Logical View (FILE).

DESCEND. If this is a key sequencing field for retrieval, retrieve the records in descending order based on this field.

DIGIT. When using this field for a key field for retrieval, the DMS is to use only the low-order four bits of each byte of the field, not all eight (for signed numbers).

ZONE. The DMS is to use only the high-order (left-hand) four bits (see above).

RANGE. DMS selects this record for your Access Path (will present it to you) only if this field is within a range here specified. On screen input, this field will have to be within this range or the record will be disallowed and the operator notified.

SIGNED. When the DMS is sequencing records based on this field, do regard the number sign.

SST. You specify that this field is to be taken from a subset of a physical file field, starting at a certain byte position in that named field and continuing so many bytes.

TRNTBL. The DMS is to translate this field using a specified translation table before presenting it to you through this View for processing.

UNIQUE. You may specify that this field, when used as a key field, must be unique within the File (record type). Then DMS will ensure that there are no duplicate key fields.

FCFO. If DMS finds duplicate key fields in the physical file or

Logical File from which you are building this Logical View (File), it will sequence those records in a "first-changed, first-out" order in this View.

FIFO. DMS will hand you in first-in, first-out order any records that had duplicate data in the fields used here as sequencing keys.

LIFO. See FIFO, but change the presentation sequencing order to "last in, first out."

UNSIGNED. If used for sequencing, this field will be treated as unsigned binary data, no matter what it really is.

VALUES. If this field is input from a screen, DMS makes sure this field matches a specified list of values (for example, valid state abbreviations or zip codes). If selecting records from a physical file for this Logical View, DMS ensures that the physical record is selected for the user's Logical View only if this field matches one item in the list specified here (up to 100 items).

DYNSLT. When creating the Access Path for you for this Logical View, the DMS will choose the records dynamically, as they arrive in the system, having the path ready for you at all times (saving execution time for ad hoc inquiry).

EDTCDE. You name the editing code word you want the system to use ($123,456.00 or DM123.456,00, for example) for external presentation of this field.

EDTWRD. This specifies the nonmonetary edit word to be used by DMS when displaying this field.

FLTPCN. This specifies if a floating point number should be single or double precision (32 or 64 bits).

PFILE. This indicates physical files from which this Logical View is to be derived.

RENAME. This uses a physical file record format, but gives it a new name in this Logical View.

TEXT. You supply descriptive text data to be appended to this record or field object, which later can be used throughout the system to uniquely describe or identify the object.

COLHDG. You may specify a column heading that will be used by the Query program or DFU file utility for quick, ad hoc output.

ALL. This will pick up all records from a physical file that have *not* been overtly marked for selection or omission from this Logical View. Perhaps you would like a count of the records of this set that you have not touched.

* * *

There are many more parameters you will use in creating Logical Views. Several relate to the relational JOIN function and to referencing previously defined Views when creating this one.

## 6.6. ACCESS PATHS

When you create a Logical View you create an Access Path, which is an index to all the records your selection/omission criteria cause to be gathered in this set. Of course, physical records are not duplicated in this View; it is only descriptive information and a split B-tree object that enables DMS to find your records quickly.

The AS/400 will reuse already existing Access Paths whenever possible. This is important because the system continuously updates them as new data enters the system, unless you specify otherwise in your FILE definition. If another user's View uses some of the same data your View uses, your View will be updated, as he updates his with new data, even if you are not running your program. For this reason there must be some design for sharing. Say, for example, you have an application that expects to query the database for regular data at four every afternoon. You want the View queried to stay constant after four until you are through looking at the data. In this case you can specify that the View be held constant, not updated further, until you say so with a special OPEN QUERY statement or the next IPL. This may be the exact same view as someone else's who wants continuous updating. You just reference that view, give it a new name, and state different update rules.

## 6.7. INSIDE A USER'S PROGRAM

To process your data, that is, your Logical View of the real physical data, you may use any of the procedural or ad hoc languages available on the AS/400 system, such as COBOL, RPG, PASCAL, PL/I, BASIC, SQL, QUERY, or any of the software packages. The data file for your program is the Logical View, with real physical data preselected, edited, and sequenced as specified in the Logical View that you choose to run the program with.

If you decide that your program should process data sequentially, this means following the sequence of the Access Path that your Logical View has created based upon data selection and omission criteria you used when defining the Logical View (FILE). Like any other system's COBOL program, you will get records within your program's reach one by one, in the sequence your program defines, but pulled from the sequence of the Logical View's Access Path, not from the physical sequence on some disk drive.

You may do all the usual things with these records: position a processing starter pointer to some specified relative record number within the Access Path or to some particular key field (composite or simple) or to some number of records before or after this point; you may begin processing at the beginning of the FILE (Logical); you may read this record, then the one before it (in the Logical FILE's Access Path) or after it or some distance away from it, or simply the NEXT record.

If you choose to process randomly by key, you may ask for data records to be fed to you by DMS that are equal to a particular key, or before or after the key that is equal to the one you proffer. In this case, for simplicity you name the record format name to avoid the time it would take—and the logic—to fathom what to do with duplicate keys from other record formats within this file (possibly within different members of the file). You can do key manipulation, such as telling the DMS to do generic key matches on the first *nnn* characters of the keys or on concatenated field keys. For statistical data analysis the choices of selection criteria plus key variation are very rich. There are ways to chain reads whereby with a single read you can pull out master records followed by all the relevant detail records to output on a display or printer. Most of the high level languages have been augmented to support these system functions.

Systems programmers should note that there is also the ability to get records in physical time-of-arrival sequence; however, you are still not controlling the disk reads and writes but only setting up another Access Path, albeit a short and simple one. You will still not see records that were previously marked for deletion.

The UPDATE option on a read causes the system to lock onto the record until the update is fulfilled by the system, on so-called hard copy (the actual physical record, not just the logical Access Path). If not done yet, the update will happen either when you

PUT the record back or when you GET the next record or end the job. If a second user asks for that same record while it is locked to the first user, that second program will wait however long the user specified in the WAITRCD option of the FILE definition at FILE creation time (or as specified in an override statement at run time) before it gives up on this record. The second user will get a message stating who has locked the record and stating file, member, and record relative record number.

When updating records, you will be controlled by the FILE entry MAX records, which specifies the maximum number of records that can be added to this file, ever. Of course, like all options, this can be overridden with a CL command before you run the job.

## 6.8. DATA ARCHITECTURE

The data architecture can be looked at this way: as layers building up from the most real—the actual physical data—to the most logical—the way an end user wants to see the data for some particular purpose. Think of it as it is depicted in Figure 6.1. Before you can run a program of your own to handle data (your programs do not actually format the physical fields or the members of the files that house the records of fields), you must go through three layers of definitions: the physical data layout (format), the logical data definitions (Logical Files or Views containing record descriptions subsetted to fields), and the device I/O logical definitions known as device definitions (Device Files in AS/400 terminology).

## 6.9. DESCRIBING THE DATA LAYERS

Physical data, that which is actually recorded on system disks, must be described to the system via DDS language statements, which can be done in a CL program or by using IDDU, the interactive prompting program for this purpose. The user, in describing physical data field sizes, thinks logically, not physically. That is, a decimal number such as 43,126.35 is seven digits, two of which are decimal places, and so that is exactly the way you describe it to the system in DDS. Your DDS statement would look like Screen 6.1.

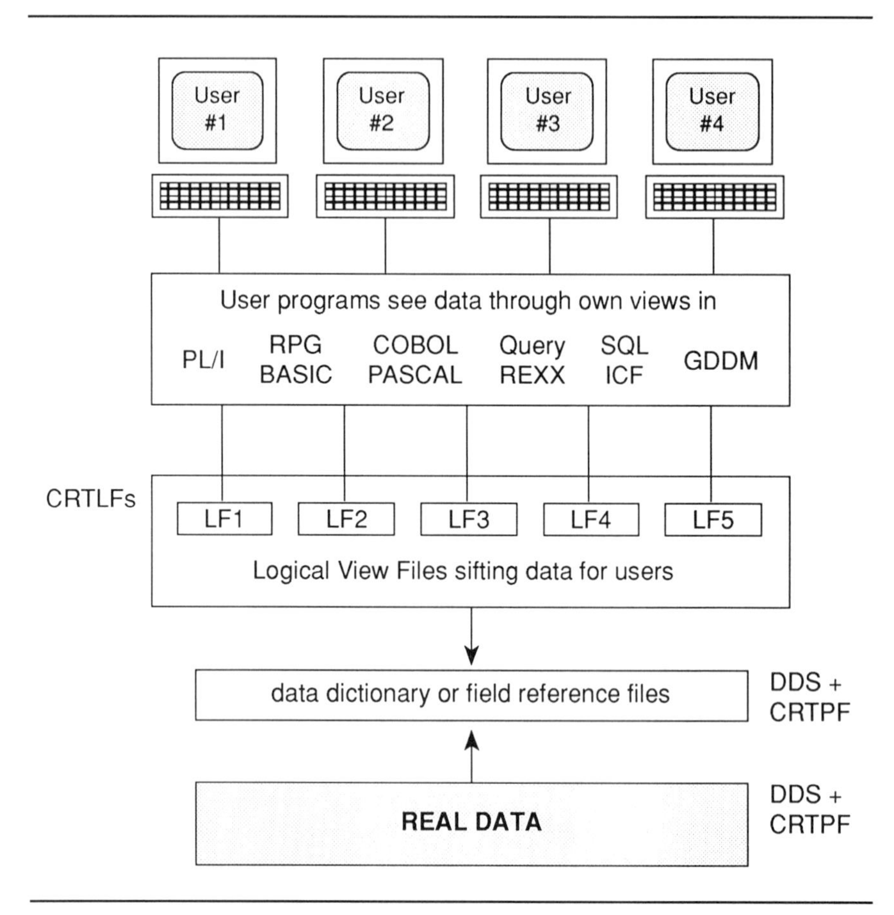


**Figure 6.1.** Layers of data definition from the most real (bottom) to the most usefully edited (top).

Although you describe the number field as seven digits, it will be stored on disk in a packed format using less space (four bytes). When edited for output, it will take up nine places, as we see it (12,345.00), or even more if you defined the editing to be done with monetary symbols such as pound or dollar signs or credit symbols. You needn't worry about exactly how the number will be stored on disk—you have no control over this. Nor do you need to concern yourself with how the aforesaid transformations take place as you had to do on other systems. This system is built for

```
Prompt Screen

Column

19..................29  33,34  36,37 45..............80

Fieldname1                 7      2    TEXT
```

**Screen 6.1.** DDS statement.

data handling: It expects to do all the data editing and other tasks you would expect a good clerk to do.

In similar fashion, a textual field (characters) would be described to DDS as shown in Screen 6.2.

You should define naming conventions for the entire system, especially if you have users who come in through different interfaces such as COBOL programmers, departmental interactive users, RPG and CL programmers, and other remote system or terminal or PC users. A naming dictionary is advisable to keep people from misusing each other's data. Put the dictionary in a special REFERENCE FILE, from which you can build all your field, record, member, file, and library object names.

```
Prompt Screen

Column

19..................29  33,34  36,37   45............80

Fieldname2                  20     (blanks)     TEXT
```

**Screen 6.2.** Textual field definition.

You precede all the data field definitions with a record statement. This is merely a DDS statement with an R in column 17, a record name in column 19–28, and any descriptive text you like in columns 45–80. These column definitions may seem old-fashioned. They are patterned after RPG, which was the original second generation system's 4GL. Think about it, though: The format is fed to you and you fill in the appropriate boxes; you cannot make any logical errors or bugs because they are not commands, just data entries the system needs to do its DMS work. Essentially you are inputting table definitions to be stored and later used by the system. Wrong entries on your part will be rejected on the spot and can be corrected any time.

Additions to record field definitions can be made later, even as programs are using the data formats, and they cause no recompiling of programs unless, of course, you want to update the old programs to use the new data fields.

## 6.10. DICTIONARY REFERENCE FILE

The ability to reference prior file/record/field definition statements when creating a new data file suggests that after you define system norms for naming objects, you should use DDS to create "ghost" formats for files, records, and field formats using standardized names. This "field reference file" is an empty system data definition set (it holds no data), to be used referentially when defining real data files. Consistency in naming conventions and relief for the end user from having to describe the detail of every record and file definition will guarantee the use of the reference file. The advantages for the user are that he may selectively use names of fields and also change the descriptions and keywords (that is, override the reference file list).

The mechanics to create a system field reference file are the following:

1. Using IDDU and DDS, create a source file called SOURCE and put it in the QGPL general purpose library. Then compile it, stating MBR=NO to make sure it is empty. For example:

```
CRTPF  FILE(anylib/anyfile)
             SRCFILE(QGPL/Source)  MBR(*NO)
             TEXT(Field ref file for apps)
```

2. Later, to create physical data files, you need only place REF in column 45, in the first statement of DDS for this new file, as below:

```
Column
45
REF  Source (file name of reference file)
```

3. Then define your records and fields simply by naming them in desired sequence, placing an R in column 23.
4. Run a CL program:

```
CRTPF  FILE(newlib/newfile)
       TEXT('my file for application 1')
```

## 6.11. REUSING YOUR DATA DEFINITIONS

In addition to having a field reference file from which those who define Logical Views can replicate structural data definitions with all the predefined attributes (which is quicker, easier, and more system coherent), and/or a system-wide dictionary of named objects, another efficient way to obtain consistency among programmers' data definitions is simply to reuse prior file definitions for new Logical Views and tailor them to the new application with slight changes. DDS has such function, especially if you use IDDU, the interactive data definition utility. This is a nice way to standardize which fields will be used as keys for retrieval or to JOIN datasets to one another, a factor you should keep in mind when opening up this almost too easy-to-use system to various and sundry data manipulators.

Another standard I would apply to this system would be the reuse not only of the Logical File descriptions for subsequent applications on the same data type, but also the reuse of Access Paths. The system builds Access Paths to reach your data based on two items in your Logical File definition tables: (1) whatever fields you have specified to be key fields (from none to every field is possible, zero meaning retrieval will only be by time-of-arrival into the database or by actual physical relative record number on the disk tracks where stored); and (2) whatever selection or omission criteria you have specified for these fields (numeric range checks, exact field content, boolean logic checks against the data fields, and so forth). If you use as a base an older Logical File, using some of the same keys, or the same comparison logic, in the same order, even if you add another decision or two, the Data Manager will use the older Access Path as much as possible. This saves internal system maintenance time (the system keeps all the Access Paths current all the time.

## 6.12. LAYERED LOGICAL VIEWS AND DATA INDEPENDENCE

If you have built Logical Files on top of each other and on top of physical files, one day you may wish to change all the dependent files. For instance, you might have a five-digit zip code that one day must go to nine digits. If you change the original physical file definition DDS, then just do a CRTLF CL command from your terminal (be sure to delete the original DDS definition). You have now changed all the Access Paths to programs that use this zip code field.

Remember the work such a change used to require—searching through miles of COBOL listings and changing every instruction that referenced the field, every data move, every GET and PUT, and every print operation, plus all the dependent fields left and right of this field, every work area in your program, etc., etc., *on every single program that ever touched this field.* As you well know, such maintenance to keep your programs up to date used up major portions of your programming time and skills. And because it was boring, you lost programmers over it. This single item of data independence could well justify changing to the AS/400. We have seen now that you derive benefits on both sides of the programming equation: keeping the old programs current and getting new programs up and running.

## 6.13. WHERE TO DEFINE WHAT DATA DEFINITIONS

*Question:* Where and how do I define which records (field sets) I want to massage, and in what order should DMS hand them to me? *Answer:* In my Logical File (Views) definition I specify:

1. What a record is to *me* (which fields *I* want to see), for example, name, eye color, age only, from a larger personnel record.
2. In what order, left to right, I want to see these fields—this will be *my record*.
3. In what sequence I want the records handed to me.
4. Which records I shall see, based on data in any of the fields in the records (even the field I did not choose to see!) and based on the comparison selection criteria I specify in this Logical File View.

# 7

# Creating Data Files

## 7.1. PHYSICAL DATA FILES

How do you create the physical files, the repositories of real live data? The place on disk where the one and only copy of the system's original data is to be housed, from which all user types will create their own personalized views of this data?

Using DDS, the language for defining data files, and the interactive source entry utility (either SEU or IDDU), you define to the system the physical formats of your basic datasets. Your data specialist must decide what your business's basic data is, from which all other versions of company records derive. This basic data is probably close to its simplest form, wherein fields that belong together *all the time* are in a basic record format. For instance, an invoice's format, the size of its data fields, and the contents of the fields, are known to the everyday user, the key-entry operator. It is obvious that the line item of a purchase and its price are an invoice's basic fields. Because many items could have the same name (two strengths of aspirin tablets, for instance), a unique number will probably represent each particular item on an invoice. Your database will probably have a physical file that accommodates only two fields, the product number and the price; these two items belong together whenever they are used. One does not exist without the other, except for description purposes. You may well have another physical file that has the same product-number field as a component, plus a company name from which you order the product. You will keep together any data that forever and only belongs with *this* concept of the product, such as its component parts or the cost of the item from this supplier. This physical file and the former one will sometimes be merged in usage, in a Logical File, for instance when you need a report on how many complaints you had from your clients about each supplier's products. To build the physical file structure you want to get down to the basics of your data, to separate it into its simplest component parts—those fields that nearly *always* belong together. Joining these small packets to other data units through Logical Views that are meaningful to certain applications is a next step in the data design.

## 7.2. CREATING A PHYSICAL FILE WITH DDS

The Command Language to actually create a file layout (spatial design) on your disks for a basic data type is:

```
CRTPF  FILE(nnn/mmm)  SRCFILE(jill'slibrary/jill'sfile)

       TEXT(aaa)
```

which means:

| | |
|---|---|
| CRT | Create a . . . |
| PF | Physical data space on disk . . . |
| FILE | For a file (of records of data fields). |
| (*nnn* / *mmm*) | Name the new file *mmm*, put it in the library called *nnn*. |
| SRCFILE | Use the source statements from a file (jill'slib/jill'sfile) named *jill'sfile*, which is in the library named in *jill'slib*. |
| TEXT(*aaa*) | Store my text (*aaa* or any fifty characters) with this file description, which I may have the system output with this data or use for comments whenever I use this data (for instance, for operator prompts when this data type is being collected in data entry). |

This command presumes that you have already put source statements into a file called *jill'sfile*, in which the entire layout of the data space is described. This command merely says to the system: Create for me, from the source statements in the source file named in SRCFILE parenthesis, a real data space layout on disk, together with all the description tables, indexes, field attribute definitions, checks, and so forth, that I specified in the source statements (*jill'sfile*), which are already in my library (*jill'slib*). The statements in the library will have defined how much physical space on disks is to be set aside initially for this data type (via the parameter SIZE), and how much more space the system should add whenever this area is approaching its fullness threshold, and how many times the system should allow this space to be expanded.

Where the space is allocated, whether or not it is contiguous (it probably is not) and how it is to be found, is not up to the user to define. A single user cannot maximize usage of shared disk space; only the system can. Having said this, I must add that the ability is there to specifically state where a certain dataset will go on disk, if by chance you have a one application system and believe you need to so allocate your own space. The one reason I can think of for doing so is that you have a number of experienced database designers who need to be kept occupied during the transition to this system. (Over time, they should be trained to think data instead of system.)

The default space allocation used by the system DBM is enough for 10,000 of your defined record size, which will be added to as you get close to filling it up, by enough space to add 1000 records, three times. After that an operator will be asked if you want another cycle of 13,000 to start, in which case space for 10,000 more records will be allocated on disk.

You can see that with a lot of different user types, disk space might go rather quickly. I suggest that the end user be asked to request space for his files from a central location; that a centralized person "own" the disk space—someone who knows how to properly define databases at their lowest levels (so-called *normalization*) and who can work with users to make the data available in the forms in which they need to see it. This means three levels of definition need to be centralized: (1) The source statement definitions for the fields and records, (2) the physical file definitions, and (3) the Logical File definitions for each type of user of various data types.

## 7.3. SOURCE STATEMENTS FOR FILE DEFINITIONS

The source statements that are presumed to exist before issuance of the CRTPF command creating physical data space on disk are entered into a source file in a library of your choice (or into the default system source library QDDSSRC, which is where DDS goes unless you specify otherwise). You create the source using the Source Entry Utility, SEU. It is an interactive tool that prompts you to fill in RPG-like record and field definitions, naming each record and its component fields' format definitions, specifying their sizes and some user-chosen descriptive text to be stored with each field in the database. You also specify with a code letter the type of field being defined, which the system will use later for checking purposes. If any fields, combination of fields, or strings of data taken from fields are to be used as keys when retrieving these records later, you so indicate here. The records will be placed on the disk in time-of-arrival sequence in the space you cause to be created with the CRTPF command.

## 7.4. FILE CREATION AND CHANGE COMMANDS

Some commands you can use from your terminal to create files and, later on, to change their attributes are CRTPF (create a physical file based on predefined source statements in a library), CHGPF (change some attributes of a physical file), CRTSRCPF or CHGSRCPF (create or change the source statements from which a physical file was built), and ADDPFM or CHGPFM (add a dataset member or change one in a physical file). Some of the attributes you would likely change on a file are its expiration date, member size, and allocated amount of storage to house it.

## 7.5. LOGICAL FILES (DATA VIEWS)

Creating Logical Views through which to peruse and modify your data is similar to creating the physical files that actually house real data. You first must create source statements and put them into a library of your choosing, and then issue a Create File command to create the Logical File view. These Logical Files (Views) are merely very fancy indexes to the data. They differ from other database management system indexes in three substantial ways:

1. There are management programs tied to them that sort, select, and sift the data live, as you ask for it.
2. There are attribute definition tables tied to the indexes that provide parameters by which this programming can know which records to select for the user view and how to sequence the records for input or output presentation.
3. Each Logical File or View is a separate index, built according to the definition you gave it, which is updated live as data records belonging in the dataset enter the system or are deleted from it. It does not belong to a system-wide single index, which would imply massive overhead for the management of items 1 and 2 above. In addition, these indexes have already done the search of your data files before you ask for the data, because they are data-driven instead of request-driven (meaning they are updated as soon as a piece of data that affects them enters the system).

## 7.6. CREATING LOGICAL FILES

The source statements used to create a Logical File define RECORDS (names and attributes), and FIELDs within the records (names and attributes). They also define which of these records are to be shown to the user of this Logical File (View) when a program reads or gets this data or when a terminal user is looking at it through some interactive interface. There is total flexibility in designing the Logical View. For instance, if a name field in a physical file is actually 20 bytes long, but for the sake of fitting a foreign form a user wants it to be 35 bytes long, he can so define the name field in the Logical File (View). When the user inquires about people in this dataset the Database Manager routines will pad the name they present to the user with blanks to extend it to 35 bytes. The other way around, putting data into the physical database through this view, would cause the extra bytes to be truncated, unless you defined how the bytes were to be selected on input, in which case the DBM would follow your instructions per the Logical File specifications.

Let's say that a key-entry person is keying in an amount field to go into this named person's file. The screen format used today has been defined so that the inputter can key in up to 4 whole numbers and 2 decimal places ($n,nnn.dd). Should the key-entry person key in $12.34, the DBM will pad the entry to fill out the 4 bytes of whole numbers ($0,012.34), per the screen format definition (the so-called Screen File Description, another table you predefined).

Assume the Logical File through which your program is reading the data defined the amount field as 10 digits: 8 whole and 2 decimal places. The input data will now be padded further to fill out that definition of the amount field ($00,000,012.34). Also assume that the physical file into which the data is eventually deposited described the amount field as 12 digits. When the data is transferred to the hard file—the physical data file—it will be further padded to fill in the 12 digits.

Why would anyone ever want to define these representations of an amount field in mismatched ways like this? We have been trained for 30-odd years to make all computer fields in the program, on paper, and in the data files match exactly—not to do so would cause a program halt, an execution bug. Well, in a true data management system, your purpose is flexible use of the data for various client types to make the most of your data. In the case here, one group of invoice data-entry operators may be dealing with customer amounts from a small store that never exceed 4 digits. A field accommodating just enough space for the real data entry makes their key-entry job easier and their screen format more like the reality of what the store deals with every day. The screen "FILE" they use is designed to match their environment. On the other hand, the Logical File used to check the data and sift it and send it to the right physical files will likely also be used by other input and output operations, so it is built to be more general purpose, to accommodate 3 or 4 applications that use essentially the same data.

Of course, the physical file has to match reality, or at least accommodate it, so its definition must have an amount field large enough to cover all the client records it houses, some of which, in this example, will be coming from a different store from that being keyed in. The levels of flexibility (data editing) are the FILE DESCRIPTION, which defines formatting for the input or output device (not described in this chapter); the LOGICAL FILE, which picks and chooses bytes out of fields and fields out of records and records out of physical files according to parameters you define in the Logical File when you create it or, with CL change commands, when you run this job; and the physical file definition, which allows some flexibility in how data and records are to be presented to you. Notice that nowhere do I say exactly how the actual data will be housed on permanent disk. It will be packed up tightly in an unedited format you will never see.

Screen 7.1 is an example of a Logical File specification screen filled out by an operator. It defines what makes up a record type for this File (View) and from what physical files the data should be drawn to compose it.

Screen 7.2 is an example of a Customer Record definition for

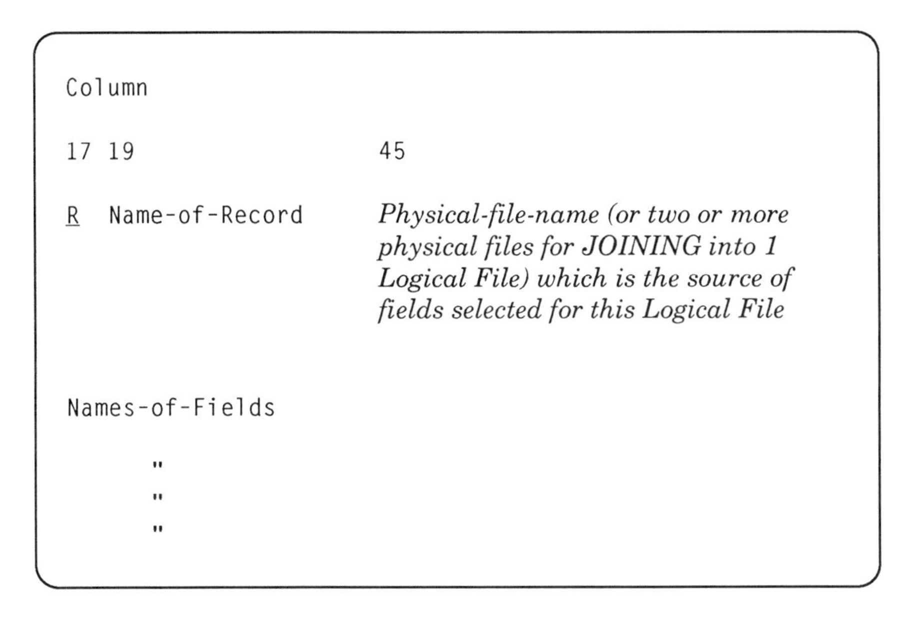

```
Column

17 19                    45

R  Name-of-Record        Physical-file-name (or two or more
                         physical files for JOINING into 1
                         Logical File) which is the source of
                         fields selected for this Logical File


Names-of-Fields
     "
     "
     "
```

**Screen 7.1.** Logical File specification.

```
Column

17  19                         45

R  Customer                     PFILE(Cust-Accts)

   Name                        (these field definitions will take
                               fields from the Physical File named
   Street                      but will redefine their attributes)

   City

   Amount-due

   Amount-overdue

   Date-last-pay

   Credit-class
```

**Screen 7.2.** Customer Record definition.

a Logical File. For each field in the Logical File definition you may change (from the physical file) the field name (necessary to accommodate older languages); the field sequence within a record; and the length of the field within a record. You may also:

- Translate a field based on a specified table or from one numeric form to another, for example, to floating point.
- Concatenate one field with others to make a new field (Month-Day-Year may be defined as 3 fields in your physical file so that you may resequence them for European reports to Day-Month-Year, or you may select or sequence records based on month or year with ease).
- Scan for certain characters in a field before including this record in this View.

- Test a field for bit values or a constant or logical values or ranges of values, or test it against a list of up to 100 specified values before including this record in this View.
- Omit a field from this rendition of the record.
- Omit or keep this record based on tests made against this field (Logical bit tests, arithmetic tests, or data value tests against a constant or a string of data values supplied (up to 100).
- Omit or keep this record based on logical equality or lesser or greater comparisons to specified values.
- Omit or keep this record based on a field being in certain value ranges.

Text data for each field can be defined in this View, which will be used by Query and other programs for column headings or as comments on the screen for ad hoc quick reports or inquiries.

You can see that in simple data presentation and gathering there is tremendous flexibility in how you make the system address the user, whether that user is a key-entry person, a programmer, a user of 4GL (Fourth Generation Language), or any interactive package user. The ease of use producible here, the customization for different "people" types, is easy to get or change (as people learn or functions change), and it can be subtle. This customization comes in at a level below the programming and thus is available even with prepackaged applications. In fact, it facilitates the use of prepackaged applications because it can modify your data to fit any rules the package demands.

The reason there are so many programming languages available on the AS/400 is that, through views, labels and names that may have been defined as 10 or 12 bytes long can be renamed at 6 bytes to match old programming languages such as RPG and COBOL, and the variations in math capabilities of the languages can be met as well. If you have ever converted from one system architecture to another, you know the value of this capability. And you can understand how easy it was to write conversion programs for this system to allow it to handle COBOL programs from any previously available system. Simply use table definitions of the differences.

Another nicety of the Logical View is that you can create a special view for the casual user that simplifies keystrokes or shields him from extra fields or comments. One viewer might want a quick request for names and telephone numbers answered without having to see the entire record of each person to be called. Perhaps he only wants the names and numbers of customers within a certain area code or of houses for sale within a certain neighborhood he is going to be in this afternoon. Another user might be a key-entry person who is paid by the item, who does not want to spend time keying leading zeroes or reading extra script on the screen, but wants as few fields as possible for quick display, quick key entry, and quick screen clearance and turnaround. That is a very different screen from the one for the casual user, who may need lots of text for prompting information and who may want to browse the entire record, looking at all the fields.

## 7.7. DATA ACCESS PATH RECORD SELECTION

The "Access Path," the order in which records will be fed to you in a program or on a screen, is figured out by the system *after* all these physical-to-logical conversions have taken place—that is, it is based on the *Logical* View, with its concatenated fields, its substrings of fields, its data and mathematical conversions of fields, and so forth. To ensure good real-time performance, this updating of your Access Paths is done as the data record enters the system, not as you retrieve the records. Note that you have the option to forestall this updating of Access Paths to OPEN file time or CLOSE file time, but I would not recommend this option because of the inherent threat to the integrity of shared data (one user may see the update before another).

There is something else I must warn you away from for performance reasons. This is the "dynamic" option for selection and omission of records based on field content, which means that the system will not analyze all data at input time to determine whether or not a record belongs in your Logical File's Access Path; instead, this analysis will happen during your inquiry, at read data time, and all of these keys will be kept in your Access Path all the time, not just the subset your selection criteria determine you need. There are two performance hits here: The size of the Access Path will be much larger (essentially covering the entire file from which the data is taken), and each inquiry will have to wait while the selection tests are performed, instead of having the subset of selected data all ready to just read, as is normal on this system. This is a slipup that database people trained on older systems might make. Although they may wish to "own" the data in this way, it violates the concept of the database machine as a shared resource and an up-to-the-minute-valid data supplier.

The only reason I can think of for violating the natural arrival-time updating of Access Paths is if you need a comparative set of statistics based on time. For example, you may do a daily 3 P.M. report on the stock market statistics, and, while you are running your report program, the after-hours trades may still be coming in. You may want to freeze the statistics as of 3 P.M., in which case, just before query time, you can use the delay option for update, one of the possible parameters in your Logical File definition, to halt the live updating of the Logical Files to be queried today. Issue an override command to change back to arrival time updating again immediately after your report.

### 7.7.1. Record Omission from Your Data Access Paths

While an access path will retrieve records selected for your Logical View based on user-defined field content, it will also *omit* records from the dataset you see based on field checks you define to the Logical View. You will not see these omitted records in your program or on your screen when retrieving data through this particular Logical View (FILE). If on another day you wish to see these omitted records, you will have to define another Logical View, give it the same name, and put it in an earlier member of the library which your program uses (ahead of this Logical File's position). Then, when running your program, the system will engage the other Logical View when you get your records and hand them to you based on the parameters you defined in this second View.

When I speak of field content, I mean that your View may state that you only want to see records where the amount field is greater than 10,000, or only those records whose amount fields show numbers between *x* and *y*. Perhaps you want to see the dataset in which the customer's balance due is over 90 days and is also over $1000 and her credit limit is over $5000. Or you may ask to see those records that have had more than five transactions this month but have not paid on their bills for over 30 days. Any combination of field analysis can be used to define the dataset that comprises a Logical View. Moreover, if a View does not exist that suits you, you can compose one interactively for an ad hoc run. Rather than do this yourself, however, you could use one of the inquiry-report tools available, such as AS/400 Query or AS/400 SQL. When using these interactive inquiry tools, the system will build the Access Path live, based upon the selection criteria you supply in the inquiry. This takes build time, but allows you to follow your original inquiry, then immediately follow it with another one based on data retrieved from the first, reiteratively following the lead of the data.

This kind of free-for-all data inquiry is very nice, but it consumes machine cycles. If you open up your system to users who need this ad hoc function, it is advisable to coach them on how to pare down the response data to the most usable, minimal amount through good winnowing procedures in the inquiries. (Design your selection criteria for the inquiries so that they return the smallest of subsets of data first, adding refinements to the inquiry against this subset next. If you have a mathematician in your shop, ask his or her help in defining which parameters to choose in what sequence.)

Some system managers use an inquiry center concept, whereby the end users call in their requests, or submit them on paper, to be entered by more system-oriented specialists. This has two advantages: One, it cuts down markedly on playing with the data, which can consume a lot of the system's and the end user's time, and, two, the centralized person sees many and varied inquiries, and can customize some Logical Views to be kept up to date by the system, substantially shortening the turnaround time for the actual inquiries and saving many machine cycles for other uses. This person also will notice if inquiries are in general slowing down, which can happen when users get careless about creating many Logical Views (to be kept up by the system all the time) and forget to erase the older unused ones. Once in a while the specialist can "clean up" the system, removing old, unwanted, or rarely used Views from maintenance.

Fields used for record selection may also be compared to one another, to an abstract value, or to a constant you supply in the View. The field used for record selection does not have to be part of the retrieved data. For instance, you could have your accounting firm retrieve records wherein the customer's credit rating is over $20,000, but the only data the accountant would see would be the name, address, and amount due, or whatever fields you want him to analyze.

During retrieval, all records that pass the selection tests will be fed to you. On input, all updates, regardless of selection criteria and regardless of where they came from (your program got them, or anyone else on the system brought them in), will be added to the physical files, but only those that pass the selection criteria will be added to the Access Path for your particular Logical View (and any other Views for which they qualify).

You may have an entire series of tests on which the DBM will base its selection and omission of records for your logical dataset. This code becomes part of your Access Path, belonging to your View. It is outside your program and will be used for all system users who have common needs, instead of being repeated in every user program application that needs to see this data (which is one reason the AS/400 can give good performance for such rich data management function).

## 7.8. RECORD SCANNING

For casual or ad hoc data scanning, there are commands you can issue in CL, from your terminal, that will hook you up with a Logical View and allow browsing of the selected records. Views can be set up with so-called "subfiles" that make this browsing function even fuller; by hitting paging keys on your terminal keyboard you can scan whole screens' worth of records up and down, back and forth, in an instant. This is a good discipline for people who do a lot of Query or SQL inquiries. The scan will give you some ideas of what kind of inquiry to make in order to get a more efficient and useful reply.

No setup is needed for the Browse function, and there is a simple command to let you browse the Logical Views themselves, to see which one you would like to work through. Three or four

CL commands are available to the terminal user that I would teach to all my interactive users. They are fully prompted and extremely easy to use.

Record selection for Views can also be made on the basis of comparison of a data field (or certain characters in one) to a list of up to 100 constants of your choice (specified in the View). You could use this facility for data-entry operator checks: for instance, to catch data-entry input as it is being entered into the system. It is much more valuable to ensure perfect data *as it arrives* than to have to correct imperfect data later on and not to know where it came from or to have it processed incorrectly.

To cause the data management system to check your data-entry input for proper state codes, the system will prompt you to fill in a spec sheet like Screen 7.3.

This kind of selection criteria can be used for two things: to subset a data file to that dataset wherein the Statecode field is one that you specify here; and to test input at key-entry time by defining it in your DEVICE FILE (description) table. You can also add another selection, which the DMS will use to further sift the data into a finer subset.

Much program logic can be pushed over to these LOGICAL FILE views, as you can see. When thinking about the system time it takes to do this data checking, remember that data check-

```
Example:    S stands for SELECTION criteria and Statecode is
            the name you supplied for the data field:
Column



17   19                                 45

S    Statecode                          VALUES(AL AR...WA WI)
```

**Screen 7.3.** Sample spec sheet set up to check Statecode values AL to WI.

ing used to be left up to all programmers, some of whom did not know much about optimizing sort routines. Also, a programmer had to call each record from disk to do the check, whereas the AS/400 does it on input and then puts the pointer to the selected record in your Access Path, to be retrieved most often by a single read for the entire FILE. Logical View time is almost always a better deal for you than having longer user programs to sort things out. Users reading every record in the physical file, selecting reiteratively on field content to find the records for update or output, cannot be expected to:

1. Maximize the sorting algorithms for the selection criteria.
2. Maximize the disk-reading formulae.
3. Expertly lock and unlock the records or files based on system regulations while still being efficient about the reads.
4. Know how to make all this code and data sharable with other user types.

If you have a programmer who will do these things, you are probably paying far too much for data manipulation programs; also, he is probably not the person who knows the most about the uses of the business data and therefore is not likely to optimize retrieval in favor of the business dollar value of data itself. Programs to retrieve data will have too long a turnaround time in development because of the encumbrances of the sophisticated programming and program testing required when each program acts like a data management system program. Some data management programmers are comfortable with this older approach because they grew up with it, but they are both too expensive and too inflexible to help your system keep pace with the data-handling needs of fast business growth. These programmers could be extremely valuable in another area: data design.

There is one note to add about the system's management of the Access Paths tied to LOGICAL FILES (Views). They are updated all the time, whether or not you and your program that uses them are running on the system. In fact, when using an inquiry tool like AS/400 Query or SQL, you may see two versions of a record in flight in one set of output. As your query is building the output stream the data could have been updated by another system user and the record could be picked up by a later criteria check based on the update, thus appearing twice. If this is a potential problem, you should use the FILE option, which "freezes" updates until your query operation is done. This can be accomplished via a File Override command at run time.

Appendix D contains all the data selection and checking criteria for sifting out and subsetting your data before sending it to a program or screen. These criteria can also be used for omitting records from your View. Multiple selection tests can be used, which the system will apply in the sequence you code them on the View or FILE specification in your DDS statements. If a record fails a selection test or falls prey to an omission test, it will be dropped from further testing. It is good logic to place omission statements ahead of selection tests in order to drop entire categories of records from further testing (and in so doing save system time).

There is another important trifle of logic in the selection/omission statements. If you put an S or O in column 17 on each criterion listed, the system will apply all the tests to every record in the FILE(s) you are basing your View upon, whereas if you put an S in column 17 on the first criterion check and then leave that column blank in further DDS checking statements, the system will do a series of tests that must all be met before selection will take place. (You may use the omission O in one statement followed by blanks in the same manner.)

With some thought, you can make your selection criteria become extremely sophisticated using these two simple DDS "fill-in-the-blanks" statement types to sift out your datasets. The statisticians of the world can get more out of this basic system function than they can out of most statistical analysis programming packages on the market today. Some well defined logical Views, combined with use of the Browse and Print commands, will replace a lot of expensive packages and are, of course, infinitely changeable.

As those of you who work with data statistics know, once you have narrowed down to a particular subset of data, a need arises to pull out another and another, because one set of numbers inspires a whole new selection path. This kind of reiterative selection is cumbersome on older systems and a piece of cake on this one.

In summary, this is how the Data Manager works: It keeps

an index of pointers to every record that meets your selection criteria, all the time. If some other user updates (changes) a data field upon which your selection is based, he is changing the real physical data, and your View (Access Path) will reflect this change, even though you are not on the system. The record will be struck from your Access Path and View if the field no longer meets your selection criteria. Should you not want to keep these Views current (matching actual physical database changes all day long), you must so specify in your View definition. Other options are to have the system do delayed updating of your View at the beginning or at the ending of your run.

The reason you might restrict updating your Views to OPEN or CLOSE FILE time is to improve the inquiry performance in between. However, other system users will pay for your performance increase by sharing the load while your OPEN and/or CLOSE are doing the updating of your Access Path pointers to your data. This tradeoff will have to be discussed, or, better yet, the different updating methods should be tried out on active days to see which one serves your total system better. If you do decide to allow the application itself to control when the updating of your Views (and Access Paths) will take place, a valuable command is the OPEN QUERY command, a CL command that can be used by anybody, even before a batch job. This command causes the LOGICAL Files named to have their Access Paths immediately updated (at OPEN time). You can precede any exercise with this command to ensure that your data is up to the minute and that you will not have to wait for the updates to be made when searching for your data.

*Beware*, however. OPNQRYF also causes your Logical View to be *deleted* the moment the next CLOSE to that file occurs, which means you will be recreating the entire Access Path from scratch every time you run this program. This is a tradeoff that I would definitely measure in real time and check out every six months or so. I know of an organization that issues a series of these commands to cover all the files that are to be used each morning and afternoon, just to speed up the actual inquiries and data runs that will be made at those times. The assumption here is that the one run against this data is all there will be today. This kind of well-scheduled system usage planned around data usage may work if all the various data users communicate with one another about what they actually do on the system; however, such communication is rare in my experience.

There is a CL command you can issue from your terminal that will show you all the shared Access Path relationships on the system. If there are more than a few shared Access Paths, do not, in your LOGICAL FILE definitions or by using OPNQRYF or FILE override statements at run time, stop the system from updating Access Paths in flight as it is wont to do. The command is: Display Database Relations, DSPDBR.

Remember as you read: Regardless of the method you choose to get your data at hand, you can access all the data on the AS/400 system. All programs and commands that store or retrieve data on the system use its integrated database management system. Thus, when you use the database to store data from one program, it can be retrieved and used by a completely different program at any time. It goes both ways, too. You could retrieve records, let's say via SQL or the QUERY interface, and write the resultant subset of data to a new file or, down a line, to a PC to be used as a daily working dataset; you could later run a COBOL or PL/I program against the new subset just as if it were the entire database. Alternatively, you could run the AS/400 Business Graphics utility program against the data subset (which is just another file) to produce a chart on the PC or to merge this dataset with others.

Notice that the various interfaces to the datasets and database are standard and interchangeable. You can go back and forth in any direction on any dataset in the system, alternately working on the data as input, then as output, with one interface and then another. Suit the "languages" to the user types. Compare this to database systems of today where you have to use Txx if you want to manipulate the data one way or even from a certain hardware terminal, Mxx if you want to save the output data, Cxxx if you want single record search capability, and so forth, and each interface has to "own" its own dataset, which is not to be tampered with via any other interface. Such systems create users who are married to their interface tools, who can only do with the data the limited function their interface was programmed to do originally, who become experts with this interface mechanism (and are therefore highly paid) upon whom you depend, and who cannot share their data with other users who want to use new and different interactive packages as the world turns. In this way your wonderful MIS system atrophies.

In the AS/400 the common microcoded data management operating system, which is shared by any and all code running on the system, does the data management work *before* the data reaches user packages or code, and feeds the final subset of data to be operated on to the program or screen. It thus solves the Medusa's head interface problem of current systems with their added database packages.

## 7.9. RELATIONAL JOIN AND OTHER COMPLEX LOGICAL FILE VIEWS

A JOIN LOGICAL FILE (View) is a Logical View that brings fields from more than one physical file (record type) or tuple type together into one record definition. The merging is done based upon a match of data found in both (or all ) of the substantiating physical record types. If, for instance, at the end of a billing period, you want to match customer charge sales to customer name and address records, these two different files could be matched on customer number. You could then ask the system in the JOINed Logical View to take any of the fields you need out of both of these singular record types to form a new record type, the JOINed one, which merges, say, all the invoices from this month's billings with the current customer name and address. Your billing program or report generator will see a newly defined record comprising only the fields you selected from as many record types as you matched via some data field. The match field does not have to be part of the new record.

The advantages of breaking your data down into these natural entities and recombining them using Logical Views are many. Paramount is that the data that lives as an entity—the fields that are born and die together, like each invoice that comes in as a complete entity, having its own timely origin and demise—can be housed with like data and can be used in various combinations or alone for data analysis. In fact, when the data dies (next month when a new supply arrives) it can be kept as an archival dataset for historical analysis of the business.

Muddying up data by merging permanent data (master records) with transient data (transactions), as we did for the last 30 years, caused us to throw away the history of our business as we "updated" the master files and then threw away the transactions that were used to do the update. By keeping the transactions in a file of their own, you can later merge their needed data fields in a higher-level View with other data to amplify a report or other data input via JOINed LOGICAL FILES. (Remember, these are only pointers, not actual duplicate data.) A wider, more flexible use of the data will ensue. It also allows great flexibility in ways to look at data. Who is to say that one day you may not want to know how many of your employees (personnel files) have purchased one of your products (billing files) or some other data combination you did not plan for when you first set up your system?

One thing to note: To keep the JOINed files clean of duplicate records that could cause questionable output later, you should ensure unique keys—that is, only one copy of the data in the key field per underlying physical file—by specifying the "unique" parameter when defining the original physical files underneath. If this has not been done, there are parameters you can define in the Logical File that will sequence the access of "identical key" records in ways to prevent you from having processing problems because of them. Even so, it is cleaner to have unique keys, which the system will check for during processing if you so indicate.

Another way to merge records in Logical Views is to define more than one record type per View. This can be cumbersome to process because your program will have to be aware that the record format changes when you get the second or subsequent record format type during processing. However, it is made to order for some hierarchical database systems that you may be emulating in single application systems—a machine parts implosion system, perhaps, in which each part is part of a subassembly, which is part of a unit, which is part of a product.

This multiple-record-format Logical File (View) can let you store the lowest-level component parts as physical records, then gather groups of them together as required for defined subassemblies, which will be the logical level. A subassembly record will have a different layout and some different fields from the actual parts records, which can be listed behind each assembly to which they belong. All the subassemblies, trailing their parts lists, form one Logical View, which makes for fast processing. Meanwhile, the individual component parts can be managed (reordered when the quantity falls below certain levels, for example) through a different Logical View designed for that parts management process, independent from the product process for which you designed the multiple-record-format Logical View.

I cannot go into relational database theory here, but you are well advised to read the simplest book you can find on it before designing your AS/400 database. This is a totally relationally managed system, which additionally allows you to define Views over the data that can mimic nonrelational database systems, for compatibility or unique processing needs. However, to do an efficient and clean job of the latter requires an understanding of the former, because of the way the system works.

Note that in JOINed data-views you can still use all the available selection and omission criteria in addition to the JOIN option, as well as such parameters as RENAME, CONCAT (concatenate this field with another), SST (the starting position in the physical field from which to take the data and how many bytes to pick up), TRNTBL (the name of a translation table the system is to use to translate this field), and the special JOIN parameters JDFTVAL, JDUPSEQ, JFLD, and JREF, which, respectively, provide default values if the JOIN finds no match for its primary physical record, use alternate sequencing fields if primary keys are matched by duplicate secondary ones, identify the fields to match to do the JOIN, and identify an alternate file from which to get a name for a field if two physical underlying record types have the same field names in them. These parameters allow you to get around some of the processing complications that other relational systems may cause.

## 7.10. SOURCE FILES

An AS/400 SOURCE FILE is a dataset with a special purpose: It is the strictly defined input for a system CREATE function, which composes AS/400 objects. On older systems there was a similar COMPILE function which also used strictly defined SOURCE statements from a library or from an input stream behind a system-supplied compiler program. It was used to create user programs written in various programming languages.

Compilers translated the programming language statements, which were fed to the compiler as input statements, into machine language instructions. Sometimes the compilations took two or three iterations because the difference between the user's language and the hardware instruction set was so vast. For this reason some language compilers were known as "High Level Languages." Of course, they were not very high, since the user was expected to know the physical methodology of the machine and had to program toward it. This was because, when the older systems were developed, no one foresaw the explosion of system usage and programming that would take place from the 1960s through the 1990s. Now most large system users are bogged down in programming maintenance, adding a new application only once in a while (for want of programming productivity). Because the only objects that changed were the programs, those older systems demanded that programs exactly match the hardware or they would not run.

The AS/400 creates self-contained objects, objects that within themselves define what they are, where they belong, how they should be used, and by whom. Objects can be inserted between two other objects, changing the relationships between them. For this reason you are given the ability to create objects, using source statements as input to the CREATE command, not only when originally setting up your system but throughout the life of the organization.

This ability to add and change objects, to insert new ones between two older ones, or to replace or update older ones, without changing other objects in the relationship, is what allows this system to be defined at first minimally, as a starter system, and then to grow as the business and its data grow, without its layouts, structure, database, programs, or interactive interfaces ever having to be redesigned. Like life itself, you just move along, phasing out one set of interfaces while adding two new ones. Data type additions are just that: new types, defined as new physical datasets, with new Logical Views placed on top of them that may combine the old with the new and later drop the old. The data growth may also be down line. That is, additional data may emerge at personal computer sites or at other AS/400 sites, which will be "added" to your system via DDM files (distributed data management file definitions in your database).

### 7.10.1. SOURCE File Usage

In past systems you once coded source statements for your COBOL or FORTRAN program and then, using a key punch machine, punched up the machine code for the letters and numbers in the statements, and then fed the cards as input into a run of a COBOL or FORTRAN compiler program. Later, interactive programming interfaces were developed that allowed you to sit at a terminal and type in your source statements, which would be parsed, checked for certain logic (not much), and translated into machine instructions, which were called an object program. These object programs would then be put into a system object library to be ready to be called back into the system and run as active programs later on. They could then be run over and over again, until some parameter of the system changed (a new disk, more memory, another terminal, a new data type, or whatever). At that time, the source statements had to be rewritten, recompiled and checked out, and finally retested. Then they replaced the old object programs in the system library. There was absolutely no system or data independence. The object programs were not really "object" programs at all, just machine language programs directly translated from somewhat higher-level source statements.

On the AS/400 other objects, not just programs, must be defined in source files and then "created" into system objects, ready for live use. Among the objects that require SOURCE are:

- Logical FILES (you supply source)
- Intersystems communications FILES
- CL commands (source is supplied by the system; and, you may create new ones)
- Translate tables (the system supplies some; you may supply others)
- Physical FILES (you supply source)
- Display FILEs (some are supplied)
- Printer FILEs (one is supplied; you may supply others)
- Assorted Job Description and Job Flow control objects

Because these datasets (source files) are not actually data to be manipulated by your programs and handled in relations, they can be inside or outside the library system. They can come into the system live (in-line) just behind the CREATE command that will process them, or they can come in as a batch, from tape, diskette, disk data files, or a remote system, and then fed to the CREATE "program" as input data. I would save all the source statements used to create the system control blocks and file definitions in libraries so that they can be updated, or used as source with some adjustment, for other function later. Naturally, it would be a good idea to have someone who understands what the system is doing, clean up these files once in a while to recover some disk space.

As files, the source statements are regular members of a database file, but there are special commands you can use to work with and on them. You can change the statements temporarily for a single job run if you like, leaving the original alone, "creating" their objects just before a program run. With CL OVERRIDE commands you can override certain parameters of the created objects *after* they are compiled but before they are actually used in program execution. You can create many objects from the same source statement set, adding and changing parameters during the Create phase. Some of this flexibility can save space, time, and frustration for the programmers and system users.

Of course, all of this function is heftily prompted from the user's terminal screen. You do not need to be an expert. You are only creating objects, not modifying running code, so you can redo as many times as you like. Also remember that the system will not execute work on an incorrect object. It checks at run time to be sure that the object is correct and that the user has proper security clearance to use it and do what he is trying to do. Screen 7.4 shows the format of an AS/400 source statement (92 bytes—two 6-byte zoned decimal fields plus an 80-byte data field). You can use the Source Entry Utility (SEU) to create these Data Definition Statements (DDS) and to enter them into a library in the system. Then you use CL commands, such as the CRTSRCPF (Create physical file source statements) or CRTLF (Create a logical file from source in a library) to create the actual system objects. CL programs from source statements are shown in the table below.

```
|---6---|---6---|---------------------80---------------|

\\      \\      \\

 xxxx.xx |yyyy.yy     SOURCE STATEMENT

 Sequence|Date of
 Number  |Last Update
```

**Screen 7.4.** Source statement example.

| **Put in Library by User** | | **Entered Interactively by User** | | **Managed by Systems DMS** |
|---|---|---|---|---|
| SOURCE statements | + | CREATE CL command | = | SYSTEM OBJECT |

You can create program objects from a string of CL commands as well as use these commands interactively. Here is how:

1. Using SEU, enter a sequence of CL commands in the order you want them to execute. Put them in your library or the system source library.
2. Interactively enter the CL command CRTCLPGM, naming the library and the file of source statements you created. Alternatively, run a batch job starting with the CRT CL command followed by your sequence of commands for the program:

```
//BCHJOB
CRTLF  FILE(CLlib/progl)  SRCFILE(mine)  //DATAFILE(mine) FILETYPE(*SRC)
source statement1  (CL command)
source statement2  (CL command)
etc.                 "
//
//ENDBCHJOB
```

In this way you can create setup and control jobs with which you can run your entire system, should you desire to automate the entire process. There is even a special command to power down the system at the end of the day.

# 8

# Security

## 8.1. WHAT IS SECURITY?

Because of the object orientation of the AS/400, you can use as much or as little security as your situation warrants. By security I mean control of access to the system: to its component parts, function, paths, and data and to their usage. Every function, every piece of data, every piece of code or user interface in the AS/400, is represented to the system by an object. For example, data is represented by many sifting levels of tabular control blocks, each of which is an object and individually controllable. From the bottom up, for data, you have physical FIELDS, RECORDS, and FILES, as well as LOGICAL FIELDS, RECORDS, MEMBERS of FILES, FILES, LIBRARIES, LIBRARY LISTS, Reference tables, and Dictionaries.

Security is based upon giving authorization to use an object, and thus allowing someone to use the control blocks that lead to the data. These control blocks can be descriptions of pathways, or descriptions of the items themselves. Authority to use the control blocks and the object itself is "granted" to user types or to individual users. It can be of various kinds, based on degree and type of use you determine. The security is unbreachable because it is not a layer added on top of an interface, which, after being unlocked provides complete system access. Rather, it is a check built into every step the system takes for you (once again, with this system you only *request* work to be done for you, you do not actually do it yourself). It is built into both the hardware and the software and it has to do with function, location, user type, and type of use. At one extreme there are hardware instructions that can never be used by external users; at the other, each user who signs onto the system is assigned 16MB of machine-protected memory (address space), which is private, under exclusive control of this user, and inaccessible by anyone else. In between there are many options, some of which I will explain here.

## 8.2. SECURITY OF ACCESS ON OLDER SYSTEMS VERSUS ON THE AS/400

Users of the AS/400 do not concern themselves with the addressing structures of main or secondary storage. Nor do they need to be aware of multiple levels of storage because all of it is allocated and managed by the hardware. In other words, it makes no difference to the user or to the machine instructions where an object (or part of it) is actually located. The entire address space (over 281 trillion bytes) consists of objects that are addressable only by any system pointers. The user is completely shielded from addressing dependencies within the system, including I/O device, channel, and communications protocols.

Perhaps you are familiar with prior systems' access methods (BTAM, QTAM, TCAM, VTAM, DAM, SAM, ISAM, CICS, IMS, and all their outgrowths on IBM systems, as well as similarly huge amounts of I/O control programming on other systems). If so, you know what it is like having to know how all this code worked, having to live within its design constraints (only getting data the way the access methods prescribed over thirty years ago), having to ensure that all of these packages of code dwelt happily with one another. Worst of all (but almost unaddressed because the access method world was so complicated), is that these access methods experts could easily breach any security system that was laid on top. There are thousands of these specialists and thousands of systems using the exact same layered access methods, which assures us of virtually no security in our current systems worldwide. Once the sign-on lock has been picked, the system is wide open in most of today's systems.

## 8.3. SECURITY ON THE AS/400

On the AS/400 all information is stored in objects. Access to that information is through hardware instructions that ensure object integrity. Any attempt to misuse an object is detected, causing the system to terminate the instruction and signal an exception condition. This gives you system integrity (it is impossible to do math to a program instruction or to branch to a storage area or outside your own designated program space) as well as security checks on who is doing what to whom.

Authorization capabilities are enhanced by the AS/400's object oriented architecture, too. Each user is identified by a user profile, which is itself an object, and objects within the system are owned by a user profile. The owner of the profile that owns (created or was given ownership to) the object may delegate certain authorities to his or her object (or objects) to other user profiles, permanently or temporarily. User profiles refer to programs, menus, job descriptions, message queues, and output spool queues. Processes (multithreaded program strings) execute under the control of a specific user profile, in the name of this user, and functions executed within the process verify that the referenced objects are properly authorized to this user. This happens *each and every time of execution*, at every step along the execution route, not just once at sign-on time.

## 8.4. OPERATING ENVIRONMENTS

The AS/400 system assumes you will have different functional environments—that is, interest in work in which transaction turnaround time is to be minimized, as well as work in which ease of operator use is more important and which requires much menu prompting, input data checking, and system warning messages.

The system resources are used (and managed) through subsystems, a concept of controlling a running environment. Three general subsystems are supplied to you in your delivered system: Batch, Interactive, and Spool control systems. They are ready to use, and (some people never add to, change, or create new ones), you can easily do so using CL. The supplied system gives you an Autostart environment to help you get started. You can use it forever if it suits you (as is often the case); or, through prompting, you can very easily add new subsystems and change how the system starts and what it allows the users to do. This system setup can be controlled from terminals, interactively, or from batch jobs on the job queues (or kept on disk as system input). Each of your environments will be designed with its own appropriate security system.

## 8.5. HIERARCHY OF OBJECT CONTROL

The hierarchy of object control is as follows:

- SYSTEM
  - SUBSYSTEMS—predefined, concurrently running operating environments, each defined by a "subsystem description" object (use CRT SBSD command).
    INTERACTIVE—as many as you need.
    BATCH (or BOTH)—as many as needed to invoke a string of jobs from a particular queue.
    SPOOLERS—as many as needed to control various output formatting methods on all your devices and remote systems, or for billing purposes.
  - ROUTING STEPS—programs that select, call programs for a job, and apply environment rules.
    JOBS—a series of programs/steps reflecting one logical use of the system, which operate within one subsystem as defined by the job description object.
      A SET of CL COMMANDS
      A PROGRAM
      AN APPLICATION comprising a set of programs

Jobs are not limited to certain data or system function by the subsystem within which they run. The subsystem is a set of rules that create the job's running environment. The hierarchical levels of control above can each be used as levels and types of security control simply by attaching particular authorities for particular users to each of the object description blocks, which the system uses when it accesses each object. The CREATE and OVERRIDE CL commands give you parameters to do this. (Appendix A contains a partial system objects list.)

You define each of the levels of system and program control. The definitions themselves are objects. At the system level, the so-called System Values Table represents the system. At the subsystem level (which you create with a CL command) the object is the Subsystem Description. At the job level, it is the Job Description, which points to a routing step. The environment for the program steps called by a routing step (what storage pools to use, which pieces of code to exercise, where the job should be invoked from, how many concurrent transactions will share this storage space and code) are defined in a class entry within the routing entry.

You decide what you want to allow a user or a set of users to do on the system. Then you design a subsystem especially for them, putting security authorization on the basic control blocks (the Job Description at least) and, I suggest, on the I/O spool queues and hardware control blocks (Device Descriptions) and the particular data, as deeply as you need to. Be aware that every security check you ask for will occur not just once per user but every time a transaction goes through the gate on which you put authorization control. This causes system overhead. Security is always a tradeoff, but on the AS/400 you can get complete, many-leveled security on some uses of the system without closing up the entire system for other, more casual usage. This is not available on any other system that I know of.

## 8.6. THE APPLICATION PROGRAMMER'S VIEW OF THE SYSTEM

It is assumed that the application programmer sits at a terminal somewhere distant from the CPU. From the terminal he or she:

- Enters source program steps into a dataset in the database.
- Requests, runs, and tests compilations of these steps in a *safe*

environment, that is, a subsystem that cannot actually change live database data or system function but mimics database updates and runs concurrently with other ongoing system processes.
- Debugs, on-line, using system-provided trap and debug facilities.
- Saves/restores the application and data objects at significant checkpoints using CL.

All these functions are menu-driven, prompted, messaged, and logged by the operating system for the programmer's edification and history. You design security control within these "usage" structural levels. Like all operator function, these programmer functions are available from any terminal. The sign-on profile determines what "system" the user sees. The profile can cause the system to show the user one specific application immediately, or it can be defined such that the programmer gets a menu of choices from which to pick an application. This start-up option is the beginning of your user security.

Programs invoked by a terminal user's sign-on and data entry, considered interactive, are run right out of their libraries (remember, a library is just a set of pointers). After defining the correct start-up option and programs for this user (or group of users) in the user profile that he must come in through, you should then follow the path of the user's application and grant authority to the library where the program resides as well as the library member that contains the data to be worked on. Both the path and the actual objects used will be authorized for this user, and in only the usage level you designate.

## 8.7. BATCH JOBS

Batch jobs will be run by the system based on the priorities you assign them and the fact that they are ready to run (the required resources are available). The system will pick off as many batch jobs to run as you specify for this subsystem's storage pool maximum activity level (MAXACT). You should be just as security-conscious about these batch jobs as you are about interactive ones. The batch job is like an internal user, which does run under a profile, albeit a system-supplied one. You should examine the path of the batch job, too, and explicitly authorize its profile—usually the system start-up (operator's) profile—to use the libraries, files, paths, and queues it needs and no others, including the explicitly defined level of dataset use.

There is a Job Description object for each and every job, which is where you will find the pointers to the objects you will want to secure. The description object itself is the starting point. Make sure only the operator, or whoever it is you want to start up the batch work queues, has authorization to these description objects. Batch programs are compiled as a sequence of requests to the system for work, are given a priority to run, and are placed by priority on a job queue (all this information is in the description object) by the input reader-spooler through which the run request came into the system. When these jobs are initiated by CL commands from a system operator (through his special operator profile) or by a CL running program issuing the commands, they are pulled off the job queues and started in ones, twos, or batches determined by the "activity" level you designed into the batch subsystems you are now using to run them.

Your security definitions for a set of batch jobs that will concurrently share the same storage pools and subsystems should match. That is, all the objects these jobs will address should be authorized ahead of time, and if two or more batch jobs use the same data or other object, the sharing level should also be predefined, such that no batch job is disallowed to run because it became eligible to run too soon or alongside the wrong program.

## 8.8. THE SEQUENCE OF STARTING A JOB

The list following presents the general sequence used by the system to start a job, which you should keep in mind when designing your security usage.

1. The Terminal user, or operator if batch, signs-on.
2. A "Work Station" Entry object for this terminal has the "start-up" Job Description pointer.
3. The Job Description contains Routing Data that points to a "Routing Entry" in the Subsystem Description object you will

use (it is actually in a "Routing Table" in the Subsystem Description).

4. The Routing Entry names the control program that will run and control this job (for interactive jobs, usually the command processor for CL).
5. This job (the CL command processor or one you wrote) will call your job and do all the subsystem setup for it.

By following the logic of job initiation, you can secure the system resources against improper usage as well as ensure the user of proper paths through the system.

## 8.9. OBJECT SECURITY CONTROL AND DATA USAGE LEVEL CONTROL

The AS/400 system has three kinds of object security control and three qualities of data usage. You define mixes and matches of these six to precisely define how an individual user or type of user or group of users is to see the system and/or manipulate it and its data. The terms used by the AS/400 literature are as follows:

- Object security:
  - Managerial—to control access to and availability of objects
  - Existence—to control ownership and creation/deletion of objects
  - Operational—to use objects and data
- Data usage level is also further controlled, to allow the authorized user to:
  - Read only—user can only look at, not change, this data
  - Read and update—user can look at, modify, and/or add to this data
  - Read and delete—user can look at and delete this data

In addition, certain commands in the system are privileged, which means that a user must be granted specific permission (authority) in his or her profile to use each of them. Some of these special commands are "Create and/or modify user profiles," "Modify resource management controls," "Create and modify network, controller, and other such descriptor objects," "Terminate machine processing (a command)," and "Initiate a process." This is a functional type of control, rather than an object "things" type of control, to prevent the very clever from "inventing" a path into the system for their own use.

An AS/400 user has explained the security of this system to me this way: "You have to learn to know French in order to see France. You have to be authorized to go through the door (an authorized profile for this set of objects) and to manipulate the data on this system."

## 8.10. GETTING TO DATA

To get to data, the user needs:

- *Operational* authority on the file-object to OPEN it.
- A *Read or Read/Update* level data authority on the data member in the file to use it (checked as the read or update is executed).

In summary, AS/400 security is based on granting the authority to get to, and use in certain ways, any and all objects in the system, including path tables to control the user's path through the system. All AS/400 programs, commands, datasets, libraries, screen designs (displays), queues, and so forth, are objects. All objects have security descriptions that define who can use them (what function of the system) and in what ways. Object use is controlled by specific authorization of the system users. The starting point is the concept of a Security Officer (whom I have been calling the operator), whose profile is built into the delivered system. It allows him or her to create, change, and delete other user profiles. Each other user profile is granted the authority that pertains to its use of the system. These profiles can be grouped by type of usage or by device (terminal type or sets) or other logic. Objects are then owned by the users, either granted to them by the Security Officer or created by them, and they can further grant usage rights to one another. Whoever grants can revoke or change the rights granted.

What follows is an example of how you could apply security to a data file using the three object security types. First, create a Logical View (File) of the data to be used and grant selected users the following:

1. OPERATIONAL authority on the Logical View (File), which allows users to:
   **a.** OPEN the file
   **b.** COMPILE a program that references this file
   **c.** Use CL commands that inform you of the file statistics
2. EXISTENCE authority on the View, which allows a user to:
   **a.** SAVE, RESTORE the FILE (the Logical View—which is just pointers; to save the real data you have to go further and grant authority over the physical files, which you may not wish the user but rather a system operator to have)
   **b.** Add to or free storage for this file
3. BOTH Operational and Existence authority, which allows a user to:
   **a.** Remove members from a file
   **b.** Delete a member from a file
   **c.** Transfer ownership of a file
4. Object Management authority over the physical file, which allows a user to:
   **a.** Create Keyed Logical Views over the physical file
   **b.** Grant authority you have to someone else (you need Object Management and Operational authority over the file) or revoke it
   **c.** Rename a file and its members
   **d.** Clear and initialize members of a file
   **e.** Reorganize members of a file

Data usage levels on physical files (Read, Update, Delete) are defined at physical file Create time. At the extreme, a data type can be specified without update or delete possibilities, for absolute, infinite integrity.

Logical field level protection can be defined in the Logical View permitted to the user, by the omission of the field in question from his or her View. By concatenating bytes (characters) within the physical field into new fields in the Logical View (File), you can carry this security of access down to the byte level.

## 8.11 THE SECURITY OFFICER USER PROFILE

When you receive your system from the vendor, the Security Officer owns everything. The password for this user profile is SECOFR, which should be changed once you decide how the system resources are to be used. The Security Officer is the only user authorized to do certain things.

Functions only the Security Officer can do:

- Display object authority information for all objects.
- Grant and revoke authority for all system resources such as devices, objects, and commands.
- Enroll users on the system by creating user profiles.
- Change a user profile.
- Display a list of user names and passwords.
- Remove users from the system by deleting user profiles.
- Display the contents of other users' profiles.

CL Commands available only to the Security Officer:

- CREATE User Profile (CRTUSRPRF)
- CHANGE User Profile (CHGUSRPRF)
- DELETE User Profile (DLTUSRPRF)
- DISPLAY Authorized Users (DSPAUTUSR)

No one can delete the Security Officer's user profile, nor can any other profile have *AllOBJ (All-Object) authority. Although the Security Officer has *AllOBJ, he or she must be explicitly authorized to and revoke from all workstations (terminals). Authorizing a terminal to (*ALL) does not include the Security Officer, because you would not want the power spread around. Nor can the Security Officer be revoked from the system console.

## 8.12. OBJECT OWNERSHIP

All objects have owners. Initially, the user who creates the object is the owner. However, *the Owner, the Security Officer, or a user with Object Existence rights can transfer ownership* to another user. The owner or the user with Object Existence rights must have Add rights for the user profile to which ownership is being transferred and Delete rights to the current owner's user profile.

## 8.13. PUBLIC OR PRIVATE AUTHORITY OVER AN OBJECT

Object use can be authorized privately or publicly. "Private" means to specific users; "public" means to all users. An object's owner and the Security Officer have All Authority over an object. They can grant to others the authority to use this object or they can revoke that authority. In so doing, remember that the other user needs authority over the library in which the object resides, over the object itself, and over the command or function that he or she will use to get to the object. Also, if it is data, you must decide what level of data usage you want to grant: Read Only, or more, and, of course, you must never grant data usage rights to the real Physical data, only to the Logical View FILES. Keep in mind that every command is only a request to the system to do something for you. You never actually do anything yourself. In this way the system can check you and your request, for everything you try to do, based on your profile of allowed activities.

## 8.14. LOOKING AT SECURITY FROM THE OBJECT OUTWARD

The owner (usually the creator) of the object has authority to do all things possible to it. (However, he or she can't do what can't be done—for example, do arithmetic on a nonarithmetic field.)

- *ALLOBJ authority over this object can be granted to a user, which gives this user "all things possible" authority. Now the grantee can further grant authority and revoke it as well, even from the original owner. (When designing your system, read the words carefully.)
- *PUBLIC authority reaches everybody and can be granted by the owner of an object at some command level to all system users.

Security over libraries can be defined at these levels:

1. *EXCLUDE—users can't get in at all (only the owner and the Security Officer can use it).
2. *USE—a user can DISPLAY the contents of a library, use commands to find objects, put the library in a LIB list, and SAVE the library.
3. *ALL—users have all the object authorities and all the data usage level authority on the contents of this library or on the library itself.

By object authorities is meant the following:

- OPERATIONAL—you can display the description. The Name and Type of the object must be unique in this library. You will see the text describing this object. You will see the attributes, including size and storage usage, if you like.
- MANAGERIAL—you can grant and revoke other users' authority over this object, for whatever level of authority you yourself have.
- EXISTENCE—you can delete the object or transfer ownership of it.

Data usage levels are defined on the library as well as on the objects within it, including data. They are:

*USE or *CHANGE

+ Read and update—you can change the name of the library or object.
+ Add—you can put a new object in the library.
+ Delete—you can delete objects from this library.

## 8.15. BUILT-IN SECURITY

The identity of the creator of an object is always retained in the Object Description (taken from the profile of the creator). If by chance the object gets copied, the copier becomes the creator. Then the original Object Description and the new copy can be compared to find out who created the copy. The copier cannot delete the original "creator" definition. Also, the system on which the object was originally created is maintained in the object's description. Even if the object is SAVED and then restored on another system, the original system ID is kept in the Object Description table (OBJD). The last day an object was used as well as a count of times it was accessed are also kept in the OBJD. At object creation time the system puts into each object the date and time of creation. It also puts in the name of the source file from which the object was created and the library name. Later it puts in the date and time of the latest change to the object. You can look in the Object Description, using the DSPOBJD DETAIL command to find any tampering.

The system keeps track of every resource it uses, even to the font and format chosen for a printout. (Again remember, you only request that work be done, the system really does it all for you.) Each time any resource (object) is touched, usage statistics are updated in the descriptive control block for that exact object (resource), its Object Description.

User profile usage counts and dates of last usage are kept on each job initiation, when any member of your user group starts a job, or when anyone grants you authority to do something or to use some object.

## 8.16. SYSTEM OPERATION PROTECTION

Certain objects on which good system operation depends cannot be operated on in ways that would cause system malfunction. Here is a sample of objects that cannot be MOVED out of their natural libraries or places of residence.

You cannot MOVE the following objects:

- Libraries
- Authorization Lists (in QSYS)
- Configuration Lists
- Data Dictionaries
- Hardware System Descriptions (Device Descriptions, Line and Controller Description Objects, and so forth)
- Edit Descriptions
- Class-of-Service Descriptions
- Display station Message Queues
- System History Log (in QHST)

- System Operator's Message Queue (QSYSOPR)
- User Profiles
- Documents, Document Lists, and Folders (from Office Work)

If when you compile a program or a CL command you explicitly define where an object is (what library), at run time your program will expect to find that object exactly where you said it was when you did the compile. It must then at least be in the same Library LIST (LIBLIST).

The table following lists objects that refer to other objects (you will need authority on the objects referred to as well as on the original object).

| A Reference to This Object | Refers to These Other Objects |
|---|---|
| Subsystem Description | Job Queue, Class, Message Queue, Program |
| Command Definitions | Programs and Message Files |
| Device Files | Output Queues |
| Device Descriptions | Translation Tables |
| Job Descriptions | Job Queues, Output Queues |
| Database Files | Other Database Files |
| Logical Views (Files) | Physical Files, Formats |
| User Profiles | Programs, Menus, Job Descriptions, Message Queues, Output Queues |
| Printer Files | Output Queues |
| Display Files | Database Files |

See Appendix E for a chart of data file security possibilities and Lock Options.

# 9

# Performance

## 9.1. MAIN PERFORMANCE CONSIDERATIONS

In the AS/400 world, instead of bit-twiddling your programs and intricately mapping out how data lies on disks, you should look at performance from a larger perspective. The first goal should be a relatively well-balanced system. In other words:

To balance: HARDWARE — SOFTWARE — USERS
By balancing: SPACE — TIME — PRIORITIES

The AS/400 has complete and complex statistical accounting schemes whereby it will count for you just about everything the system does, nanosecond by nanosecond, all day long. Some of this tallying goes on all the time whether you ask for it or not, and much of it you have to specify that you want. Some of the accounting is actually done within the so-called vertical microcode, below the machine interface (within the hardware). Tables of statistics are gathered and placed in data files if you so request. There are programs to show you the data, either on your screen or in a printout: reams and reams of it or just some particular item you are interested in. There is a "Work Management Guide" to help you analyze all this data and decide when your system is overloaded in one area or another. I will not go into a study of page faults and the like here.

The elements of space, time, and priority are user-controllable on the AS/400 (although you are not required to go into this at all). If you do not want to concern yourself with this, there is a parameter in the System Values Table that, if set to 1, causes the system to configure itself, designing its own storage pools and setting maximum activity levels each time you IPL (start up) the system. If you are happy with this, read no further here.

## 9.2. SPACE

Space on the AS/400 can be looked at from different viewpoints. First, there is virtual address space, or single level store. This means the 281-plus trillion available characters or bytes of addressable space within which this system executes its instructions and places and retrieves data and other objects. The entire system floats like a cloud in this vast space, carving up big virtual 16MB chunks of it for every activity it undertakes. This is virtual space. Real instructions and real objects use virtual addresses, which are all you can ever get hold of.

The system itself "encapsulates" objects to make them real, within the vertical microcode, below the machine interface, where you can never get to. This is why it would be futile for system programmers from other systems to try to performance-tune the AS/400 by trying to rearrange *where* things are put (as they do on the older systems), including where on disk data might be placed.

In addition to AS/400 virtual address space, there are main memory POOLS of space to work in, allocated by you the user, and disk space—as much as you decide to get—on which to permanently store objects and data when they are not in use. How you allocate this space (at a very high level) determines to a large extent how your system performs.

The system controls the where and when of object and data movement and placement. It collects statistics on how often it has touched data and other objects, and figures out the clusters of objects that are used together. With this information it decides where to place everything and when to actually bring all of it in and out of main memory pools and when and what to read and write to disk hard copy. It separately counts virtual paging "faults" as well as pure data (and other object) faults, all the while adjusting how much it reads and writes at one time and from where. It can read in from disk in one read anywhere from a single 2048-byte page to 10 whole tracks—a cylinder of information combining data and other objects.

The system keeps track of what is in main memory and does not need to reread what has already been read in. It writes updated pages out to secondary nonvolatile storage when it needs more main memory for something else, or according to "purge" parameters you have supplied on FILE definition statements. The control is there, if you want it, to force a disk write of every single update that occurs, to force a write when all the parts of a transaction have been completed ("commitment control" options), or to let the system write out whole strings of data and objects whenever it deems the space is needed or it is an opportune moment for such a write.

For some applications (for example, financial) you may choose to have the system write out immediately every single update, but be aware that there are other options to ensure no loss of data, even with power outages, that use logging (journaling) facilities that can be dedicated to this one data type. On the AS/400 you may request individual logging of data types; you do not have to define just one log option for the entire system as you may have done on other systems. Of course, every read and write to disk is a potential performance hit because disk controllers use many MIPS when they interrupt the CPU and because disk access time is magnitudes different from CPU time.

All of this leads up to how you control the use of space on the AS/400.

## 9.3. SUBSYSTEM DESCRIPTIONS

When you define a subsystem (or use one of the predefined subsystems supplied with your system) you state how many pools you want main storage to be carved up into, how big they should be, and whether or not they should be shared with other subsystems. You also define the maximum number of concurrent jobs the system will start in each pool at any one time. Sharing pools across subsystems allows different terminal activity to share this main memory.

Sharing will improve overall terminal response time. The system itself shares its "machine" across subsystems so that it can run code reentrantly for many different subsystems' usage. This saves you from having to invoke redundant code within the system.

There is a System Values Table that houses parameters used to control events across the entire system.

Main storage (in your CPU) is divided into pools, some shared, some not, that house programs, data, and control objects. Your system is delivered with default pools to match your CPU size and the predefined batch and interactive subsystems. The System Values Table contains entries that define the size of these pools, which are described below:

QMCHPOOL — The entry in the System Values Table that specifies the size of the storage pool used to run system software. It is also called pool #1. Remember, unlike other systems, this system pages everything, even system code. The system sets this pool at 1.5MB. Be generous with it. Use the CHGSYSVAL command to change it.

BASPOOL — Called pool #2 in CL commands, it provides the space for your batch programs and objects and the system monitor. Set its *minimum* size. All unassigned main memory will fall to it. The system sets this pool at 0.5 MB.

QMAXACTLVL — The system-wide maximum number of active jobs at any one time. Set at 100 unless you change it.

QBASACTLVL — The QBASPOOL (batch) active job maximum, which includes many system jobs. Set at 6. You should reset it higher if you run batch job strings, or if you use TIMESLICE on interactive jobs, which dumps them in this pool if they exceed the slice.

QACTJOB — The number of jobs for which you want the system to allocate disk storage (for paging, spooling, and so forth) at first. QADLACTJ is the number to increase this by after you reach the QACTJOB number. Set by the system at 20 and 10. About 110KB per job is assigned.

QINTER — The subpool to run your interactive jobs in and the system's interactive monitor. You define the pool for these jobs when you define the subsystem. Use CHGSBSD to change it.

SPOOL — The pool for the output writer, also defined in your subsystem description.

There are default specifications about how many jobs can be run in each pool. When one job is in a "long" wait, the monitor will start another job. (See Section 9.5, on Time.)

## 9.4. STORAGE POOLS

Main storage is divided into the following pools:

| STORAGE POOLS | SIZE defined in System Values Table or Subsystem Description/use this command to change value | What is IN POOL |
|---|---|---|
| *Machine pool | QMCHPOOL/CHGSYSVAL | System Programs |
| *BASE pool | BASPOOL/CHGSYSVAL | Subsystem Monitor, Users' Batch jobs |
| *INTERACTIVE pools | SBSD/CHGSBSD (permanent) /WRKSYSSTS (temporary) | Users' Interactive jobs |
| *SPOOLS pools | same as above | Spool Writers and Readers |
| *SHR pools #1–10 | SBSD/CHGSHRPOOL /WRKSHRPOOL | Users' Programs and Data |

## 9.5. TIME

The magnitude of time usage for various actions on computers differs tremendously. Mechanical actions of I/O devices, such as reads and writes to disk, are done at disk rotation speed—about 9 milliseconds per track of data—while the arm access mechanism takes ten times that. User think time and key-entry time are infinitely slower still. The system knows when it has sent a request or data out to a terminal, that it will have infinite amounts of time to do other things before it hears back from that terminal. Such operations are considered "long waits," and the time is used to do other work.

The AS/400 automatically overlaps the time that one program is waiting for a disk operation, or any other time-consuming event, with execution of instructions from another program. There is a concept of short and long waits. Any disk operation or interactive terminal request is considered a long wait. (Other I/O, such as printer or tape output or input, which are not interactive, are spooled events, handled asynchronously, for which the system does not wait.)

You define (in the MAXJOBS parameter in your subsystem description) how many jobs you want the system to run in each of your memory pools. It will keep that number constantly running, pulling another job (by priority) off the job queues each time one of the running jobs goes into a long wait. In an interactive subsystem, every terminal sign-on invokes a new job. It does so using a reentrant copy of the program that other terminals are using, but for scheduling purposes that copy is still a new job. (There are ways to run a group of terminals under one "job," but in general, each terminal can be thought of as a job, and every data request as a wait, when another job will be started.)

Another time control is the time-slice. If you have long-running jobs that are not I/O dependent, but considered CPU bound (they execute millions and millions of instructions for each and every input item—usually mathematical calculations), there is a time-slice parameter you set at a number representing the seconds your job will be allowed to run before the system puts it arbitrarily into a wait state to allow other work to go on. The System Value is QTSEPOOL (*BASE). A common number to use is two seconds. This says that after two seconds of running, this job will relinquish its place to another waiting job of equal or better priority. If only lower priority jobs are ready to run, this job will get another time-slice of two seconds to run. Remember, instructions execute in billionths of seconds. The batch CLASS (environment) and controlling subsystem description supplied with the system, QBATCH and QCTL, have TIMESLICE(5000) and (2000), respectively, when your system is delivered, allowing the system itself to switch from function to function within its own priority level.

You can help to minimize time on the AS/400 by:

1. Adding more system memory to allow more code and data to stay in memory and avoid paging.
2. Adding more disk controllers, with disks spread evenly among them, to overlap disk I/O. This is more important on this system than on most, because it is completely virtual—*everything* is paged.
3. Controlling your maximum activity levels in each subsystem. Try two or three numbers while running to see if visible results ensue.
4. Sharing as much as possible—storage pools across subsystems, Logical Views (Files) over the databases among different active applications, and all sorts of Job and Subsystem control blocks, if possible.
5. Not giving every application highest priority. Not all interactive work is high priority, either.
6. Don't let system hogs have completely free access to the system. System hogs can be the occasional Query or SQL users who ask for ALL. Help them limit their inquiries with sequences of Select and Omit options and good thinking ahead of time. The hogs can also be poor programmers who recompile seven times to correct seven errors, or very-long-running mathematical routines that may just as well be run during off-hours.

A quick way to judge who is monopolizing the system is to take a look at the paging rates per system storage pool every five minutes, three or four times, to see whose paging rates are excessive (anything over 15 in the standard system status report is probably excessive). If everybody is too busy, look at the statistics for the arms (actuators). A number under 40 percent is good. If an arm is too busy, a pool is busy, too. Look for a balance of statistics.

Here are the commands to use to examine performance:

WRKSYSSTS—work with system statistics to examine pools
WRKACTJOB—work with job activity levels
WKDSKSTS—look at disk statistics

The machine pool (pool #1) should be almost "fault"-free and have no tasks ready-to-run-but-waiting (INEL). It houses the highest priority system-shared code that should never be held up. Other pools should show balanced page fault values, with no one bearing the brunt of the faults. Disk arm tables should be close to one another in percentage utilization. If one is much higher than the rest, the pool is too small, the maximum activity in the pool is too high, there is too much stale code lying around in the pool (redundant or leftover, out-of-date, but still system-maintained Logical Views and Job Descriptions), or there are too many disks on one control unit.

## 9.6. PRIORITY

I won't say much here about the priority of jobs you run, except that the system plucks jobs to run from queues, based on priority, and every time your job goes into a long wait (disk or terminal operation, wait on locked data, and so forth) somebody else jumps in and runs, and your priority, not your readiness to run, determines when you run again. These priorities are worth thinking about.

## 9.7. MISCELLANEOUS

OPENs and CLOSEs build the indexes that are Logical Views on the AS/400. They sometimes do recovery work, too, if so specified. Queries and SQL rebuild these indexes rather than reuse them, presuming ad hoc inquiries. If you do reissue the same queries often, or very similar ones, consider using the special OPEN, the Query OPEN, before your users sign on to do the query, so that the index building will be done ahead of time and the users won't have to wait for it.

Control how much locking your programmers do. The system will lock data when two users are vying for one piece, if you specified Shared-for-Update in your data specs. Exclusive locking should not be necessary. Such locks last the length of the job and are designed for data that is to be worked on by only one application, for security or other reasons.

Buy plenty of memory. Compared to programming and interactive user time, it is very cheap. The AS/400 system loves memory and balances itself beautifully if there is enough. What, after all, is the price of a system programmer?

# PART 2

# Add-On Interfaces, Natural and Unnatural

The AS/400 has a number of user "add-on" interfaces that are above the machine interface. Their individual purposes vary, but there are some general reasons for their use:

1. *Unique application.* Some interfaces serve a particular user type, in his or her own world, in a language or a methodology attuned to that type's usual way of doing business. Often these interfaces are so-called 4GLs (fourth generation interactive languages) or application "packages," written exclusively for a particular industry or user type, such as manufacturing or scientific APL users. They usually make a number of assumptions about what the user does *not* want to do, eliminating from view what are considered to be unnecessary choices (thus making things "easier"), and they try to speak to the user in his or her assumed voice. These interfaces frequently expect a dedicated system, unshared with other user types.
2. *Emulation.* Such interfaces make this machine look like some other one you are used to working on (say the IBM System 36). They can share the system with normal AS/400 users, but provide different, incompatible end-user interfaces (that is their purpose), which complicates a shop.
3. *Compatibility.* There are an increasing number of user interfaces to the AS/400 that mainly serve the purpose of mak-

ing a function on the AS/400 look just like it does on a large IBM mainframe. Among these are the SQL (database query) and GDDM (chart and draw graphics) packages. Usually such interfaces were afterthoughts to the AS/400, demanded by IBM large-system people, in order to attempt to make this machine "strategic," that is, look like a 370, from which, of course, it is a far cry.

4. *Interactive Productivity*. There are a number of interactive interfaces supplied by the system designers that complement the basic MI (machine interface). They are designed to use every function of the system, including multilevel Help, which responds to the HELP key on the terminals; system security; and normal system object management; and to make full use of the data management facilities—in fact, to enhance them. These "natural" interactive interfaces should be the backbone of your system setup.

In Chapters 10 through 16 I will describe some of the user interfaces that were designed with the original machine by the original system designers. They are a natural and useful part of the system as a system. In Chapters 17 and 18, I will give examples of two mainframe compatibility interfaces. One of these, SQL, is close to the AS/400 in concept, being a relational database language; the other is an extreme example in the other direction, very far from the AS/400 concept of an integrated high-level ease-of-use system. My hope is that you will get a feeling for the variety of interfaces available as well as a hint or two about how to select those you would like to use and eliminate those you would rather steer clear of.

Some of these are natural interfaces in that they come in through normal AS/400 object management, allowing the system to invoke them just as it would any other interaction from a user, sharing system resources among all users. Others try to force-fit the AS/400 into some older, less flexible style of architecture by disallowing the natural sharing of resources that the AS/400 has designed into it. The latter have two great disadvantages: They become system hogs and, worse, they require "bit and parts" large-systems-type programming.

In my mind, compatibility is a tradeoff between maximizing new function and older styles of doing business. This particular machine is such a light-year leap forward in productivity and in ease of achieving rich function that the compatibility question needs to be rethought. If a program can be written the new way in one-tenth the effort of the mainframe way, why opt for compatibility? Most of the programmers I have seen who migrated to this machine from the older architectures have, in less than two months, become strong supporters of the new AS/400 methods, and all have become at least two to six times as productive as they were on the older system. The only exceptions were in a couple of shops where teams of specialists refused to let the machine do its own thing: They insisted on controlling where data was to be housed as they had had to do on 370s for performance reasons, and they insisted on designing applications that owned and controlled the data and devices just as they had done on other systems, instead of breaking apart device and data control from the applications, freeing it up for the AS/400 to manage (and shortening their programming effort considerably).

## CHOOSING INTERFACES

When choosing these add-on interfaces, it is important to examine carefully what your goals are. Don't let yourself get sold on the idea that, because you know the old system's way, it would be easier to use the AS/400 in some kind of emulation mode. This machine, as far as production of applications goes, is so easy and quick to get running that trying to produce your own application will often be easier than trying to work with a package.

As far as programmers go, there is the famous case of the first AS/400 user in St. Olaf's, Minnesota, who was a retired milkman. He was trained and productive—really so—in six weeks. One reason this was possible is that RPG, the forgotten language from the 1960s, has been updated to do everything you can do on an AS/400 and can still be learned in only a three-day class, requiring no prior computer background. Take a look at it again.

The database seems remote from these packaged add-ons, but in most cases it is the essential underpinning for other function provided. In general, however, the users of these APIs (Application Program Interfaces) do not need to know anything about the database or how it works. They see data as desktop items, invoices, and the like; that is the purpose of the API. These users are usually not programmers. The machine is a tool for them, to do a piece of business work. They are not sitting all day long at terminals and cannot be expected to understand computer jargon.

Because on older mainframe and minicomputer systems this level of support was not common, the industry got into the habit of trying to amend each so-called HLL (high level language—COBOL, PL/I, FORTRAN, PASCAL, BASIC, and others) with the ability to supply new function over the years as new computer uses came about. However, the underpinnings weren't in the "operating system" code to support the new function, so massive chunks of self-contained nonshared, nonuniversally similar (in fact, system-dedicated and particular) system code was separately piled on top of the existing operating system (which runs the hardware and partially manages memory). New words were added to each HLL to call and transfer to this new bundle of code for each piece of the new function the user needed to invoke in his program.

GDDM, for instance, originally the name of the IBM System/370 large mainframe graphics "package," was literally millions of lines of code. A COBOL call to GDDM is further encumbered by reams of new parameters that must be passed to the added bundle of code. In this particular package the parameters you pass are the binary bit values, in long hard-to-code-without-an-error hexadecimally specified strings, which you actually send down the line to the graphics device as-is, to control all the hardware that turns on and off millions of pixels (screen dots). You may wonder at this when you realize how little graphics function it provides, especially since the PC world has passed it by with many PC-run graphics offerings.

This very large amount of code for little new function is illustrative of what has been happening on these older systems, whose original hardware as well as operating system design was at a level so low (compared to the AS/400, certainly) that it took millions of lines of code to lift the user even a little way above the hardware interfaces. The newest, latest computer function suffers the most from this syndrome: Today that means graphics and remote communications (teleprocessing).

You can usually tell when an interface has not been sufficiently brought up to date by the price you must pay for programmers. One day, once the function has been brought up to the level you would like to use it at, you will not need a specialized communications programmer. This has happened over the years to the disk drive, tape, printer, and other media interfaces. Why should remote data exchange be more difficult than its local counterpart? Only because we still program all the tiny electronic and mechanical things that are needed to establish a link to the other side: Are you ready, is the in-between box ready, did the other guy answer my last message, were there any errors, what is the path to the other side of this conversation, and so forth. Once we programmed this level of control for disk and tape units as well, but over time the hardware–software functional interface became higher-level, and low-level choices of the way function worked were removed, thus eliminating miles of intricate, error-prone machine-level code. Programming to the hardware (the operating system) was moved up to a data input and output level of operation. Then access method code was supplied, which took the user up to a level where you simply GET and PUT records. Faster hardware, less system code, easier user function availability—we're not there yet with graphics and telecommunications. You can tell by the price of the programmers.

Some AS/400 add-ons mimic that large system low-level interface code for compatibility's sake. Even so, the code added to the AS/400 system is much less than the comparable code on older systems. This is simply because of the AS/400 architecture, which was built to allow dynamic passing of attributes, program commands, and I/O commands and control, and because everything on the AS/400 is queued, with full device support for the terminals and printers separated from the users' programs in every case. There is no direct control of terminals from a user program, so it is natural on the AS/400 to "pass a request" across the program interface to the system manager. It is too bad, however, that the implementers of the packages that are trying to be compatible with the 370 mainframes had to force the COBOL and other HLL programmers to code the bit string parameters within their programs, as they had done in the past in order to add code for the 370 "new" function. This is compatibility gone awry. Fortunately, not too many AS/400 shops are trying to make their systems compatible with the larger mainframes—the users know why they bought the machine: It was for productivity.

Even though these interfaces look a lot like those on the larger older system, they usually perform better on the AS/400 than on the older system. They also use less machine because whenever possible they are using the shared resources of the system rather than taking over and becoming a new operating system with miles of code, cutting other users out, as in other systems, especially mainframes and PCs.

## THE UNNATURAL ADD-ON INTERFACE

In Chapter 17 I describe the SQL interface to the AS/400, an example of an add-on user interface that is only 3/4 natural. It does use the system Data Manager to manage the processes, but the implementers, not quite believing the AS/400 could do all it can do, decided to "control" their own library, unshared with the rest of the system, and then added redundant algorithms with which to search for record fields that are not shared with the rest of the system. Of course, this decreases performance for the rest of the system, but not too much. Some day the designers will surely go back and correct this interface to make it a true AS/400 shared resource. Still, by mainframe or minicomputer standards, it is a very good interface: easy to use, very powerful, and compatible with the mainframe SQL it was designed to mimic.

In Chapter 18 I discuss an interface at the other end of the spectrum: the AS/400 GDDM, a mainframe graphics programming interface, which is an exact copy of the mainframe model. It shares nothing with the rest of the AS/400 system, has dedicated files and I/O interfaces, and actually physically controls the terminals you choose to draw upon—a real AS/400 no-no. Reading about these two examples will, I hope, help you judge a package that perhaps could solve a unique requirement you may have for your system. At the least, these two chapters should aim you toward the right questions to ask of the vendor who offers you a solution package for the AS/400.

Take a good look at any add-on package. If the documentation is over 150 pages, be suspect. And if it doesn't use the AS/400 HELP function *at every level* (meaning right in the midst of defining a statement), be very suspect—it probably does not share in the AS/400 data function or ease of use, and it probably closes off the system from other users. This kind of package may have been designed to be used as a dedicated system. What a shame to waste the AS/400 this way. It may require expensive system programmers to use it, and even if you have such people already, they are more valuable designing your data definitions.

On the other hand, your package builders may have realized what the AS/400 is all about and may have used it as a very high level base for their product. If this is so, the package should contain a great deal less code than it does on other computer systems (ask this question of the vendor), because it should be using the natural data management and interactive end-user facilities of the AS/400. Ask two questions: Does it provide HELP at every level, even while running, and does it share all its data with any other system users? If the vendor can answer yes to these two questions, you most likely have a truly integrated add-on to the AS/400, which will supply you with all the AS/400 superlatives plus the specialties of the package, and also will not hamper your other AS/400 users or operations.

# 10

# Interactive User Tools: Overview and the HELP Function

The natural AS/400 system add-on interfaces comprise a set of tools to help the user define and manage data. They were designed and built by the original Rochester, Minnesota, laboratory as an integral part of the system. This means that they use all the machine-level function built into the AS/400, including the multilayered Help functions that allow you to inquire about any parameter, any statement, any interface, or any function, anytime; to find out information about that item from the level of "How do you code it and what is it for?" to "How many times has it been used lately and who owns it?" Remember, the system keeps statistics about every object, and every item and function is either an object itself or described by one. The AS/400 is rich with heretofore unavailable or lost information. Recall that most programming bugs on former systems came about because the system threw away valuable information about objects you carefully described to the language compilers used by your programs, right after compilation, so that at run time the system had no way of knowing if it was being asked to work on invalid data types or to branch to invalid locations in memory. These are errors the AS/400 cannot make because it keeps the attributes of the objects you supply to compilers and can refer to them at run time. It will warn you if you mistakenly attempt to access the wrong data or area of the machine or try to misuse an object. You will not be able to do something to any object for which it was not designed. All your program instruction and data definitions are kept, complete with attributes, just like any other data in the machine.

## 10.1. THE "NATURAL" ADD-ON INTERFACES

Listed below are the main data management and programming "natural" interfaces provided:

- SEU (Source Entry Utility). An interactive terminal interface that is both a programming and a data management tool. It is used to define the DDS (Data Definition Specifications) from which you create data formats comprising Field, Record, View, and File definition. It is also used to define input/output devices to the system at both a hardware level and a data editing level. SEU is the interactive programming tool for all the HLLs.
- DFU (Data File Utility). An interactive tool for the creation of quick and easy data applications for interactive data entry, simple inquiry, interactive data updating, and interactive maintenance of databases.
- IDDU (Interactive Data Design Utility). An interactive tool for defining the names and formats for database definitions: Fields, Records, Files, and Views. It is used to create dictionaries of common cross-system names associated with formats. IDDU makes a repository of predefined formats. It also will be used to "create" (compile) the actual View or File from these formats, complete with the predefined or new attributes for the Fields and Records. (SEU can also be used for this purpose, but does not give you a dictionary.)
- SCA (Screen Design Aid). A What-You-See-Is-What-You-Get interactive tool for screen design. This involves the specific attributes of each field of input or output and the control that is to go with these fields, including split-screen imaging and scrolling.
- QUERY (Ad hoc inquiry program). A matrix-oriented inquiry system that allows a completely casual user to retrieve very specific data records based upon field selection criteria (the

user is prompted for this), or entire classes of data in lists complete with predefined headings and some formatting and notation. The query will be generated live, but can also be saved as a program for repeated execution at a later time (as can the output). The advantages over other methods of inquiry are these:

1. It is extremely easy.
2. You cannot make a mistake.
3. The end user can easily be prohibited from seeing data he is not cleared to see, but can see whatever portions of that data that have been okayed for him.

- BGU (Bar Graph Utility). An interactive utility that prompts you to define an interactive graphing program that will be driven by the system Data Manager and use as input data from any database you say to use at run time. Since it can run off a Logical View, that data can be redefined whenever you choose without your having to redo the graphing program you created here.
- Office Vision Programs. A set of ready-to-use interactive interfaces for the person who has a computer terminal or PC on his or her desk and uses it for everything from the daily calendar of appointments to sending messages around the building to other like-minded people.

## 10.2. THE SYSTEM HELP FUNCTION

The HELP function on the AS/400 is a system function—that is, it is an integral part of the machine and is always available. You can invoke Help from every system screen by pressing the hardware HELP key on your terminal. This means that no matter where you are or what you are doing: creating a program in SEU, doing retrieval within DFU, filling out a Query input screen, invoking a CL command from your terminal—anything you do interactively is supported by the multilayered system HELP facility.

In general, there are four levels of Help:

Educational
Specific functional
Specific statement
Parameter

The educational level is an entire topic in itself. You can educate yourself on any aspect of the system and its added interfaces from your terminal, at any time. In addition, all the support manuals (system reference library (SRL) materials), are available on an on-line CD disk to be perused from any terminal, anytime.

## 10.3. HELP FOR COMMANDS

For general functional help, place your terminal screen cursor right after the functional word or definition you are interested in and press the HELP key, or if you are in the midst of invoking a function, hit the HELP key only. For example, if you are looking for help in creating a CL command, type in the category of function, say the CREATE function, and then press HELP. You will be shown all the possible CREATE CL commands. For example, keying CREATE and then hitting the HELP key gives you a list of all the CREATE CL commands. You will get instruction in what Create is for, a prompt screen of choices to fill in for CREATE commands, and levels of screens to back you up until you have properly entered a CREATE command. You can merely scan through the Help screens, or, filling them in, actually code the CREATE command you are interested in and execute it (compile it, put it into a library, and run it now or later).

To explore a particular CREATE command, type in the specific command, then hit HELP again.

To explore the Logical View (File), command, key in:

```
CRTLF (Help key)
```

which gives you a parsing breakdown of the complete command with all its parameters. Place your cursor over one of the parameters and again hit the HELP key. Your next prompting screen will specifically address that one parameter: all its options, what it is for, how to use it. You can select from the options and move on. A handful of terminal function keys are always available (listed at the bottom of each screen) to lead you through usage of Help. Never do you run to the end of the HELP function and get stuck, as so often happens with the program HELP function of other systems (especially PCs).

From anywhere within Help, for any function, you can always do the following by hitting a function key:

- Escape back to the Main Menu.
- Return to your prior work screen.
- Return to the first Help invocation directly (one keystroke).
- Return to the previous Help screen.
- Return to where you were prior to hitting HELP the first time.

Note that this Help, because it is not just an add-on in an external system interface or program but is integrated into the basic machine, is not just explanatory; it is active. That is, this system Help is interactive, accepting input to *do* whatever it is you are asking about. Thus, it is a tremendous learning tool—you read about it and do it on the spot. And since everything you do from Help is through prompt screens wherein you select from menus or fill in predefined boxes, and everything is syntax-checked and validity-checked as you go along, you will not damage the system by using the Help menus to enter real work. It is a great learning tool for new users. Most AS/400 shops I know of are void of those stacks of reference manuals you see in other computer organizations.

People find the Help interface much easier than SRLs. Instead of being a separate function that takes you away from the thought process of what you are doing, this integrated, interactive HELP function becomes part of the system's daily use. A user takes it for granted that in entering a CL command, for instance, he will use Help to define his parameters properly rather than rely on memory or on a manual.

The same Help applies when writing a program in RPG or COBOL. You refresh yourself on parameter usage for your statements with Help rather than waiting until Compile (Create) time to discover that your memory is not perfect. This constantly available prompting across all system function and all natural add-on interfaces contributes greatly to the fact that AS/400 programmers and users branch out to become more generalized rather quickly.

Here are the hidden benefits of a system-wide HELP function:

1. Dedicated COBOL (or other) programmers become skilled in all the interactive data-handling tools; also, as they try out

routines in other fully prompted languages, they pick up these skills, too.

2. External data definitions become standard even for hard-nosed large-systems programmers who migrate to AS/400 because of their PL/I or COBOL skills, because the system prompting makes it so easy to change your ways, learning on your own and in private.
3. The HELP function moves at the user's pace. That is, you can learn enough early on to write your programs, define some data, and get these things operational. Then, over time, you explore the depth of function of the system, finding out about such large-system concepts as multitasking and multi-threading, queued data between functional uses or operations, late binding of data to programs and of editing to data, and so forth.

### 10.3.1. Search for Other Help

If you are sitting on a DFU (or other) screen and need help on some other function, the AS/400 has a special "Index Search" HELP function that will get you other help, outside the function you are working within. From anywhere, just press the HELP key and then the f11 function key. A prompt screen will come up asking you to type some words at the bottom of your screen, which the system will analyze. Press Enter and the system will search for topics related to the words you typed in. It will then give you a list of topics thought to be related to your words.

For instance, if you type in "What do you use CL for," you will be fed a list of help topics related to CL. If, after F11, you press Enter with no words typed in, the system will give you a long list of general titles for all the topics about which the system prompts you for help. Other standard system function key usage includes F12, which cancels the current operation, and F13, which gets you to a user-supplied help routine if you have one. Add-on packages sometimes use the F13 interface to provide their own unique help if they are not "fully integrated" into the system. Ask your vendor about this if you have such packages. As always, the system will take you by the hand and pull you properly through the Index Search function.

After being given a list of titles regarding your help request entry, you select some of them for further information by putting a number beside the entry in the list on your screen. For instance, place a 5 next to the entry and you get a display of all the topics the system will discuss on this one item. Place a 6 there and you get the list printed out. These choices are listed for you on the screen prompt.

A topic such as DDS will show you a first prompt screen of some 20 items about which you can ask for prompting. You place a 5 on one or two of them and you get screens of further subsets of information. Help is as deep and as specific as a topic requires, and it covers various levels of inquiry.

# 11

# Source Entry Utility (SEU)

SEU should be called the "programmers' interactive interface" because of all the support it provides to the programmer.

## 11.1. STARTING UP

The AS/400 SEU can be reached by typing STRPDM (Program Development Manager) on the command line at the bottom of your AS/400 Main Menu. This system interface is a built-in, on-line screen editor for all the languages you will use on the AS/400, including the special ones—CL and DDS. It is designed with reuse in mind, meaning you will save your source statements in the database. Like the data records they really are, the statements will be retrievable and can be reused and modified as you see fit for the next usage. This is a must for data definitions (DDS), especially Logical Views, because many of them will be only mildly different from an original View. It is also a great boon to a well-organized programming shop. Routines composed by your crack programmers can become system standards, to be incorporated into others' programs. And because the AS/400 encourages inclusion of modules of code written in any of its languages within programs written in any other of its languages, this is a possibility that really should be pursued.

Languages Supported by SEU:

COBOL
FORTRAN
RPG
PASCAL
PL/I
BASIC
C
CL
DDS

Interactive SEU Function for All Languages:

COPY
MOVE
INSERT
DELETE
FIND/REPLACE STRINGS
BROWSE
PROMPTING

## 11.2. SEU FUNCTION

With the commands listed above, you can work on a set of source statements—in any language—moving them from place to place, creating new ones (insert with prompting), dropping some, and editing others. This allows you to take a file of source, say a Logical View definition, give a new name to it, and thus create a new View. These functions can reach into any of your libraries and pick up any source statements to work on or to include in the new set you are creating, whether it be a data-view, a file definition (even an SQL dataset), or a COBOL program segment.

SEU saves much repetitive work in defining fields and records with all their attributes, or in defining such things as COBOL data definitions or standard program routines you have previously saved in your libraries. Programmer productivity is greatly enhanced by such reuse of source statement resources. On this system, source is saved in libraries rather than thrown away at compilation time, as on other systems. (I can't say this enough—it is very meaningful.)

Each language has its own special parser and screen formats to prompt you. For instance, for fixed-word placement languages like FORTRAN and RPG, the screen will automatically jump your cursor for input to the correct "column" for the next entry. You cannot misplace a word or forget a comma or semicolon as you were wont to do on other systems. You can program nearly as well on days when your mind is dull as when it is sharp. The trivia of coding will not trip you up.

Below are listed some extra things you can do while you are working with (creating) source statements:

- Create a new source member in a library.
- Save your source statements as is, in a Save File.
- Print the source statements.
- Edit the statements.
- Change the text descriptions (comments) that go with each statement (these statements are system objects, remember, each with its own text description, security, title, type definition, and so forth).
- Delete the statements.
- Rename the statements.

Remember, you may be entering the source statements in any of the available programming languages, or you may be defining data formats with which to create physical files or Logical Files and records with DDS or CL.

Whatever language you work with, this full-screen editor will, before compilation, properly parse each line statement by statement, interactively, to give you clean compiles. There is a modicum of logical check within the source to ensure that, among other things, you don't branch to a nonexistent instruction or to a noninstruction.

Because this tool is a system function, you do not have to buy a different interactive programming editor for each language that your programmers will use. If you come from other large systems, you know how cumbersome and costly this can be. A fallout of this fact is that programmers begin to realize how languages that are different from their own work just by looking at the prompts in this tool. With the built-in HELP function, they can actually learn a new language from the parser plus the HELP function. Another benefit is that you only have one version of each HLL language, not one for batch processing and another for interactive users. Lastly, the high level languages are simpler, cheaper, and faster because they do not have to include the burden of the interactive parsers and editors.

## 11.3. THE BROWSE AND COPY FUNCTIONS

The Browse function deserves special mention. Pressing your terminal's function key number 15 (F15) from an SEU screen temporarily gives you a special screen that prompts you to name an object you would like to browse through. This can be any library or member of a library, any spool files (in or out), queues, and so forth.

Your screen will be split horizontally, providing a browsing window on the lower half. You are prompted to specify all the options you want regarding the data you want to see. You may browse, hitting the Scroll (ROLL) key on your terminal, and slowly peruse miles of code or DDS or Logical View statements. As you browse, you may also COPY into a new dataset of source statements, any portion of the data you see that serves your purpose, as you go along. (Since to the AS/400, all is data and commonly managed by the system Data Manager, you actually can pull statements into your browsing panel from anywhere, even from the input queue for some remote system if you so desire.)

Items you might browse through include:

- Parts of the Field Reference File—copying source or data definitions from here is one way to standardize data references within an organization.
- DDS source files—for copying and modifying when you are creating an external file for your programs or for your interactive interfaces.
- Job output on spool queues—browse before you print it or put in onto disk storage.

These very easy to invoke Browse and Copy functions are the catalyst to the reuse of resources in which your shop has invested time and intelligence. Over time, programmers will reinvent the wheel less often because the Browse option allows them an effortless, errorless, nonthreatening way to access code already in the libraries. After using it, they will become less guarded of their creations and more willing to share their own code and use that of others. The creative resource, ever valuable, will become richer when pooled. Also, a bond among the programmers will develop and replace old rivalries.

The COPY command allows you to reproduce any source lines from the browse area (the lower portion or your screen) in the source you are creating in the upper half of the screen. You can move the screen browse window up or down (making it a larger or smaller proportion of your screen) by pressing function key 6 (F6) on your keyboard. To exit from this operation, press F3. To cancel what you are doing, press F12. These function key options are noted on the bottom of each screen and are the same ones all the system interactive interfaces use.

This Source Entry (Programming) Utility is convenient, does everything you want it to do, and cleans up any casual (careless) errors that on other systems would end up incorporated into your programs as bugs. It is also the preferred interface to use when creating logical views, not only because of the ability to reuse prior Logical Views as a base on which to construct new ones but also because SEU is the way to add keys to the data-views.

It would be silliness not to use SEU.

# 12

# Interactive Data Definition Utility (IDDU)

## 12.1. WHAT IS IDDU?

IDDU is the interactive interface you use from your terminal when you are defining your database. You define the format for physical files, which house the actual data, by defining data field formats within each record type (a relational tuple form definition); then you define the file structure the record type is to be housed in. What you are doing is setting up an edifice that will, from then on, be the shape for the repository for a certain data type. Before data of this type is entered into the system, you must create this set of rules. However, unlike on other systems, you do not have to define the entire database at one sitting, nor do you have to design the disk layout for the database. This is amazingly different from the lengthy planning needed for database software packages on other systems today. The AS/400 system is an integrated database system; the system, not the user, designs how data will be placed on disk drives.

Another huge difference is that you only have to define the data format you will be using, not a format for data to come later, because you are permitted to add new data formats (record types) any time, either creating a new file or, if you are trying to clone an older hierarchical database, even adding a new record type to an existing file. All this you can do without reorganizing your older database or your disk drives in any way. You do not manage the disk drive layouts. You never have to reorganize them. (Older systems people and other database users will understand the cost savings in time, intelligence, and experience that this single sentence represents.)

IDDU will also be used to define the Logical Views or Files that tell how you want to mix and match fields from physical database file records, to reformat and resequence them, and to feed them as new record types to application programs, 4GLs, report generators, Query programs, or interactive terminal user browsing operations.

IDDU is very interactive. Help is provided every step of the way. Your terminal screens are preformatted and preprogrammed for proper cursor placement and movement. You key in the necessary characters to name data and define attributes; the cursor jumps you from one screen input area to the next proper place. At any point you may hit the HELP key on your keyboard and temporarily jump to another prompted screen to get help on whatever you are trying to do.

Help is not just a list of instructions but an active prompting mechanism to move you along and explain what is going on. HELP will respond to IDDU menus, help fill in input needs, and give you already coded common choices or choices from the dataset you are using as a base; it will get you from screen to screen and then back to where you were working. There are Help prompt levels within HELP prompt levels in case you have forgotten everything you ever knew about the AS/400. You can hop back to where you came from with one keystroke, or you can page back through all the Help levels you came through using a different key.

The first menu you see allows you to:

- Pull down the menus for defining database DDS for fields and records.
- Create a data dictionary.
- Work with existing database files.
- Work with existing device file definitions.
- Work with existing libraries.
- Work with existing office tasks.

To get to this first IDDU screen menu, type STRIDD at the bottom of the AS/400 Main Menu.

## 12.2. DATA DICTIONARIES

Since a library is the largest grouping you can manage as an entity on the AS/400 (being an object), you can Save and Restore a library using a single CL command. What you do is create a dictionary of names to cover each library that will define all the names used for Field formats, Record formats, Data File Members, and data files. You define the attributes that will go with each name. In the case of fields, this means what sort of data will be housed in the field. For example, is the data numerics, alpha characters, or mixed; how long can the field be; if numeric, is it binary, floating point, or decimal; what range of entries is valid; and what description should go with it when it is used in a program listing or on a report or query output. The prompting for these items makes IDDU almost mistake proof. Plus, you can go back and change it any time—interactively, of course.

Other users of this dictionary will be saved the keystrokes they may have needed to define all the attributes of each data field for each external file definition, and these entries will have been checked out to be correct so they save time and redos. The primary advantage of using a library dictionary, however, is that each user of this library data will use consistent names and attributes for the system data, even if it gets shipped elsewhere. If these names are too long for some language compiler or conflict in any way with rules for some language, names can be equated external to your program. Then you can see in a cross-reference listing (an option on your CREATE command used to compile your program) both the dictionary (system) name and the name used internally by this particular program. It still pays to enforce the discipline of commonality of names for use of the database, since by definition the database is shared by the entire system.

After defining all the names and formats for Fields, Records, Files, and so forth, IDDU is used to create the actual Files of Records. The Data Manager will create space on secondary storage to house the data that will later fill in these formats. The

Data Manager will assume space needs unless you tell it how much you need (the CREATE command) and will allocate large chunks of further space as needed unless you tell it not to. Since it manages all data in the system, it will also decide the most expedient and efficient place to assign this data.

## 12.3. USER SEQUENCE FOR IDDU

The user should follow these steps when creating a database:

1. Define and create the dictionary for names and attributes of data Fields, Records, File Members, and Files.
2. Add the detailed Field definitions, with all their attributes, descriptive text, and rules for data validity checking when the field is in use. You will group these fields into Record format type as you define them.
3. Create physical data files (physical formats and the space allocations to house actual data entered later).
4. Create Logical Files (Views) if you know what they will be, or if you are defining some standard ones to be used as prototypes for your users (a good idea because you will need to control the proliferation of Logical Views, which eat up a lot of space and even more system performance and time in their continuous automatic maintenance by the Data Manager.)

The files so defined are now available to be quoted by and retrieved from by any data interface to the system, be it a user HLL program, some obscure 4GL, a dedicated package, Query, BGU, SQL, or simply the Browse function from your keyboard—as soon as you enter some real data into the files, that is.

## 12.4. MENUS

Screen 12.1 shows the first menu you will see after your STRIDD CL command is issued.

You will type a 2 after the ===> on the input line at the bottom of the screen to ask for the Dictionary Menu.

The Data Dictionary design screen is shown in Screen 12.2

```
IDDU      Interactive Data Definition Utility (IDDU)
Select one of the following:
 1. Work with data definitions
 2. Work with data dictionaries
 3. Work with database files
 ...
20. Work with libraries
21. Work with files
...
30. Office tasks
...
70. Related commands

Type your Selection or Command:

===> ________________________________
F3=Exit F4=Prompt F9=Retrieve F12=Cancel F13=User support
  F16=System Main Menu
```

**Screen 12.1.** The first menu after the STRIDD command.

```
            Work with Data Dictionaries

  Position to........         Starting character
  Type options (and Data Dictionary), press Enter.
   1=Create  2=Change  4=Delete  6=Print

        Data                  Data
   Opt  Dictionary     Opt  Dictionary
```

*(here you list the Dictionary names for which you will further define Fields, Records, etc., on another screen)*

```
  F3=Exit  F5=Refresh  F10=Work with database files
  F11=Display text  F12=Cancel  F13=Display libraries
  F21=Work with definitions
```

**Screen 12.2.** The Data Dictionary Menu.

(you keyed a 2 on the prompt line of the IDDU screen shown in Screen 12.1).

After you have named the Dictionary on the Dictionary Menu, you press the function key F3 to return to the first menu, where you select the Data Definition Menu (Screen 12.3) by typing a 1 in the Selection line at the bottom of the screen.

The Data Selection screen looks like this:

```
              Select Definition Type

Type choice, press Enter.                   1=Field
 Definition type .............(1)          2=Record format
                                            3=File

 Data Dictionary ..... (you use name from prior screen)

                                            F4 gives name list

F3=Exit  F4=Prompt  F10=Work with data base files
F12=Cancel  F22=Work with data dictionaries
```

**Screen 12.3.** Data Selection screen.

Next you will be shown the Field Definition screen (Screen 12.4). Here you will fill in the blank lines with your company's choice of field names, type indicators taken from the menu above (for numeric, character, or double byte you type a 2, a 1, or a 3, respectively), and add field max size, number of decimal positions, and Y if there are more attributes to be defined on a further screen—for example, the precision of a floating point number or whether decimal numbers are "zoned" or "packed." On the optional screen you will be able to define alternate names for this field (aliases), column headings to be used with this field if used in output listings from Queries, Reports, and so forth, and editing options for use with monetary amounts and other kinds of editing

```
              Create Field Definitions

Type information, press Enter to Create.
Field type...:  1=character, 2=numeric, 3=Double byte
Field size...:  if char: 1-32766  num: 1-31  DB: 4-32766
Dec. positions: 0-31 for numerics, blank for char & DB
More options?:  Y=yes

- - - - - Field - - -  Dec More

Name       Type  Size  Pos  Opts  Text
_________  ___   ___   ___  ___   ________________

_________  ___   ___   ___  ___   ________________

_________  ___   ___   ___  ___   ________________

(More lines)

F3=Exit  F12=Cancel  F14=Copy previous line
```

**Screen 12.4.** Create Field Definitions.

for numeric fields when used for output. Screen 12.5 is the optional editing screen you get when you put a Y in the "more options" column on screen 12.4, "Create Field Definitions."

You have a variety of editing options to use in outputting this field, which should accommodate U.S. as well as other countries' currency symbols, credit and negative number notations, and magnitude value delimiters (commas or periods).

Similar levels of screen menus are given to you for defining files and the rest. At any time, anywhere on the screen, you may place your cursor over a word or an input area and by pressing the HELP key on your AS/400 keyboard, obtain assistance in filling out the screen. You can also at any time cancel what you are doing or save your work partway through.

```
        Describe Numeric Field Editing

Definition ..........:  (name the field)
                        Dictionary: (name the Dictionary)
Type choices, press Enter
Decimal point ..........(1)  1=.  2=,  3=:  4=$  5=none
Thousands separator ....(2)  1=.  2=,  3='  4=blank 5=no
Show negative sign?     (Y)  Y=yes  N=no
  left negative sign?   (Y)  Y=yes  N=no
  right negative sign?
Show currency symbol    (N)  Y=yes  N=no
  left symbol           ($)  you place any symbol here
  right symbol
Print zero values       (Y)  Y=yes  N=no
Replace leading zeros   (Y)  Y=yes  N=no
  replace with          (1)  1=blanks  2=asterisks **
                            3=floating currency symbol
  single leading zero   (N)  Y=yes  N=no
F3=Exit  F12=Cancel
```

**Screen 12.5.** Numeric Field Editing.

Later you can browse through the record definitions you have created as well as use any of them for prototypes for further definitions. At any point in the future any and all of the work you have done may be cloned and then further edited to create another set of definitions.

You use IDDU to define the format of your original datasets when you start up your system and later when new data types are added to your processing needs, without ever having to redesign or reorganize your original data definitions. However, if you ever need to redo an original definition (say a 5-byte zip code turns into a 9-byte field due to a change in government procedures or regulations), you need only go back to the original data definitions for the dictionary, change the 5 to a 9, and reinvoke the Create from the menu. A version level check is done when you run programs using these definitions, which will warn you if any program you run is not able to accommodate the 9-byte field. Since the AS/400 references data by name and not by attributes, picking up the attributes as it executes, and since the system assigns all work areas to work on data outside your program, dynamically, in its own expandable areas, you often have to change nothing but the original definition of the field attributes in the dictionary.

# 13

# Data File Utility (DFU)

## 13.1. PURPOSE

The purpose of DFU is to create and maintain data applications, interactively, for:

Data entry
Inquiry
Database maintenance

In addition, you can use DFU directly, interactively (without creating a program), to:

Update databases.
Log all changes to databases for history.
Recovery purposes.

## 13.2. MENUS

The DFU Main Menu is shown in Screen 13.1. If you press 2 on your keyboard, "Create a DFU program," you get the prompt screen, shown in Screen 13.2.

Using this screen, you name your program and select the database (file) it will work with. Pressing F4 while the cursor lies

```
                AS/400 Data File Utility

 Select one of the following:
   1. Run a DFU program
   2. Create a DFU program
   3. Delete a DFU program
   4. Update data

Selection or command
   ===> __________
F3=Exit  F4=Prompt  F9=Retrieve  F12=Cancel
For HELP place cursor over desired word for HELP
```

**Screen 13.1.** DFU Main Menu.

over the “Program” or “Data File” Name position will show you a list of all the DFU programs in the named library, as well as your data files. This will help you choose a unique (new) name for the program and to select the proper name for the dataset that you want to work on.

```
                Create a DFU Program

Type choice, press Enter.
   Program ..........DFUx __________    Name, F4 for list
     Library ........ ______________    Name, *CURLIB
   Data File ........ ______________    Name, F4 for list
     Library ........ ______________    Name,
*LIBL,*CURLIB

F3=Exit  F4=Prompt  F12=Cancel
```

**Screen 13.2.** Program creation.

Pressing Enter takes you to the next screen. Now you fill in prompts that define your:

- Job title
- Screen format type
- Audit control rules
- Error options
- Numeric editing choices
- Whether to generate data record numbers as the data is entered through this program
- Whether to allow updates on scrolled data screens
- Whether data is to be retrieved sequentially or randomly (direct retrieval by key or number)

After this you will walk through more prompt screens. You will select (by placing Xs next to words and fields on the screens):

- Record formats you will work with
- Each field you want to work with
- Sequence in which the fields should be displayed to the end user (key-entry person)
- Format in which the fields should be displayed
- Editing to be done on each field, if any
- Headings to be put over the columns of fields on the screens

Finally, you will be given a last-chance screen to review your program. You will be asked if you want to save the program and/or its generated source statements, and where (which library); what the authority needed to run it will be; and if you would like a sample run, for prototyping or for real. It is a good idea to save the source statements because this is a real program, even though you didn't have to code it. You might like to embellish it later with calls to other routines, say to add a logo to the top of the screen or to print a summary sheet for the user after the key entry is done, telling him or her how many records have been updated, how much time it took, and how much he or she will be paid for the work.

## 13.3. RUNNING THE PROGRAM

To run this program as a data-entry program, press F9. The record format, with all its field names, will appear on your screen in the manner you defined. If you let the system default work, and you used a single record type, all the fields will be listed down the left side of your screen in a column, with entry blanks to the right with exactly the right number of spaces for the field to be filled in, as in Screen 13.3.

```
Fieldname1 - - - -           (a 4 character field)

Fieldname2 - - - - - - - (a 7 character field)

Fieldname3 - -               (a 2 character field)
```

**Screen 13.3.** Portion of Single Record Default screen.

Your cursor will automatically jump from one field key-entry space to the next as you key in the last stroke. Pressing Enter refreshes your screen for the next record entry. You can define as many columns of fields as your application calls for, in whatever positions on the screen. You can make the key-entry fields correlate to the document from which the operator is transcribing the data.

After a run of this program, at program end time, you will be given statistics about data record changes that have just been done.

Notice that this program generation tool gives you a second way to scroll through (browse) your data without any effort (the first was SEU).

## 13.4. RUNNING THE SAME PROGRAM IN UPDATE MODE

You can change the mode to update, rather than data-entry by pressing F10. F10 allows updating of the records by:

1. Record number
2. Key
3. Scrolling through data records

For each record you want to update, you can update either by record number (the logical sequential number of the record you want to update) or by using a field of data as a key, typing in the exact data that is in that field in your database on the proper prompt line. You can also update by scrolling through reams of data until you see the record you want. This is done in F10 mode by holding down the ROLL key on your keyboard until you see the data you are interested in, then stopping and typing over the data, and then hitting Enter to accomplish the update. In this way you can update a number of records before hitting Enter, to save time, if the updates are clustered in nearby records. I would not give security clearance for this Scroll function to any and all key-entry operators, but it can be very useful for a database specialist or a programmer who is creating temporary test data of various kinds to give a live test to a program.

## 13.5. ADDING A NEW RECORD

To add an entirely new record to the database, use the F9 function.

As you can see, DFU can be a real productivity boon to the data entry operation. Remember, every record change or new record entered will automatically be recognized by the system Data Manager, and if it qualifies, will be added to all the Logical Views that are collecting data of this caliber. For instance, if a key-entry operator enters a record through this interface that has a payroll field which causes an employee's pay to go over a social security limit being checked for in some Logical View, that Logical View will be updated by the system, as will the person's record itself. The next time a paycheck writing program is run, it will use that Logical View to calculate that this person no longer needs to have social security deductions taken out of his or her pay.

These "simple," naturally integrated AS/400 database programming tools should be considered while keeping the power of the AS/400 Data Manager (under them all) in mind. The tools look simple because the power of the machine is great. In fact, a good rule of thumb in selecting packages for the AS/400 is: If it has thick manuals and complicated interfaces, it is probably not using the AS/400 as a database machine. Beware.

# 14

# Screen Design Aid (SDA)

## 14.1. PURPOSE

SDA is an interactive interface that is part of a program set called Application Development Tools, used to:

1. Design input and output screens for your application programs.
2. Compile (CREATE) and test these generated screens.
3. Create user designed menus for application or system use.

SDA is probably the most important "extra" program on the AS/400 if you do any of your own application programming. Screens today do a lot more than simply display the words you send to them. They have hardware controlled but programmable attribute control bytes for each field you display, which ought to be used to provide your end users with truly friendly screen formats. In addition to blinking, underlining words, and using more intense lighting for certain fields, the hardware can do such things as build boxes around a field, change or reverse coloring on a field, put column lines between data columns, and, of course, display your data using all the options you defined on the AS/400 Device File Description which you have selected to go through on this particular output operation—those options being both hardware *and* software attributes.

Remember that you can do such things in your FDs as have the system display a red CR symbol (or a minus sign or whatever) next to a number, should it be an arithmetically negative number in your dataset. Any of the hardware attributes of these new screens can be turned on or off based on data types flowing from the output queue through the particular Device File Definition you chose to run with for this program execution. The power of the AS/400 system design, combined with the possible combinations for display output—the Logical View selection of data from physical data definitions; the Logical View editing of data or adding of data as it passes through the View; the checking that is done as defined in the Device Description; the sifting and editing of data as it passes through here; and the Device Description selection of what data will or will not be displayed, in what fashion (software editing), with what device hardware characteristics, whether or not the cursor should be moved and where, and whether or not the keyboard should be unlocked yet. These provide a layered set of data flow control that you cause to happen if you set up the proper controlling objects (Logical Files, Device Files, Screen Designs) and select them at run time.

SDA is the tool to design menus and screen layouts that will get you to really use the options of your terminals and the data control of this system.

## 14.2. TO START

To invoke SDA, type STRSDA at the bottom of your AS/400 Main Menu.

Each user group on your system should at least have its own general-purpose menu by which to reach and invoke its commonly used function, both system- and user-supplied, along with one menu to reach all other function it is cleared to use.

This user group menu does three good things:

1. It tailors system entry to the particular group's mentality.
2. It gives users the feeling that the entire system is their own and easily accessible.
3. It prevents users from bumping up against security locks inadvertently, which is time-consuming and painful.

```
                         Design Menus

Type choices, press Enter.
   Source file . . . . . ____________ Name, F4 for list
     Library . . . . . . ____________ Name, F4 for list
   Menu  . . . . . . . . ____________ Name, F4 for list
```

*(here you choose a name for the generated source for this menu, what library it will be kept in, and a name for the menu you are creating, or key F4 to see lists of those system objects that already exist)*

```
   F3=Exit  F4=Prompt  F12=Cancel
```

**Screen 14.1.** Menu design.

## 14.3. DESIGNING MENUS

It takes less than two minutes to build a good menu on the AS/400 with SDA. SDA assumes that you are designing a menu in order to get to a certain dataset in your database, and that this menu will be housed in a particular library, probably the same one the dataset resides in or your user library. The first screen you will see asks if you want to design screen formats or menus or test one of your designs. The first screen you see after you select "Design Menus" is shown in Screen 14.1. You enter your name for the new menu and hit Enter.

The second screen you see will be a prototype of your new menu, your name at the top, with menu selection numbers down the left side for you to fill in with the names of the function you want this user group to have access to. It looks like Screen 14.2.

On the next screen, reached by pressing key F10, you put a CL command next to each "option" number that matches your menu numbers on the prior screen. These CL commands will be used at run time to call the optional function from the previous screen (Screen 14.2).

You type in your line numbers from the prior screen next to the CL command that will invoke the wanted function. For in-

```
                "your menu name" Menu
"your menu name"
   Select one of the following:
   1.
   2.      (you fill in your list of function for this menu, then
   3.      press F10 to get to the command screen on which you
   4.      enter the CL command to call each of these functions,
   5.      one for each numbered function on this screen)
   6.
   7.
   8.
   9.
  10.
```

**Screen 14.2.** Prototype menu.

stance, you type in a 1 under the "Option" column and start the IDDU utility (STRIDD) under "Command," as follows:

```
1      STRIDD
```

## 14.4. USE OF FUNCTION KEYS

Common function key usage for all these interactive interfaces is shown in Table 14.1. SDA is used in the examples. Notice that pressing Enter always takes you to the next thing to do, whatever that may be.

You can add your own Help, including other menus, by pressing F13 anytime. The help you supply will apply to whatever function you are performing just then.

## 14.5. SCREEN DESIGN

In addition to creating menus, you create all your screen layouts for programs you will write using SDA. You can also create screens

```
                Define Menu Commands

Menu . . . . . . . .: (name your menu)

Type commands, press Enter.

Option          Command

  _ _           ________________________________________

  _ _           ________________________________________

  _ _           ________________________________________

etc.
```

**Screen 14.3.** Command definition.

to be used by the system, which will show the user a system interface differently from how it is normally shown. For instance, if you have one set of users who work in Spanish, you might create Spanish-language screens for them. Of course, there is a Spanish option for the system, as well as many other language interface options, but you may only want to translate one particular set of functions for one operation or user type.

The database this interface feeds or retrieves from is, of course, the same one everyone else uses; only the interface to the user set is different. Another user set could use the regular system menus and screens.

## 14.6. AN AS/400 "SCREEN"

A window on an AS/400 screen is composed using one "record" definition to that screen. Thus, for full screen layouts to be com-

| Pressing Key | When you are here | Does this function and moves you further as indicated |
|---|---|---|
| Enter | On Main Menu and in general | Exits this prompt screen. Takes you to the functional menu you indicated with the cursor, or the next sequential screen. |
| Enter | On repeatable screen | Keeps work from this screen. Renews screen for further work. |
| Enter | At end of this screen function | Takes you to next screen in this job flow. |
| F12 | Anywhere, on any screen | 1. Exits, after prompting you to save your source statements. Using work done here, creates objects to be used by the menu or screen you are creating.<br>2. At this point, with proper security clearance, you can replace existing system menus with this new menu (i.e., the programmer menu). |
| F3 | At end of prompt screen | Returns to (SDA) Main Menu. |
| F4 | In mid screen | Prompts you for whatever functional level you are in. |
| F4 | Cursor is placed over a command parameter | Explains use of parameter. Gives help in defining it. |
| F4 | Cursor follows command name; no parameters given | Gives uses, options, and defaults for this command. |
| F13 | At user selected screen location | Lets you define your own HELP for your screen function |
| Field Exit | In mid screen | Finishes this screen prompt early, keeping what you have done so far. |

**Table 14.1.** Function key use from prompt screens.

posed in one operation (one write, one read), a single record is considered to cover the entire screen. You define fields within that record to format different areas of the screen in different ways. If you want to section a screen into windows of unique control, such as split screens or four-part screens, you define more than one record type per screen layout. Each area will then be controlled separately as far as input and output go. You can (in this way) leave a permanent heading over a screen while changing the format of a section of it.

## 14.7. SCREEN "FIELDS"

The "fields" within the screen "record" can be separately designated for:

Input only
Output only
Either Input or Output ("Both")

Fields can have any length: up to full-screen size or down to single-byte size, and they can have all the normal field attributes of data plus all the attributes that are specific to the display screen architecture.

## 14.8. THE DESIGN PROMPT SCREEN

Your first screen design screen, which you get to by keying a 1 in the SDA Main Menu option, appears in Screen 14.4. You are creating DDS source statements that will be placed in the library you specify here and that also will be compiled into a runnable code object and screen control objects for later use in creating the screens you design here. All of this work will be done for you by the SDA.

You will be asked if you want to use an older design as a base to work with or want to design a completely new screen. When reusing an older definition, you will be prompted to give it a new name, delete or add fields, change field attributes, use different

```
                        Design Screen

Type choice, then Enter.

   Source File _ _ _ _ _ _ _ ____________Name, F4 for list

      Library _ _ _ _ _ _ _ _ ___________Name, *LIBL,*CURLIB

    Member  _ _ _ _ _ _ _ _ _ ___________Name, F4 for list

F3=Exit  F4=Prompt  F12=Cancel
```

**Screen 14.4.** Design prompt screen.

data keys to get and put data to the screen, add new comments of help prompting, and so on.

Some aids to design are a ruler across the screen for measurement of character field placement and line numbers down the left side of the screen (press F14 to get the ruler). If you press F10 while on this screen, a list of database files and field references you may use will be displayed. (The HELP key will supply you with all these uses of the function keys.)

## 14.9. CREATING A KEY-ENTRY PROGRAM SCREEN

Suppose you decide to create a key-entry display for a certain data type used in an invoicing process. You want input fields on the screen with certain descriptive information for the key-entry operators. The first SDA screen you will use to create this input display is the Select Database Files SDA screen (Screen 14.5), which you get by pressing F10 from the original SDA menu screen. The first screen you will see looks like this:

```
                    Select Database Files

Type options and names, press Enter.
   1 = Display Database Field list
   2 = Select ALL fields for input  (I)
   3 = Select ALL fields for output  (O)
   4 = Select ALL fields for both input and output  (B)

   Option    Database File    Library    Record type Name

      1       file name         lib-name   record name

(here you type in the names you want to see and a 1 to get the list of
all the fields in this record type)

F3=Exit F4=Prompt  F12=Cancel
```

**Screen 14.5.** Select Database Files.

Hit Enter after you have put a 1 in the Option column and have filed in the names for the system to find the record definition where the fields are kept. These fields are the ones the user's key-entry program will be keying in later when your screen is operational. Here the system will show you not only all the fields defined in this record type but also what types they are (a=alpha, n=numeric, z=zoned decimal, and so forth) and the lengths as they were defined.

The field definition screen is shown in Screen 14.6. One by one you decide which fields you want on the screen and put in the lengths, types, and a 2 to define the fields as input for the key-entry operation.

## 14.10. FORMATTING YOUR SCREEN

When done here (you can choose more fields using the page-down key on your terminal), press Enter to return to the prior file

```
        Select Database Field

Record . . . : (your record type name from prior screen)
Type information, press Enter.
  Number, fields to roll. . . . . . ____________
  Name of field to search for . . . . ____________

Type options, press Enter.
  1=Display extended field definition (all attributes)
  2=Select field for Input  (I)
  3=Select field for Output (O)
  4=Select field for Both   (B)

Option   Fieldname   Length   Type   Column Heading to use
_____    _________   ____     ____      (text you want to
_____    _________   ____     ____      appear with the
_____    _________   ____     ____      field on the screen)
etc.
```

**Screen 14.6.** Select Database Fields.

selection screen, then Enter once again to see your sample data-entry screen (the "work" screen). All the fields you have selected will be lined up horizontally along the bottom of the screen, waiting for you to indicate to SDA where you want it to place them on the input screen you are creating with it. The fields will be preceded by 1, 2, 3, and so on, numbers you will use for placement indicators on the screen shown above. Now, compose your key-entry screen as the following paragraph describes (the pound sign (#) means use the number to the left of each field).

Type &#, &#L, &#R, or &#C where on the screen you want that numbered field to reside. The letters "L," "R," and "C" mean left, right, and center. This means you want the "Column headings" information from the "Select Database Fields" screen to be used which R, or C in relation to the field. Also, you can add new fields not in this record definition by typing anywhere on the screen +3333 (as many 3s as field positions) or +66666s or +999999s, meaning here is an input field (3s) or an output field (6s) or a "Both" field (9s), which is numeric. Or you can type +IIIs for alpha input fields and +OOOs for alpha output fields, and—guess what—BBBBB for both input and output. For a decimal number, "666666(4,2)" means six digits, two of which are decimal places. What kind of editing you want for that number is defined elsewhere, for output fields.

A key-entry screen being composed might look like that shown in Screen 14.7. You have typed instructions to the operator plus &# where you want SDA to put the input fields to be filled in by the key-entry operator.

Your SDA generated screen will look like Screen 14.8. The operator's cursor will jump from field to field for him as he inputs each data field.

## 14.11. USING DISPLAY HARDWARE ATTRIBUTES

After you have selected all the fields from your record types that you want to use on the display, you will have the chance to select hardware display characteristics for each field to be put on the display. Suppose you are working on the Item Price field and want it to blink if the amount goes over a certain number (or a program indicator is set to a condition 44, for example). Screen 14.9 is what you will see, once per field. This screen will react to a field containing price amounts over a figure you determine by making the field blink and underlining it. This could be a warning to the operator to check his invoice for correctness.

## 14.12. ADDITIONAL FUNCTIONS

Other things you can do for your screen with SDA are as follows:

- Sound alarms on certain conditions.
- Move the cursor right to left instead of left to right.
- Move the cursor down to up instead of up to down.
- Specify input defaults where there is no data input.
- Generate error messages for the operator or for the system.
- Allow graphic output.

```
. . .10. . .20. . .30. . .40. . .50. . .60. . .70. . .80

                          Invoice Record

Enter customer name and number:
      &1L                       &2L

Enter Item number, Item name, Quantity and Price each:

      &3L    &4              &5L      &6L
                                     Total sale  &7
Hit F3 to end.
Fields selected on prior screen:
1 CUSTOMER  2 CUSTOMER NO.  3 ITEM NO.  4 ITEM  5 QTY
6 ITEM PRICE  7 TOTAL INVOICE AMOUNT
```

**Screen 14.7.** Key-entry screen being composed.

```
                        Invoice Record

Enter customer name and number:

Name _ _ _ _ _ _ _ _ _ _ _ _ _ _ No _ _ _ _ _

Enter Item number, Item name, Quantity and Price each:

Item no._ _ _ _ _ Item ________ Qty_____ Item Price_____

                                      Total sale ________
Hit F3 to end.
```

**Screen 14.8.** SDA generated screen.

```
              Select Display Attributes

  Field . . . .:Item Price    Usage:  I   (input)
  Length. . . .:6,2           Row:    10
                              Column: 70
 Type choices, press Enter.
  Field Conditioning          Keyword   Y=Yes   Indicators
  Display Attributes:         DSPATR
    High Intensity              HI       ___     _________
    Reverse Image               RI       ___     _________
    Column Separator            CS       ___     _________
    Blink                       BL       _Y_     _44______
    Don't Display               ND       ___     _________
    Underline                   UL       _Y_     _________
    Position Cursor             PC       ___     _________
    Set Modified Data Tag      MDT       ___     _________
    Protect Field               PR       ___     _________
    Operator ID mag.card       OID       ___     _________
    Select by Light Pen         LP       ___     _________
 F3=Exit   F12=Cancel
```

**Screen 14.9.** Select Display Attributes.

- Validity check any/all input for valid data type and valid ranges of data against a list of possible inputs for correctness you supply.
- Print results to printer queues (thence to some printer).
- Add your own Help anywhere.
- Change the size of the display area.

Hit F12 to see the last screen of the design you are making for the key-entry screen. It is the Exit screen, where you decide in which library you want to keep the DDS Source you have generated and where you will keep this Display Device Description and Device File (perhaps a different library). You also answer prompts about whether or not you want to create a job from this SDA work and what Save options the system is to use for it when it is in use.

This generated screen definition is external to your program's definition and can now be used by any programs you write that have to store or manipulate this particular invoice data as it comes into the system. The screen (as well as the control objects SDA created for it) is a door through which data passes to your program. You name this display "file" as the externally defined device for your program when you run it. The program could be a DFU or COBOL program you wrote or any other. This is now a system-controlled and shared object, to be used by anyone you authorize to use it (you are the creator, so you own it).

A third option on the original SDA screen (in addition to the design menus and screens) is to "test display files." This is a built-in function that allows you to use the screen in test mode, meaning test data will be protected from the updating of your real databases. It will come from and be stored in special test files for your perusal with the Browse function (see IDDU and SEU) or the F9 Retrieve function from the original SDA screen. Because SDA facilitates creation of the screen and objects that can prepare data for direct entry into your database (your program behind the screens could be merely a GET–PUT sequence) or for formatting output and sifting data for reports (plus another GET–PUT sequence), you should use this test facility to hone your SDA screens to make good interfaces for such function.

# 15

# Query

## 15.1. OVERVIEW

The AS/400 Query is an interactive menu-driven tool used for "load and go" inquiry programs, which can be run ad hoc, that is, at once and not to be repeated, or cataloged in your library and run multiple times, or both.

Query is system-wide, meaning it can reach any and all data in the system without having to "import" the data into a special program area, as other systems usually do. Reiterative in nature, the prompts are designed so that after you have defined your inquiry and seen the output of its first pass, it is very easy to go back into Query definition mode, hop to a particular prompt screen, and modify some of your prior prompt choices to try the inquiry again.

When you get the inquiry results you are seeking, you can save the Query to be run as a regular program either in batch mode or by using the CL interactive command RUNQRY. The basic definitions you make through the prompt screens are:

1. What data you are interested in
2. Data sifting rules and data analysis rules
3. Output formats and devices
4. Relation to other AS/400 system interfaces (do you want this output inputted to the Office or Business Graphics programs,

or kept as a new dataset for use as input to another part of the system?)

Query can be *run* from any display device, as a CL command set (it generates a CL program), or as a batch job. You create the program interactively, from a terminal, using the Query prompt screens. These prompts generate and run the inquiry as you work. It generates the Logical Views (Logical Files) with which it sifts for the proper set of data for you, based upon the answers you give to the prompts it provides.

## 15.2. QUERY OPERATION

Here is how Query works:

1. The raw data is drawn from the already existing physical database file you name on the prompts.
2. The Logical View (the path to the desired data) is built on the spot. If a data path exists that will serve, it will be used (to save time).
3. Output definitions you supply are used to build output Device Descriptions automatically, complete with data editing for the Query output.
4. The "dynamic" Logical File (from item 2 above) is used to find the data you want (winnowing out the unwanted), sort it according to your prompted definitions, and JOIN it to other similarly massaged data as you defined it should.
5. Your output prompts are used to design the report output format, the device is prepared for output, and the inquiry data is put out to you.

Query input is database physical data of any kind. Query output is listings and reports, or files, of dynamically selected, massaged, and edited data housed in forms you design here and now, interactively.

## 15.3. QUERY OPTIONS

If you are a programmer, you may want to speed up the process. Once used to Query, you can bypass the menus. You can compose

Query programs simply by using the CL commands it generates. Or using Query CL programs cataloged previously, modify them for some other use, either using CL commands, or by rerunning the prompting mechanism.

The CL command RUNQRY can be used to run queries written earlier that were cataloged in a system library to be saved for later use. You can invoke such Query programs, then use any of the prompt menus to modify them for today's changes or to work on other datasets. This can be a very productive tool because Query can create almost any kind of report you can conceive, and its output can become input for transmitting elsewhere or for further massaging. You can get data from today's operation and marry it to yesterday's output, and you can also create live data to be merged with the Query output on the fly.

At any time you can change the titles and points of subtotaling or other break points in the data output flow. All sorts of statistical mathematics can be added to the data analysis after you have determined that the query gets you the right data. This is light years better than having to plan an entire analytical program at once, batch mode, and rewrite the entire thing until it comes out seemingly correct. Here your mind will not be caught up with the programming but rather with the ramifications of the data you are exploring.

## 15.4. QUERY INPUT

Data to answer a single inquiry can come from:

- Up to 32 different database record types (files, datasets).
- Up to 100 "JOINS" (merging of more than one data record type to form a new record type on the fly).
- A combination of different kinds of JOINs.

## 15.5. QUERY OUTPUT

Your Query output will be a report or listing for which you define both the format and the content. Here are the ways output is derived:

- The end user defines which fields will show up.
- The end user defines how data fields will look on the output device.
- Up to 500 field types are allowed per Query output.
- Fields are edited to your own purpose.
- Data can be resequenced, sorted, reorganized however you decree.
- Output fields can be highlighted, clustered, titled.
- New fields and editing symbols can be added live, dependent on data output content.
- Math can be applied to data output content, after which decisions can be made, breaks in data created, and sums, totals, averages, and so forth, added to output.
- Output may be ordered any way you want.

## 15.6. SELECTION OF DATA RECORDS (INPUT)

Query uses all the AS/400 selection criteria (see Logical Views in Part 1) plus 10 types of data "tests" for relevancy to your purpose, with as many as 100 of these tests allowed for one single field type.

You can specify the selection criteria for the data you want to analyze through the Query definition. Or, for quicker response, you can use an already existing Logical View (File) from the database, wherein the data sorting and sifting will already have been done. For the output, you can define new output editing in Query or use already defined database defaults.

In general, this is true: You have all the original choices for data selection and massaging through Query that you had in originally defining your data to the system, for Logical View and for printer or display output files. It is your choice whether you want to use preexisting definitions (they are quicker, at Query time) or define new data selection, editing, and usage. The only thing that must exist before you do your Query inquiry is the data, which must be already housed in your database in some physical file.

Query works on physical files, through either its own generated Logical View (paths) or one you predefined for this or other purposes. It has its own special automatically generated "OPEN," which is where it does all the work of creating the path tables and sifting and sorting Views.

## 15.7. CONCEPTS OF DATA SELECTION

Query data selection is a two-step process:

1. You test certain data fields (you specify which) in a database record type for certain attributes. If the fields pass the test, the record "passes." It is considered to be chosen as input for the Query function.
2. You:
   - "Select" fields from the chosen records to create a *new record* for *output*.
   - *Sequence* the *fields* how you wish.
   - *Sort* the new *records* for output based on any fields you wish, concatenated for the sort if you name more than one field.

Add to these basics the JOIN function (see following) and you get a very rich data-sifting mechanism that you can use from your terminal (wherever it may be), to examine one set of data or many, from many points of view, ad hoc and dynamically.

The analytical possibilities are myriad.

## 15.8. INPUT JOIN

To interrelate various datasets in the system you may want to use the AS/400 system's built-in data management record JOIN facility.

Here are the JOIN methods you can tell Query to use:

- ALL OR NOTHING. This option tells Query to select (primary) records (the record type to which you want to anchor (join) other "secondary" record types) with their "matching" (secondary) records (from other datasets) *only* if *each and every* (secondary) record type (file) you specified for the search to match a field does contain a matching data field (the data contents) match the primary search field).

- ANY ONE. Query will select only those (primary) records that have a matching field in *any one* record type of the chosen secondary records.
- ALL. Query selects all the primary records and will JOIN them to matching secondary records if there is a match. If not, it will join them to a default you choose, blank or otherwise.

Note that the AS/400 can also select matches outside of conventional relational theory; that is, you could select those records that do *not* have a JOIN matching field, or all the secondary records that do *not* have a primary match, and so forth. This function is sometimes essential for statistical analysis.

## 15.9. FORMATTED OUTPUT REPORTS

You define formatted output reports by answering prompts through which you define new headings and footings, along with column headings, for your live report. You *can* use words that were predefined as the "Text" when the files were defined to the database originally. The output may be ordered any way you choose. You can apply mathematical formulae to the Query-selected output to find data break points or to create new data to be included in your report. Query will find the break points and place the subtotals, averages, means, or whatever at those points for you. It will also do printer control (ejecting paper, skipping lines, and so forth) at those points if you so indicate.

## 15.10. THE QUERY PROMPTS

You start Query by typing STRQRY on the command input line of your Main Menu. The first Query prompt menu you see looks like Screen 15.1. If you type a 1 ("Work with queries") on the command line, you will then receive the next prompt screen (Screen 15.2).

The third screen you will see (Screen 15.3) asks you to tell it which query definition screens you want to be prompted about,

```
                         Query Utilities
QUERY
Select one of the following   (for end users)
   1. Work with Queries
   2. Run an existing Query program
   3. Delete a Query program

Query management              (for programmers)
  10. Work with Query management forms
  11. Work with Query management queries
  12. Start a query
  13. Analyze an AS/400 Query definition
  14. Start a query, allowing AS/400 Query definitions

Selection or command:
 =====> _(1)_ then ENTER
F3=Exit  F4=Prompt  F9=Retrieve  F12=Cancel  F13=user
F16=System MAIN Menu                              exit
```

**Screen 15.1.** First Query Menu.

```
              Work with Queries

Type choices, press Enter.
  Option ____(1)___   1=Create     9=Run
                      2=Change
                      3=Copy
                      4=Delete
                      5=Display
                      6=Print definition
                      8=Run as Batch job
Query________(your chosen name) Name, F4 for list
                        of catalogued query programs
  Library ____(your lib name) __  Name, *LIBL, F4 for
                           list of libraries
F3=Exit F4=Prompt F5=Refresh F12=Cancel
```

**Screen 15.2.** Work with Queries Menu.

```
                Define the Query

Query __________(your name) ____       Option:  CREATE
   Library ________________

Type options, press Enter. Press F21 to select ALL options.
  Type a 1 for selection
    _1_  Specify File selections
    _1_  Define result fields
    ___  Select and sequence fields
    ___  Select sort fields
    ___  Select collating sequence
    ___  Specify report column formatting
    ___  Specify report summary functions
    ___  Define report breaks
    ___  Select output type and output form
    ___  Specify processing options

                          F21=Select ALL
 F3=Exit  F5=Report  F12=Cancel  F13=Layout  F18=Files
```

**Screen 15.3.** Query Screen selection prompts.

including input, data massage, and output definitions. Now you will be fed prompt screens to:

1. Name the datasets (files—up to 32 of them) that you want to inquire within (F4 gives you all possible data files for your use).
2. Indicate the fields to be tested for attributes you are looking for, from the field lists fed to you (from your named datasets).
3. Give the sequence you want these fields to be in.
4. Select the "records" you want by specifying tests against the data field content in these records, i.e., all the records in which the person's middle initial is "W."
5. Create derived ("result") fields from data within fields—for

example, do math on numeric fields or concatenate data from these fields into new data and new fields.

6. Search for exact matches and inexact categories. For example, you can search data for logical comparisons like height greater than six feet; eyes equal to brown; or logical truths or falsities. You can also search for mathematical ranges of data or for similarities such as Name LIKE'%Smit%', which gives you such names as Smith, Smithson, Smithers, Smite, Smitt, and Arrowsmith. Or you can search for all the names that have an "A" in the second position, specified thus: Name LIKE '—A%'. This gives you Matthew, Mark, Larry, Jasper, Casper, Varesh, Sadish, Tamor, Laurence, Barbe, Marnie, Karl, Kaija, Tamaroff, and Kanzi.

And you will be asked to define output specifications such as:

7. The sorting sequence of output records using as many as 32 concatenated fields if you wish (for example, Day within Month within Year, then the Zip code, then Last name, and finally First name.
8. Output headings, column spacing, and any other layout rules.

## 15.11. INTERMEDIATE RESULTS

Pressing F5 during the Query process on any of the prior screens lets you see your Query output results so far. If you press it after sorting by data, zip code, and names, you might have intermediate output that looks like Screen 15.4.

You can page up and down with Page keys on your terminal, and left or right (if your report is wider than your 80-column screen) by using function keys F19 and F20. If you use F21, overly long lines will wrap under the first half of the line.

Now you take a look at the output, decide if it is formatting to your liking, and then continue to define what you want to the Query process, including altering what you have done so far. It is nice not to have to wait until you have completely finished defining the inquiry to see how you are doing.

The output field editing screen for numeric fields looks like Screen 15.5.

```
    QUERY                   Display Report

    Date of Purchase         Areacode     Name

00010  1 Sept 1992            10105        Andrews, John
00020                         10105        Zitwitz, Alex
00030                         28609        Bentham, Jeremy
00040  5 Sept 1992            10025        Barkley, Arthur
00050                         20209        Andres, Corinne
00060                         20209        Smithson, John
00070                         20210        Anjou, Kirin
00080                                                     more
00090 F3=Exit F12=Cancel  F19=Left  F20=Right  F21=Split
```

**Screen 15.4.** Query intermediate output.

```
                  Describe Numeric Field Editing

Field____________________   (type in field name)
Type choice, press Enter.
  Decimal point          ___   1=.  2=,  3=:  4=$  5=None
  Thousands separator    ___   1=.  2=,  3='  4=Blank
  Show negative sign?    ___   Y=Yes  N=No
    Left negative sign___      (key in sign)
    Right sign           ___   (key in sign)
  Show Currency symbol___      Y=Yes  N=No
    Symbol on left       ___   (key in symbol)
    Symbol on right      ___   (key in symbol)
  Print Zero values      ___   Y=Yes  N=No
  Replace leading
          zeroes         ___   Y=Yes  N=No
           with          ___   1=Blanks 2=* 3=Floating sign
  Use one leading zero___      Y=Yes  N=No

(you get these choices for each field of numeric output)

F3=Exit  F5=Report  F10=Process/previous  F12=Cancel
F13=Layout  F16=Remove Edit  F18=Files
```

**Screen 15.5.** Describe Numeric Field Editing screen for output.

## 15.12. MISCELLANEOUS QUERY FUNCTION

Here are some other, miscellaneous Query functions:

- Totals, averages, minimums, maximums, record counts—the summary report screen prompts you to define on which fields you want these functions.
- Report break points—the "Define Report Breaks" screen prompts you to define fields you want analyzed for changes in data on which to base breaks in the report formatting. A following screen prompts you to supply text to put at the break points, summary type data to be printed, what level of break it is (nine are possible), and so forth.

## 15.13. RUNNING THE INQUIRY OR SAVING THE QUERY DEFINITION

Pressing F3 (Exit) after you are done takes you back to the "Define the Query" screen. From here, F3 takes you to the "Exit this Query" screen, which gives you the options of saving the query definition, running it, or doing both. You get a chance here to add some descriptive text and to define once again what library you want to house it in, as well as what authority you want it to be run under in the future and in what mode (interactive or batch). I suggest *not* filling in these items until you have seen a sample run of the inquiry. Afterward, go back and describe it as the user will see it.

Now you are done. Exit back to the AS/400 Main Menu (F3) and sign off (option 90 on the Main Menu). Your Query definition can be recalled to be modified any time, from Query's original prompt screen, option 1 "Work with queries," using the Change option from that follow-on screen.

## 15.14. QUERY OPEN (OPNQRYF)

The Query OPEN has a special nonquery function that is worth noting. Query OPEN can be used in front of other, nonquery programs or applications to dynamically create and build access paths to your ad hoc specifications. It will use an already built path if one exists that will serve.

Query OPEN will use the relational functions:

Order
Selection
Projection
JOIN

It will add output control function as follows:

- Add new fields derived from old
- Group records by data class
- Average fields
- Do totals and subtotals
- Do sophisticated mathematic function such as hyperbolic arc tangents based on the data in fields

This Query OPEN creates a temporary Logical View that will be destroyed when you close the file in your program or end this job. However, it is perfectly feasible, indeed smart, to use the work it does on the data to get your data ready for some batch mode program or some interactive application. You can save a great deal of data-preparation programming by learning to use the Query OPEN for other than query purposes.

The rules for using OPNQRYF in a regular program are as follows:

1. Use Override SHARE(*YES) for the database file to be opened, so that your program OPEN won't take precedence and nullify the Query OPEN options.
2. Issue OPNQRYF, responding to its relational operations and selection of record definition prompts.
3. CALL your program.

Your program input will only see the records selected by the Query OPEN, all sorted, sifted, and selected as you specified in the OPEN prompt.

Here is an example of Query OPEN in batch mode:

```
OVRDBF      FILE (logical file name)
            TOFILE (physical file name)
            SHARE(*YES)
OPNQRYF     FILE(*CURLIB/physical file name)
            QRSLT (all your selection items)
CALL        your program name
CLOF        physical file name
```

*Note: The CLOF will delete the paths to data created by OPNQRYF.*

To use the Query OPEN interactively, just key in the comma at the bottom of your main menu, precede or follow it with an override statement, and then call your program from your terminal using the CL CALL statement as shown here.

# 16

# Business Graphics Utility (BGU)

Like other natural AS/400 interfaces, the BGU is interactive, entirely menu-driven, and sharable across the entire system. That is, it can reach any data files on the system, it can share them with other interface users concurrently (under the system protective control of who gets to use what, when), and its output can become input to any other natural system interface or HLL program. In similar fashion, the output from other natural interfaces can be used as input to the BGU when appropriate. For instance, output from Query (some subset of data records reshaped and rebuilt somewhat by Query) can be input to the graphing capabilities of BGU. You should think of all of these interfaces as sharable in this way.

## 16.1. BGU CHART FUNCTION

You can invoke BGU from any attached terminal. It is a chart-making tool that takes data from your database and charts it on your screen in response to answers you supply to prompt menus. Using the system COPY function you can send the output charts to any and all screens on your system when they look right to you. You don't do any of the drawing of the graphics, so you don't have to know which terminal you are doing charts for. Any AS/400 terminal or plotter that is all-points-addressable (and some printers) will do. As with all AS/400 natural interfaces, the hardware characteristics are not the user's concern but are taken care of by the machine itself, automatically. There are no bit strings to deal with. You select options on menus for the parameters of the graph, the text you want to explain it, how you want to place it on the screen or page, how many graphs you want on one display, and so forth.

The graphs you can create are as follows:

- Bar charts
- Line charts
- Surface charts
- Histograms
- Pie charts
- Venn diagrams
- Text charts

Charted (input) data can be from any database files, at the physical level or, preferably, from Logical Views, or you can key in data from your terminal. Data from different Logical Views can be joined and shown on one graph, and different graphs of the same data can be shown on one output.

Like the other natural interactive interfaces, you can Save the output of the menu-driven creation process, which is a CL program, and you can run it later as a program either interactively or in batch mode. Also, once you become skilled in the use of the tool, you can use the CL commands directly, without going through the prompt screens, to create a chart-drawing program. Another nice thing you can do is create analysis charts at one location, on one AS/400 data system, and then send the program itself to another system to analyze its data or to be used by that system's interactive users to analyze their data. The users can modify the program as they run it to reach their own libraries and data or to change any of the titles or formatting on the output screen.

The charts that are the output of the programs generated by BGU can be saved also, as a GDF (Graphics Data File), or they can be transmitted to other systems or merged into Office Vision documents, Query output, or other interactive or HLL programs. BGU is an integrated interface.

## 16.2. SUPPORTED DEVICES

The devices supported by BGU (they must have graphics capability) as of June 1992 are these:

- 5292-2 terminal
- PC with VGA, EGA, CGA with 5292 emulation (all graphics-capable)
- PC with PGA (graphics printer)
- PS/2 with workstation emulation or AS/400 PC package
- 5224, 5225 printers
- IPDS graphics-capable printers (3812, 3816, 3820, 3825, 3827, 3835, 4028, 4224, and 4234)
- 7371, 7372, 6180, 6182 plotters

I list these devices because point-by-point graphics programs, requiring "all-points-addressable" hardware, cannot by definition run on all AS/400 devices (actually, they can, but the results will not be as expected). This is one case where the AS/400 is hardware dependent.

Graphs are in color or just two-tone if your device is not color-capable.

The prompts for BGU are much like those for Query, only there are fewer, and the results, as in Query, can be permanent or temporary as you wish. I will not draw pictures of all the prompts here; by now you know the drill. Try out BGU by keying STRBGU from your command line, and follow the prompts to see all you can do with it. Then read Chapter 18 to understand the power you have with this little BGU package. Notice that the BGU output comprises GDF files that can be shipped around the network, just as the GDDM files can. If BGU does not give you all you want in graphics, I say again, as I say in the GDDM chapter, consider a PC package that can produce output that can be shipped freely around your network via the AS/400 to other PCs on this or other systems.

# 17

# SQL

It is important to know the history behind SQL in the AS/400. SQL was built for IBM mainframes and later retrofitted to the AS/400 database machine. This semi-Structured Query Language, SQL, was added to the AS/400 so that the system would have a query language compatible with the large IBM mainframe 370 series of computers. In the very large systems the mainframe query language sits atop the add-on database, DB2. In the smaller 370-type systems the product runs with the disk access method VSAM. None of these underpinnings approach the high level of machine interface the AS/400 provides to the programmer, but in *this* case it works well anyway because of the inherent relational structure of the entire AS/400 machine. In fact, I believe SQL works better on the AS/400 than it does on the older systems it was designed for, because the latter had to do a lot of work (programming) to get to the level of relational support that SQL was meant to bring to the user. Also, the older 370 architected systems had to accommodate running SQL concurrently with their former separate-but-equal chained and hierarchical database designs, which were layered on top of the operating systems like access methods. The midsized 370-type systems also had to build SQL by using the already available, nonrelational access method, since it was thought that such systems could not accommodate the very large, complex bundles of code that the relational database DB2 entailed.

## 17.1. SQL RELATED TO THE AS/400 AND SET THEORY

The SQL package on the AS/400, compared to other midrange SQL systems, is, in my opinion, the best choice for both function and performance, because the AS/400 underpinnings fit very well with the SQL language, needing no new access methods or new database packages to accommodate it. The question for AS/400 users is not "Is SQL going to work well on my system?" (the answer is yes) but rather "Is SQL the best of the query interfaces for my purposes and for the experience level of my end users?" To do the best queries using SQL, one would be well off to be a logical mathematician well versed in set theory—pure set theory is what the language itself is. You choose elements of data from sets and subsets using AND-OR logic, restraining your query by set theory bounds. For *good* query results you must abide by set theory's relational rules of union (JOIN), intersection, difference, and complement, which embody the arithmetic rules of commutation, association, distribution, idempotent, complementarity, dualization, and involution. Appendix H presents my oversimplified sixth-grade-level review of all this math, which I imagine you forgot long ago.

Regardless, you can get very useful and quick information about your data using SQL without having to know logical algebra at all, if you remain aware that you may get odd results if your logic is incorrect. If your end users know their data well (say they created it in the first place or they work with it in nonautomated ways a great deal of the time), they will recognize a strange response from SQL.

## 17.2. WHERE TO USE SQL

The best thing about SQL is that it is designed to be reiteratively interactive—that is, you do a query, look at your results, and then narrow down your quest by using more delimiting parameters and redoing the query until you get it right. I think the first use of this language, or any other reiterative language, should be by teams comprising your business data analysts plus your SQL teacher, not one or the other alone. One will pick up logical errors by the seat of his pants, the other by the theory of the language. Together they will devise rules for some fine query usage for your business analysis people that will serve as a base to develop further use of SQL. This can be very valuable indeed in helping to provide information about your business to help guide your growth.

The SQL language can be used quite simply for ad hoc data gathering or to develop slide presentations with convincing backup data. It can also be used a little more intensively by semiprogrammer types with a bent toward logical thinking (old FORTRAN or PL/I users, for example) to analyze business data from new and interesting points of view. Alternatively, it can be used by relational theory experts to build intricate models of your business, which the AS/400 system can keep current automatically via its ability to keep all your Access Paths and Views (pointers to data that falls within your sets) dynamically "au courant."

Inevitably, end users will get better and better at using SQL and will find out what power really lies behind it. For this reason, it is very important to put security holds around all the function and all the data, assigning very carefully who can do what to which data. Recognize that a relational machine, in achieving ease of interfacing to data and in opening up the entire system (which is one grand database in the case of the AS/400) to an interactive terminal user (even a remote user), can be a wonderful benefit as well as a terrible danger. Even if you have never before needed to use the security functions of the AS/400, you *will* need to do so with this product. Don't let your data leave home without it.

## 17.3. INTERACTIVE SQL

You can use SQL interactively, entering pure SQL statements from your terminal, or you can imbed SQL statements in a COBOL or other HLL program, using a preprocessor for the statements before you compile the HLL program itself. Since SQL is a data analysis and retrieval language, designed to give you listings of tables and answers to search questions (queries), it makes sense to use it interactively. Often you will get an answer to a query about your data that only clarifies what it is you really want to know, at which point you will want to enter another query about the same data. In such a case you don't want to go through multiple compilations per inquiry and have batch output put onto some printer. This is not to say that once you have refined a query to the desired output, you can't then make it into a batch program to be rerun on some periodic basis. You can do so if it suits you. However, even if my goal were to have a report based on a certain dataset printed out every week, I would still test out the query interactively at first just to give myself the chance at many iterations until I got it exactly right, without having to adhere to system work schedules.

## 17.4. PROMPTING

The AS/400 SQL language is prompted just like any other AS/400 natural interface. This means you can type an SQL statement with no parameters and then hit F4 (function key 4) to be prompted for all the parameters of this statement. Or you can type the SQL statement with your parameters, put the cursor over the parameter you need prompting about, and then hit F4 to be prompted for what and how that particular parameter works and how and if you should use it. You can get to the SQL prompt screen from a prompt on your programmer screen. Once there, if you want to see the entire SQL command set, type F4 before you do anything else. Then you can select any of these commands and go from there.

You can teach yourself all of SQL except, of course, good logic. Let's say you choose the SELECT statement from the SQL prompt screen by putting an X next to it on the screen. At this point F4 will tell you how to use SELECT and what all the parameters are. Then you type in the parameters. To be prompted about one particular parameter, put the cursor over it and hit F4. You will be given all the rules about its use. This can be done in the middle of entering your interactive SQL statements. SQL is truly interactive and almost completely integrated* into the AS/400 system

*With one exception: SQL requires a dedicated library.

(unlike most of the so-called compatibility interfaces added to the system).

AS/400 natural prompting levels within SQL:

| SQL statement: | Result on screen: |
|---|---|
| SELECT (F4) | Prompts about SELECT |
| SELECT par (F4)er1, . . . | Prompts about parameter1 |

## 17.5. GETTING STARTED

You get to the SQL screen by typing the CL command STRSQL on the command line at the bottom of your sign-on screen. Name the library (in SQL, the "Collection") from which you want to see data as follows:

```
STRSQL      LIBOPT(*my_SQL_lib)
```

This STRSQL command lets you build, edit, enter into the system, and run an SQL statement or a set of statements, interactively. Hitting F4 after typing STRSQL will give you the entire parsing breakdown for this command.

The first SQL screen is shown in Screen 17.1.

```
Enter SQL
Type SQL statement, press ENTER:
--->________________________________________________
____________________________________________________
____________________________________________________
____________________________________________________
____________________________________________________
F3=Exit  F4=Prompt   F6=Insert line  F9=Retrieve
10=Copy line  F13=Services  F14=Delete line
F15=Split line  F16=Select Collections (libraries)
F17=Select tables (files)  F18=Select columns (fields)
```

**Screen 17.1.** The first SQL screen.

You then type:

```
SELECT      (F4)______________________________
____________________________
____________________
```

Typing the SELECT then F4 as above gives you a prompt screen to help you define all the parameters of your SELECT command. This level of prompt exists for every SQL command, just as it exists for all the AS/400 CL commands.

The SELECT prompt that F4 gets you to appears in Screen 17.2. From this SELECT prompt screen you can define your complete SQL SELECT command from the data tables (files) you want to work with, including what criteria to use for data selection or omission, the arrangement of the output tables, and even whether or not these tables should be "joined" relationally with other tables before the resulting tables are drawn up.

```
Specify SELECT Statement

Type information for SELECT statement. Press F4 for list.
 From tables. . . . . . . ___________________________
 SELECT columns. . . . ______________________________
 WHERE conditions. . ________________________________
 GROUP BY columns. . ________________________________
 HAVING conditions. _________________________________
 ORDER BY columns. . ________________________________
 FOR UPDATE OF columns ______________________________

Type choices, press Enter.

 DISTINCT rows in result table. . . . . . .N  Y=Yes, N=No
 UNION with another SELECT. . . . . . . . .N  Y=Yes, N=No

F3=Exit  F4=Prompt  F5=Refresh  F6=Insert line
F9=Subquery  F10=Copy line  F12=Cancel  F24=More prompts
```

**Screen 17.2.** SELECT prompt.

This prompting goes on and on, supporting every SQL command at every level and function. You can learn by it, use it for a while until you are used to SQL, then drop it and just enter your SQL commands cold on the first screen once you know what you are doing. This means that you do not need to be an expert before you start using SQL; you can learn as you go. Keep in mind that the system uses a lot of cycles to support this kind of interaction. I suggest you assign your "learn-as-you-go" SQL users to lunch-hour usage or some other not-so-busy time of day on the system.

### 17.6. TYPES OF SQL STATEMENTS

There are three types of SQL statements you enter from your terminal:

1. SQL database definition statements
2. SQL data manipulation (retrieval and update) statements
3. SQL program flow control statements

### 17.7. SQL DATA MANIPULATION COMMANDS

The SQL data manipulation commands are SELECT, INSERT, and UPDATE. And here are the commands you use to control the flow and understanding of your "program":

| | |
|---|---|
| COMMENT, LABEL ON | To identify your statements. |
| GRANT, REVOKE | To give to someone else, or revoke usage authority over tables and views you create. |
| DROP | To drop a column or row. |
| INSERT | To add a column or row to a table. |
| LOCK TABLE | To keep all others from using this table while you are updating it. |
| COMMIT, ROLLBACK | To hold back on updating the real tables (physical files) until all the pieces of your transaction are completed; to roll back to the beginning of your last transaction if a problem arises. |

## 17.8. INTERACTIVE TABLE CREATION COMMANDS

Here are the interactive SQL commands you use to create your relational data table's structures:

CREATE
  COLLECTION (an AS/400 library)
  TABLE (an AS/400 physical file)
  VIEW (an AS/400 Logical File)
  INDEX (an AS/400 access path plus parts of the physical file or Logical File setup)
DELETE (the same items as above)

## 17.9. MORE ON DATA MANIPULATION COMMANDS

An end user can learn to use the data manipulation commands SELECT, INSERT, and UPDATE almost immediately. Trial and error will self-teach. To set up the database using the CREATE commands requires a database specialist who is trained in relational theory, working with a business expert (perhaps the end user) who knows what she wants to milk out of the data both now and later on. This should be a combined effort, with the businessperson asking a lot of questions of the database specialist such as "Can I do this or that with it afterwards?" "How can I mix together different kinds of data?" "Suppose the business goes in this direction—can I find out the following?" "Could I go back to using it this other way?" and so forth. Be sure all these questions can be answered yes, because the AS/400 can do just about anything with data that you want it to do, and if SQL cannot, you should be using the native database interface on the system.

## 17.10. USING INTERACTIVE SQL

You can type in a single SQL SELECT or UPDATE statement, just as in the AS/400 CL language, and interactively execute it. Or you can type in a group of statements to be executed as an SQL program. After you see the results, you can save the statement or statements you just ran, and you can also redirect the data output to a database file if you like. Later you can run these statements again, modifying the set of statements to run on different data if you wish (change the Collection parameter) or with different options for output (say a different terminal or a printer). You can also run the "program" in a different manner, say with commitment control this time.

To modify or save your statements, you press function key 13, F13. SQL statements you successfully tested and ran can now be saved in your database for later insertion into a HLL batch program or for shipment down line to another system to be executed there later in batch mode. (For now, you cannot do SQL interactive queries across the AS/400 Distributed Data Management interface (DDM) on a remote system from your local terminal, except across a LAN network to a data-server, which is beyond the scope of this book.)

Note that you should use F13 no matter what, just to specify to the SQL parser that you would like it to check out that your statements can successfully reach the objects your SELECT or UPDATE criteria aim you toward. Remember, you have to have security clearance for the commands, the libraries, the views, the real data (tables)—everything. F13 lets you know your logic is right *before* you try executing the request.

## 17.11. INTERACTIVE RETRIEVAL

Here is all you do to retrieve data using SQL from your terminal:

1. On the SQL Menu, type the SELECT statement.
2. If you need to review it, hit the F4 prompt key.
3. Hit Enter to compile the statement.

You will be interactively prompted to correct any errors. You are putting your statements through a syntax checker every time you hit Enter. Thus, your errors will be pointed out and you will be shown interactively how to correct them. Hit F21 now if you want to see a parsed SQL statement as far as you have gone.

To quit this mode hit F12 or F3. F12 cancels your efforts, taking you out of prompting mode; F3 exits this process and takes you back to where you were before you started the SQL operation. If you correct the statement, F12 (or F13) adds the correctly parsed statement to a statement list SQL is building for you, making a program. If you don't correct the statement, it will not be added to this list. This means that you can work along making one good statement after another, and if you make a bad one, it will not be added to the good ones that you have collected so far. When you figure out what it is you should be doing with this statement, you can pick up again later on this program without losing all that went before. This is a nice feature. When you hit Enter, if the parser deems your statement to be correct, it gives you positive feedback by moving it up the screen a notch, placing it next to those statements already successfully parsed.

At the end of your effort, use F13, the services prompt key, to save your entire interactive session on paper and/or in a database file. This is a good idea for new SQL users because an SQL specialist can look over the work later on and give suggestions for improving your queries (perhaps for data integrity but also for performance, that is, turnaround, reasons).

## 17.12. RUNNING SQL

If you know what you want, define your database file (what library—"Collection" in SQL—your query can be answered from) in your original STRSQL command. If you want to know what data you are authorized to look at, enter SELECT FROM and then hit F16, F17, or F18. You will be shown all the objects you are privileged to see.

F16 tells you your allowed *"Collections"* (libraries).
F17 tells you your *"Tables"* (physical files) and *Views* (Logical Files or Views) you can use.
F18 tells you your allowed *"Columns"* (some fields may be denied you).

You will now be able to pull any of the listed data objects (collections, tables, views, and columns) into your SELECT statement at the location at which you place the cursor.

If for some unknown reason you do not get back the data you think you asked for, go back to prompt mode and hit F4, and you will be given a list of objects available to you. Your STRSQL statement may not have named the correct library (Collection) for you, in which case you will have been defaulted to your profile name, or to the *CURLIB or *LIBL normal AS/400 system default library search objects, because the system didn't know what data you wanted. Pressing F13 puts you into the corrective control mode, wherein you can ask the prompter to check out your statements for proper object (data) usage, without actually running the statement or program.

Later, when you have used the SQL command and table selection prompting mechanisms for a while, you will get familiar enough with the system to correctly type in your full SQL statements list without prompting, using the bare-bones SQL language. You can still go back to the prompt mode any time, anywhere in the process, just as you can on all the other AS/400 natural interfaces.

SQL is fun to learn in this prompted interactive way and once you have learned the language, fun to use.

## 17.13. DATA INTEGRITY AND PRIVACY

Here is a word of caution about unleashing your databases to casual end users via SQL. There are two SQL statements you can use interactively (from any terminal) that grant and revoke authority to another user to use your physical files (SQL Tables) or Logical Views (SQL Views). The AS/400 does *not* allow you to go through SQL to change authority on objects that were not created with SQL. In other words, opening up SQL to end users does not impair the security of your system database. However, if you do use SQL to create the *system* database, these two SQL commands can be interactively invoked from the terminal to grant and revoke security authorities. With these, the creator of the SQL objects (data and Views), or anyone the creator has passed authority on to, can grant or revoke authority to another user to use his or her physical files, the SQL underlying tables of real data, or logical views (from which, in SQL, updates can be done). If there is collusion among end users, this can lead to a serious breach of data security, especially since SQL makes it so easy to retrieve and alter the actual data in the SQL database, not just mirror images of it (as on some systems). Therefore, I suggest you not give to any end user the authority to create, and therefore own, the physical data tables. Create them under the Security Officer or Database Manager's control. Give the end users the authority to create and own Views, which are merely templates through which data is seen. Give them Read Only, not Update authority over the physical tables, because they must have this to see the data, even through a View.

If users must update their data, and if it is mostly data for their usage and not for other system users, you can devise a library a user group owns completely, that is not shared across the system. You can also devise a system in which you download to a PC copies of the files they want to work with and then let them manipulate these copies all day long. If you have PS/2 PCs with SQL on them, you can run the logging option while updating at the PC, and use this log later to update the company database back at the AS/400. There are AS/400 users doing all this across LAN networks, and it works easily and very well.

Using SQL, normal AS/400 system-controlled authority checks are made during each stage of the SQL job: at statement parsing and prompting time, at compile (process) time (that means when you hit the Enter key after entering a SQL statement), and at run time.

Note: Views are a good place to put security in order to shield interactive SQL users from seeing data you want to protect. Define the views they can use at a system level and have your database specialist or security person do the actual CREATE and provide the authorizations, which can be field by field if need be. Do not authorize the end user to use the CREATE function.

Authorization checks that are done as you use SQL:

1. The SQL compiler—have you been authorized to use it?
2. SQL commands—which ones are you authorized to use?
3. SQL Views of data—which ones?
4. Data—the fields (Columns), record sets (Tables), and libraries (SQL Collections) your inquiry reaches down to—are you authorized to see it? touch it? change it?
5. If you are using the COBOL or other HLL SQL CALLS, are you authorized to use the preprocessor and the HLL compiler?

You can see that security is an elaborate AS/400 function, as well it should be when you are using such an easy, available interface to system data.

## 17.14. INTEGRITY

Data integrity means insuring that your data is never incorrectly changed by failing or halfway-done operations, by improper updates, by hardware or disk paging problems, or by data sharing by two or more concurrent users. Every time a user sees data, it is the most up-to-date, the only, and the correct version of that data in the system. The AS/400 system prevents data integrity problems by managing all data activity within the hardware itself, treating all user activity as mere requests for data change. The system never really changes data before it has insured its integrity. The functions it uses to insure data integrity are journaling, commitment control, save/restore, damage tolerance, index recovery, atomic operations, and concurrency control. If you are interested in these topics, a good database design book will help you. Suffice it to say here that the AS/400 is state of the art in this area. It absolutely insures the integrity of the SQL catalog in each library (SQL Collection), no matter where an update comes from (SQL, system, or other user).

For SQL use, the AS/400 Database Manager implicitly acquires locks on all tables (files) and rows (records) to prevent concurrent users from changing the same data at once. So-called "deadly embraces" are also prevented because the system data manager sees your entire program sequence ahead of time (remember program "encapsulation" back in the database section?). It only starts the processes that can see their way clear to completion without contention for data with someone else. If within your own program you manage to lock out a future statement of your own and a deadlock structure ensues, due to timing of the data requests, the AS/400 will only keep the lock shut until the specified or default time (taken from your database definition way back when); then it will voluminously notify you and unloosen the locks to continue. You have a logical error in your program, which is serious in data operations, so you should remove the program, study it, and correct the logic. If you have half-completed data updates, the Rollback function of commitment control will allow you to reset your database (tables) back to what they were when the defective operation started. An operator prompt helps you to accomplish this.

You can lock the entire physical file set if you are using SQL to update your database. I am not in favor of updating your files from the SQL interface. I cannot think of a reason why you could not use the normal AS/400 interactive database tools for the actual data update, which would ensure data integrity, concurrency, and sharability. Why leave your company database purity up to end users who have a single user view of the system? As I said earlier, if your end user has his own subsetted copy of a portion of your database, you can let him fiddle with it any way he wants, but when it comes time to update the system database, use the update journal, rather than the updates themselves, as source data. And have your database person do the system updates. This can be fairly easily automated.

## 17.15. SQL SUMMARY

SQL is a very good tool for casual retrieval, ad hoc queries and reports, and data analysis. Once learned, it is closer to the end user's data-use mentality than to the computer programmer's mentality, which is why it was built. Because it so effortlessly opens up the data interface, making entire sets of data available for perusal, it can pose a security risk. For this reason, it is littered with locks on the data to protect you from yourself. If you use the batch mode HLL interfaces to SQL, the lock protection is invoked every time you open a file. Since you open a file on every HLL call to SQL, this means just about every statement. On the interactive SQL interface you can have some control over the locking by specifying your files outside of SQL, defining your own lock status, and defining all your interactive users as Read Only with no live updating of files. In addition, you can soup up performance a little by teaching your end users to build their queries, compile them, house them in their library, and invoke the already compiled queries from their terminals, rather than reproducing them from scratch every time.

## 17.16. SO-CALLED "DYNAMIC" SQL PROGRAMS (HLL)

In addition to interactive and batch-mode high level language CALL interfaces, SQL has a third, so-called "dynamic" interface, which is meant to be used with an HLL program but not precompiled. This interface is a set of SQL commands you can build into your PL/I or C program to make it a kind of "load and go" SQL program. That is, during the actual run of your compiled PL/I program, your SQL statements will be preprocessed and compiled, the data binding will occur, and then the SQL statements will be run. This is in comparison to the normal way of precompiling the SQL statements and then compiling the HLL program they are within. In this third option for SQL, you tell your HLL compiler that you are using the "dynamic" SQL interface. This is such a bad method for the normal AS/400 shop that I hesitate even to mention it.

Disadvantages of the SQL "dynamic" interface:

1. It requires PL/I or C language skills because COBOL, RPG, FORTRAN, etc., do not have the ability to manage address variables, which are required for this interface.
2. No reiterative process allows you to preview your output.
3. It is definitely *not* an ease-of-use interface.
4. It requires complete knowledge of error-code handling, which is rare in the AS/400 world, as it should be.
5. It opens up a wide area for errors in execution, which then impact total system performance and other system users.
6. CPU utilization is terrible for this load-go mode.
7. SQL was designed for live, decision-making terminal users, not for static programmed batch interfaces. This interface has the negatives of the batch interface, while at the same time it does not supply the versatile function of the interactive interface.

Supposedly this "dynamic" SQL interface was designed so that a person on one computer system could invoke a query on another system by dynamically supplying the parameters to be plugged into the ready-and-waiting SQL program on the other system. Since the AS/400's latest release of DDM (Distributed Data Management) now allows cross-systems SQL interactive queries, this was a way to achieve them. This cumbersome interface no longer requires this kind of activity—the casual, ad hoc, or analytical inquiry. The new DDM interface that reaches across LAN and longer distance networks obviates the need for this older interface.

Should you need to do queries across systems using SQL, a nice way is to attach your AS/400s to a LAN ring, to which you also can attach PCs that will do the actual inquiry. Many people are doing this—SQL is compatibly available on PCs, AS/400s, and larger systems. There are cross-systems–compatible data design CASE tools available for SQL databases as well.

## 17.17. PERFORMANCE

SQL builds indexes to data columns and rows (in views) dynamically. That is, each piece of data entered into the system that is addressed by this view has its address added to the view as soon as it enters the underlying physical file (at data entry time). If you choose not to use journaling, SQL also rebuilds all its views' indexes entirely on each IPL after any abnormal system termination. If you are subject to system failures (power failures and the like) and have no battery backup, be sure to tell SQL to use AS/400 journaling. Now your indexes will not have to be rebuilt in their entirety on restart.

You use the CL command STRJRNAP to journal SQL indexes. In a heavily SQL oriented system this should be done at least every evening. Also, when you SAVE your data objects, *SAVE YOUR INDEXES* as well, using ACCPTH (*YES) on the SAVOBJ or SAVLIB command. Then at file RESTORE time the indexes do not have to be totally rebuilt, a function that takes a very long time. Any rebuilding that is necessary because of the way you aborted will be done properly, not as a blind rebuild of the entire index set.

Other performance considerations: When using SQL through a COBOL or other HLL, be aware that file OPENs and CLOSEs happen all the time. Almost every SQL CALL generates an OPEN. These OPENs build your entire SQL index scheme from scratch, locking the entire file the whole time. If possible, it is a good idea to place all your SQL statements within one CALL–RETURN sequence, to avoid OPENs.

When you specify UPDATE in your operation, SQL locks onto Views, rows, and even files. For performance reasons, keep your updates to a few special programs not run during prime time, if possible.

While safer for complex transactions, commitment control causes SQL to lock onto whatever rows (records) you are accessing until you release it, to keep other jobs from accessing the partially changed data before a "recoverable unit" is completed. It also requires journaling. All these things are performance hits. You always trade performance for data integrity and ease of use.

SQL automatically creates a journal when you create a Collection (an AS/400 library for SQL). The so-called journal Receiver (buffer) is created within the Collection. For improved performance, put the journal in your own auxiliary storage pool (ASP). You can turn off journaling if you do not need commitment control.

The way to improve performance for SQL or any other AS/400 operation is not to rearrange your database as you may have in past systems. First, try more system storage in the pool you are running in. Then be sure the machine pool that gets the leftovers is at least 140K. Examine the page fault records to determine if your pool is stressed. If system code is being paged out and in from the machine pool, the entire system will be impacted. If your SQL storage pool is cramped, you might run your inquiries at times of day that are less congested. Or you could download your SQL files to a PC and do your queries locally, at the terminal, with no updating.

After you get SQL-smart, you will learn better ways of sequencing your Select/Omit criteria that will cause the query to drop the largest portions of the database first, doing subsequent selections on lesser domains.

Since SQL is interactive, try a few things. That is what it is designed for.

# 18

# The Graphics Data Display Manager (GDDM)

## 18.1. HISTORY

The GDDM package, written originally to be layered atop the MVS operating system for the IBM 370 mainframe computer, gives you the ability to write programs that will produce pictures and charts for graphic representation of your data (pie charts, bar charts, even Venn diagrams), for presentation illustrations for instance, overhead projection slides, or to put pictures within data output. These pictures can be made on devices that have the special graphics hardware capability to address every point on the face of the display or printer or plotter (all-points-addressable). They cannot be made on devices that just print or display lines of alphanumerics. You have to have special hardware and special software to draw curved lines or draw between normal print lines. Plotters, laser printers, terminals, or PCs equipped with graphics adaptor cards will do. Don't expect that because you grew up on a PC that draws pictures, all display terminals can do that.

## 18.2. SUPPORTED DEVICES

On the AS/400, the following types of devices can be used with GDDM software:

1. Graphics-capable display devices (with so-called "workstation function") or PCs
2. Graphics-capable printers
3. Database files

The last item in the list, database files, is important. This means that even though graphics data is like no other data in the system, it can still be stored in the database, in a special format provided just for this purpose, called the Graphics Data Format file (GDF). Once you have created a picture you like, you can keep it for later use on this system, or, because it is a system file, it can be shipped down line to another system, or up to a 370-type system, to be displayed on a device on these. This is the major reason for the existence of this software package.

You might want to use an AS/400 as the creative workplace to house certain corporate data and to make the pictures and graphs (and other forms) you use regularly in your business. This is no trivial application, because graphics capability on your large system takes away a lot of performance from other work. Offloading this function to an AS/400 might be a good idea for mainframe organizations.

## 18.3. SOME ADVICE

If your AS/400 is the main computer for your company, I do not recommend the GDDM package because there are much better ways to meet the same requirements. You are better off not sharing your daily work system with this graphics package but rather using attached PCs, supplied with graphics cards and interactive graphics tools, of which there are many. An interactive tool makes sense because you always want to redraw a line, rearrange a title, change a color, or cut out some information from the chart—dynamically—each time you look at or present it. Having to reprogram for changes is cumbersome, the language itself is difficult (compared to other AS/400 function and certainly compared to the same function on a PC package), and the machine performance utilization is too much. You are warned in the manuals not to fill in fields with solid color and not to mix ordinary text with the pictures if you want good performance. Think about the fact that for every slightest change to the pictures you will have to recompile, whereas on the PC packages you usually just answer a menu concerning how you want the data displayed or use icons to help draw the pictures.

In current technology it is true that drawing a pixel-by-pixel picture on a screen or plotter is extremely CPU consuming in time, space (lines of code), and CPU utilization. But it makes sense to offload that utilization to a PC, not to combine it with your normal workload on your main computer. Also, there are more and better packages coming out for the PC every day. Usually no systems programmers are needed. It is worth the search to find the one to suit your needs. Then standardize on it, stay with it, and be happy with it. Don't allow a mixture of graphics packages in one organization. This technology just costs too much CPU.

Should you want to know a little about how GDDM works and what you can do with it, read on.

## 18.4. USING GDDM

The GDDM software will reside in the IBM-supplied library on the AS/400 called QSYS, in a display (and plotter) file called QDGDDM and in a printer file called QPGDDM. You describe your display device to the system in the normal way, using DDS (data definition language specs), probably via the interactive SEU system utility supplied for this purpose. Then, in the normal way, you create the display file using the CRTDSPF command. You specify the parameter ALWGPH, which means "allow graphics." This causes the display to be set to graphics mode when input and output operations occur. A small G will show up at the bottom of your screen. the graphics picture will be displayed as a background, dot for dot, with no regard to the screen format you may normally use for such things as delineating where input words will be put on the screen, securing output from the view of certain users, defining page control, and the like. In other words, graphic mode is quite different from normal input and output (verbal) mode.

You may have words in your picture, but they will be out of the graphics font library, not from the terminal's normal alpha character set. They will be drawn characters, dot by dot, along with the entire picture, just part of the bit map for the screen. You *can* overlay normal script on top of the picture using the display file definition for this device to house the words. In this case the words will be sent out to the terminal after the picture has been drawn from the previous bit map sent out, and these words will act as an overlay, obliterating whatever is underneath.

If you want your letters to be part and parcel of your picture, then use the graphics fonts and incorporate them into your picture. The graphics mode terminal actually changes hardware format, giving you less space between print lines. This shouldn't matter, because you can enlarge any font you choose from the graphics list to any size you like; you can even turn and twist the characters or draw them backwards. You can use Farsi, which reads right to left, if that is your choice.

## 18.5. DIFFERENCES FROM NATURAL AS/400 INTERFACES

Here are some things you need to know that are different from normal AS/400 interfaces:

1. There are no OVERRIDE commands (OVRDSPF—"Override the Display File") to change parameters dynamically as is usual on the AS/400.
2. Device errors are considered unrecoverable (severity 40).
3. If someone uses the Systems Request function to start a different job, any other job, from this terminal, even if the new job does not use graphics terminals, whatever *terminals* that new job uses *will be put in graphics mode.* If your system spits out weird printer output somewhere while someone is using GDDM, suspect this culprit.
4. The system will not take care of your mistakes in handling this device. For example, if you OPEN a device for graphics and forget to close it again when you are done, the next person trying to OPEN it will not be able to do so.

These rather horrendous omissions in the code are based upon the fact that the code is designed to mimic the 370 code it came from, which tends to take over the system rather than use the resources in the natural AS/400 shared way. Thus, it cuts itself off from the normal device handling of the AS/400, which would never leave you hanging in these ways. (This is why I prefer to stick to the natural AS/400 interfaces, which are designed to use the AS/400 function, not to mimic some other system architecture.) After all, the AS/400 machine was primarily designed for easy user interaction and productivity, with data and operating system function mostly buried in the hardware microcode.

Should you want this machine to make graphics in the exact same way your larger mainframe does, or if you have a worldwide mainframe-controlled (centralized) organization and you want to create standardized forms from the central system, you can generate them on an AS/400 at one site, then ship them out to all locations, to both 370-type and AS/400 computers, and keep the GDF files in the local sites, providing they all had compatible terminals and printers (perhaps you have an expert GDDM programmer hanging around!). If this is the case, read further—this package may be for you.

## 18.6. THE GDDM METHOD

You invoke GDDM through high level language (COBOL, PL/I, RPG, BASIC, PASCAL) CALL and TRANSFER statements imbedded in your program. Immediately following the CALL statements you supply GDDM with binary bit strings (the real bit string that will turn into both the commands to the external graphics device and the actual on–off bits for the picture to be drawn). As an option (in a second operation) you may overlay the screen with normal lines of text. This is tricky because this text comes not from GDDM but from your AS/400 Display Device File definition Table.

You must think about the following four things while using GDDM:

1. How the screen or device really works internally.
2. The sequence in which you must supply proper data to the screen.
3. How to code hexadecimal renditions of the bit strings the device requires to do what you want done on it (it is like writing the I/O code).

4. The sequence of control within your program (the back-and-forth exchange between the HLL parts of your program and the GDDM actions).

### 18.6.1. The GDDM Programming Routines

Essentially, the GDDM programming routines send the device a bit stream. The graphics control within the device needs separate hardware from the normal alphabetic control) interprets these bits to generate a picture. You can also retrieve this "data," the graphics control bit stream, and store it in the GDF file in an otherwise normal database. Then you can retransmit the whole file down line to another system for use on its graphics devices. You and they will then be showing your users (the graphics terminal operators) the same screen.

There are three important rules:

1. When you create the Device File Definition for the graphics device using DDS, you must use the parameter ALWGPH, which causes the device to be thrown into graphics mode on any I/O operation.
2. Do not use any OVERRIDES on this graphics file at run time.
3. If you want to put normal (nongraphics-created) script over the picture, do so second, only after the picture is completed. If you do the script in graphics mode (with graphics fonts from the graphics library file), the colors will blend into new colors (see 18.10.1, Color Mixing). If you lay normal device mode script over the picture, it will replace the graphic pixels that lay underneath.

Regarding rule 3, here is how the normal and graphics modes will interact. There are two output commands in GDDM—ASREAD and FSFRCE. Essentially ASREAD writes out a picture and then asks for operator input, while FSFRCE just writes out a picture. ASREAD clears the screen of any prior output from the nongraphics mode (but keeps it), puts the screen into graphics mode, puts out the picture to the display, puts the display back into nongraphics mode (restoring to the screen the saved nongraphic alphanumeric data from the prior operation), and then unlocks the keyboard waiting for normal mode alphanumeric operator input (interactive). FSFRCE just puts out the graphics picture, in the midst of the normal (nongraphics) output you have just displayed on the screen.

You could add your logo to your bills in this way, by calling a GDDM subroutine your graphics programmer wrote from your billing process. If your prior alphanumeric script output does not get put back onto your screen after the graphics operation, and/or the keyboard does not unlock, then the Device File Definition for the display you have used does not have the ALWGPH parameter specified in any of the record formats that you have written out to this display. The graphics will be written out anyway because GDDM takes over from the normal AS/400 device management routines and does whatever the bit stream it created tells it to do. However, this is not good.

To put graphics output on a graphics capable printer, GDDM uses another special file, QPGDDM, from the library QSYS. This file is a Printer Create command, CRTPRTF FILE (QSYS QPGDDM), with the following specifications: (1) DEVTYPE(*SCS); (2) PAGESIZE of 99,132 lines (dots); (3) 9 lines per inch; (4) 10 characters per inch; (5) no level checking; (6) no sharing; (7) character set ID of 101,037; (8) no replacement for unprintable characters; (9) spooled. Again, you can see that the graphics output is going to go out and bludgeon the printer, allowing no flexibility of what you do on the page. No sharing means you give up much of the normal printer spool-print control—basically, this job takes over the printer until it is finished. That is how older computer systems worked, anyway.

There are as many little rules for defining your graphics printer and using it as there are for the displays. They are too many to go into here; just understand that it takes the same kind of expertise, especially if you are trying to create your own forms on a page size different from normal computer printer output. It is possible, but you must be GDDM-trained.

## 18.7. GDDM GRAPHICS SYMBOL SETS AND FONTS

To find out what symbol tables and fonts (*GSS objects on the AS/400, housed in the library QSYS), you use the CL command

DSPOBJD. To get fonts off another system, dial up that system and read the GSS file from the GDDM library, which, remember, is QDGDDM (for displays and plotters) or QPGDDM (for printers), and is housed in library QSYS. You can get fonts from a mainframe 370 also and then use the CL command CRTGSS to convert them to an AS/400 object. You will be prompted on how to do this from your terminal if you put it into command mode. Once you have the file in AS/400 object form, you can save, rename, copy, grant authority to, or send it further to another computer, or you can use any other appropriate AS/400 CL object control function.

These tables have character sets (fonts) as well as small icon-type pictures of various denominations. They can be of two types: so-called "image," meaning built from dots or pels; or so-called "vector," meaning drawn with tiny lines. The default is image (mode 2) for plain picture making and vector (mode 3) if you are using any of the IBM "Presentation" graphics business chart routines.

You can code characters yourself by entering hexadecimal for the old EBCDIC code for the characters (left over from card punch and 360 days). Here is the hex code for letters A through Z.

| | | | | | |
|---|---|---|---|---|---|
| A | x'C1' | J | x'D1' | / | x'E1' |
| B | x'C2' | K | x'D2' | S | x'E2' |
| C | x'C3' | L | x'D3' | T | x'E3' |
| D | x'C4' | M | x'D4' | U | x'E4' |
| E | x'C5' | N | x'D5' | V | x'E5' |
| F | x'C6' | O | x'D6' | W | x'E6' |
| G | x'C7' | P | x'D7' | X | x'E7' |
| H | x'C8' | Q | x'D8' | Y | x'E8' |
| I | x'C9' | R | x'D9' | Z | x'E9' |

The CHRID parameter on the special graphics printer file selects the printer font. There are numerous English, European, Arabic, and Asian fonts you can choose from for your own pictures. The default is IBM's own "multinational" set. See GDDM manuals and your graphics device hardware manual for details.

GSLSS is a GDDM program routine you invoke to download your chosen font onto the graphics device. It is advisable to use vector sets on plotters because continuous dot movement tends to wear out the pens. Following the GDDM command, the sequence of commands you will put into your HLL graphics program to prepare the device is:

| | |
|---|---|
| GSLSS | Downloads the *GSS symbol set to the device; this set will be used for the character strings you specify on GSCHAR and GSCHAP routines (which allow you to put words around your drawings). |
| GSCS | Selects the character set once it has been downloaded to the output device. |
| GSCM | Sets character mode (2 for image, 3 for vector) to be used to draw the characters. |

The names of the IBM fonts (character sets) from which you can choose begin with the letters ADM, followed by the following letters:

- D, for any national unique character set.
- M, for the standard IBM multinational set.
- VM, for certain vector sets (plus SS, standard simple; SB, standard bold; OB, open-block; FB, filled-in block; RP, Roman principal); monospaced (all letters take the same space), using only standard characters from the IBM multinational set. For example: ADMVMSS means vector, standard simple.
- WM, same as above, but proportionally spaced.
- UV, for vector special (not abc's), monospaced.
- UW, same as above, but proportionally spaced; followed by the country character to select the national character set:
  E UK English
  F standard French French
  G German
  I Italian
  K Katakana
  S Spanish

Vector sets contain the western 26 letters—upper and lower case—the 10 numbers, and the following 16 special characters: $&*()–+!:;',.?/ and blank (but not @#%^_~'\ | <> or any others such as the British pound sign). For other symbols you must select a specialized set and not rely on the standard IBM multinational. Symbol sets can be created for GDDM on the mainframe 370-type computer using its GDDM symbol editors, then shipped to the AS/400 and used there. If I were running a very sophisticated print shop, I would consider such things.

## 18.8. BASIC GDDM COMMAND TYPES

In-line, in your high-level language program, you mark the beginning and end of your GDDM commands with two delimiters: FSINIT and FSTERM. You cannot issue a graphics command outside of this area of your program. To give you a feeling for the type of function and level of support GDDM supplies, here is a list of the basic commands you use after the FSINIT command:

| | |
|---|---|
| GSLW | Sets your line width for the next drawing you will do. |
| GSCOL | Sets the screen colors for the next drawing. |
| GSMOVE | Sets your drawing "pen" (locates you) at some specified X–Y coordinate on the picture surface. |
| GSCHAR | Draws whatever alphabetic or numeric characters you say. |
| GSLINE | Draws a line from one X-Y coordinate to another, as you specify. |
| CHPLOT | Draws the plot (chart) of your supplied data on the y axis of your display area. |
| GSENDA | Fills in a figure you have drawn with solid color. |
| ASREAD | Sends your picture to a display and awaits operator response from the keyboard. |

Using these commands, your graphics program insert, placed within your high-level-language program, will do the following:

| | |
|---|---|
| FSINIT | Gets the graphics code into the AS/400 system from its library and makes the machine connection to the |

device, allowing you to supply parameters to this command that change how the device interface will work this time. This device is no longer under AS/400 normal management.

Set attributes and select fonts: colors, line thickness, type of graph to be drawn, font type, language, size, and so forth.

Draw the actual picture—using supplied subroutines to assist, so that you do not have to turn on every dot or pixel on the screen.

ASREAD Sends your picture to some output queue to be displayed, printed, plotted, and so forth.

FSTERM Disconnects the device and releases GDDM code.

## 18.9 HLL—THE HIGH LEVEL LANGUAGES TO USE

The High Level Languages currently supporting GDDM imbedded statements are BASIC, COBOL, PL/I, RPG, and PASCAL. Since you mingle the graphics statements among your normal HLL statements, you can also use AS/400 function for your graphs and charts.

Some AS/400 things you can do within your graphics program:

1. Use database Logical Views as the data for graphs and charts. Data can be character strings, 4-byte binary numbers, floating point numbers, or decimal numbers.
2. Put graphics into your DDS files used for display formats and menus. That is, put your company logo at the top of a menu, or add your help center phone number at the bottom of data-entry screens, or graphically represent normal help screen or prompting information, or add Spanish or other foreign-language words of help plus pictures for infrequently used workstation menus.
3. Draw organization charts that will circumscribe your name lists and departmental breakdowns with large arrows to take the user from section to section at the strike of a paired prompt key.
4. Display a series of pictures at the touch of a prompt key to teach, help find an item of information, or get the user from

function to function within the AS/400 (intermingling your own created graphics with the AS/400 Prompting and HELP functions).

5. Change attributes of the pictures on the basis of the data or code sent to the screen; that is, negative balances can be discovered and displayed in red, plus a picture or words can be displayed or not displayed based on this balance.

## 18.10. COLOR OPTIONS

GDDM color options depend upon the capabilities of your output devices. GDDM itself can change three aspects of color: hue (the pureness of the color), light-to-darkness (the amount of grey), and saturation (in art, the amount of pigment). These selections were meant for display devices, but they also affect printers in different, unexpected ways. (Plotter colors depend on the coloring pens you physically insert in the plotter.)

The colors on the IBM screen are:

Blue
Red
Pink
Green
Turquoise
Yellow
Neutral

Notice that these are not your normal artist's color wheel. Even more surprising is how they mix together and what you come up with when you mix or overlay them.

You use a GDDM-supplied program routine, GSCTD, to define the color tables to be used for your output. There are seven basic colors per table form. You choose them by building a numeric array whose numbers represent combinations of the three attribute types: hue, lightness, and saturation. Later, when defining your pictures or graphs, you choose colors by selecting one of your color tables and using numbers from its array. If your formula selects an invalid number, a default color is used instead. GSCT is the graphics command you use to select the color table.

### 18.10.1. Color Mixing

The GSCOL command picks the number from the table that represents the color you define. If one color is to cross over another on the chart, there is a GSMIX command that controls which color will dominate (use option 2 to dominate). This is important because there is often a fair amount of criss-crossing on graphs and charts.

GSMIX plus option 2 causes the designated color to dominate when two or more colors cross over each other. GSMIX plus option 1 allows color mixing. It does not allow blending because the result is not always what you might expect. The mixes are based not upon color blending but on logically OR'd selection bits.

Here are GSMIX resulting colors when two colors are overlaid by GDDM on IBM screens:

| | | |
|---|---|---|
| Blue + Red | gives | Pink |
| Blue + Pink | gives | Pink |
| Blue + Green | gives | Turquoise |
| Blue + Turquoise | gives | Turquoise |
| Blue + Neutral | gives | Neutral |
| Blue + Yellow | gives | Neutral |

You can see that blue does not dominate here. But look at pink; it replaces itself, and red, in a mix, as neutral replaces itself, and yellow, in any mix.

| | | |
|---|---|---|
| Red + Pink | gives | Pink |
| Red + Blue | gives | Pink |
| Red + Green | gives | Yellow |
| Red + Yellow | gives | Yellow |
| Red + Turquoise | gives | Neutral |
| Red + Neutral | gives | Neutral |

Again, red, like blue, does not dominate. Pink does again, as does neutral.

- Pink + green, turquoise, yellow, or neutral gives neutral.
- Yellow + blue, pink, turquoise, or neutral gives neutral.
- Turquoise + anything other than blue or green gives neutral.
- Neutral plus anything gives neutral.

Each picture GDDM draws for you can have up to eight colors (including one for the background color of the display, giving you a choice of seven). The IBM standard selection numbers are as follows:

Background—8
Green—4
Red—2
Blue—1
Yellow—6
Pink—3
Turquoise—5
Neutral—7
(White)

You may reassign these numbers to colors you choose from among those your device can handle. And you can select hue and intensity by assigning decimal numbers between 0.00000 and 1.00000 with an array you build for the three parameters: H (hue), L (lightness), and S (saturation). IBM's default for blue, for example, is:

| | |
|---|---|
| Hue—0.0 | meaning hue is the lowest possible. |
| Lightness—0.5 | meaning a moderate amount of whiteness in the color (0.0 would mean no whiteness, almost black). |
| Saturation—1.0 | meaning the most saturation—the purest form of the color with no white or grey dilution. The color almost disappears to become grey with 0.0. |

### 18.10.2. Sample Program

Here is a sample program sequence that defines the color your graphics will be using:

| | |
|---|---|
| `INTEGER COLOR` | *defines a variable parameter named COLOR* |
| `LET COLOR = 2` | *choose red (2 = red)* |
| `CALL GDDM ('GSCOL',COLOR)` | *call the GDDM routine called GSCOL and hand it the color parameter called COLOR, which I set up with a 2 in it in my HLL program prior to the GDDM CALL* |

From here on, red will be used for all the lines and dots I draw pictures with unless I change it later. In a similar parameter-passing manner, you supply GDDM with your choices of mixed color defaults and your tables for hue, lightness, and saturation for each use of the color.

These "attributes" for color must be set up ahead of any picture drawing you will be doing within your HLL program.

## 18.11. LINE-DRAWING AND PICTURE ATTRIBUTES

There are a few other attributes you must set up ahead of the drawing sequence. They define widths of the lines you will draw (wide or narrow is the choice), patterns to be used to fill in drawn areas (cross hatchings, "x"s, dots, and so forth), and solid color fill-in if you choose. Here are the commands to use to define these attributes:

| | |
|---|---|
| GSLW | Sets your line width to narrow (option 1) or wide (option 2). |
| GSPAT | Selects one of 16 possible fill-in patterns for your enclosed areas. |
| GSAREA | Lets you fill in an outlined area with solid color. |
| GSENDA | Terminates the definition of attributes for your coming drawings. |

## 18.12. CHARACTERS

To put alphanumeric characters on the graphic display, use the normal AS/400 DDS by which you define the display file

(DEFDEVSP command) to define the characters and their screen locations. The characters will be the normal hardware character set (same size and type you normally see on the screen in nongraphics mode). For plotters and printers, use the GDDM symbol set provided, which allows you to control size, type style (font), and place on the device. Now you can make dot (image) or line (vector) characters. Because they are drawn graphically, vector characters can be placed so that they face in any direction, even upside down or slanted, and they can change size along a path.

The AS/400 operating system, OS/400, supplies an object, *GSS, which contains a selection of predefined graphics fonts. If you want to use a font that is not the built-in standard for your output device, you use the GDDM command GSLSS to download your selected font set to the device. This step is necessary before you try to use the font on the device. (Note: don't use dot image fonts on plotters, because they cause the pens to go up and down continuously, which is wearing on the media. Use vector fonts.) You can have more than one font at a time in most graphics devices, so next you have to use the GDDM command GSCS to select the font you want to use. Lastly, you choose dot image or vector mode (mode 2 or mode 3) using the GDDM command GSCM. To set your cursor or drawing pen use X and Y coordinates, X being horizontal, left to right, and Y being vertical, bottom to top. In other words, the lower left-hand corner of your drawing is location 0,0. Use the GDDM command GSMOVE to put the cursor there or wherever you want it.

Screen 18.1 is an example of four-corner X,Y coordinate specifications for a 8 × 16 character picture. After placing your drawing cursor where you want it, you can draw a straight line from there to another X,Y coordinate of your picture by using the GDDM command GSLINE. To find out where the cursor last lay, use the command GSQCP.

For example, CALL GDDM ('GSQCP',X,Y) will find out where the cursor lies and put its X,Y coordinates into two variables predefined by you in your HLL program, named X and Y. Prior to drawing the line, set its width to wide or narrow by using the command GSLW, and set up the method of drawing the line

```
0,7          A             15,7     X = across, Y = up
             A
             A
A A A A A A  A A A A A A A A A A
             A
             A
             A
0,0          A             15,0     X = 15, Y = 0
```

**Screen 18.1.** Coordinate specifications for an 8 × 16 character image.

by using the command GSLT. Solid lines are the default, but they could be specified as one of seven different types, as follows:

| Option on GSLT Command | Type of Line to Be Drawn: On a Plotter/Printer | Type of Line to Be Drawn: On a Display |
|---|---|---|
| 8 | (invisible) | (invisible) |
| 7 | solid (default) | solid |
| 6 | — — — — - - | —··—·· |
| 5 | — — — | — — — |
| 4 | — — — - | .. .. .. |
| 3 | _·_·_· | _·_·_· |
| 2 | - - - - | - - - - |
| 1 | . . . . . . . . . | . . . . . . . |

## 18.13. SOME LINE-DRAWING OPTIONS

Here are some GDDM commands to draw lines, arcs, and the like:

CALL GDDM ('GSLINE',15,7) — Draws a line from wherever the cursor is to the upper right-hand corner (X = 15, Y = 7) of the square in Screen 18.1.

| | |
|---|---|
| CALL GDDM ('GSARC',...,...) | Where ...,... is an angle and a point the arc circumscribes. |
| CALL GDDM ('GSELPS',X,Y,n,m) | Draws an ellipsis or circle from the cursor position to X,Y, with major and minor axes of n and m. |

## 18.14. ADDITIONAL FUNCTION

Here are some other GDDM commands:

| | |
|---|---|
| GSPFLT | Meaning poly fillet, curved lines within a specified set of tangent lines. |
| GSPLINE | Draws a polygon based on an array of X,Y coordinates you supply for the line endings. |
| GSVECM | Draws a set of independent vectors, using end points taken from an array of X,Y coordinates you supply, each preceded by a 0, meaning move the cursor without drawing a line, and/or a 1, meaning draw a line to the X,Y specification that the 1 follows. |

Of course, you can also prespecify the color for these lines using the GDDM command GSCTD ("Set up a Color Table Definition"), GCST ("Select the Color from the Table").

To add graphics mode characters (draw them from the graphics fonts available) use the commands listed below. (Do this *after* you have drawn your pictures and lines. In fact, take a look at your pictures before bothering to add lettering. You may save some time.)

| | |
|---|---|
| GDDM ('GSCM'....) | Sets the character mode for graphics symbol drawing for the device you are working on. If you did not download any fonts to this device, the default set will be selected now. |
| GDDM ('GSCS'....) | Selects a symbol set (U.S., Spanish, International, and so forth) from those you previously downloaded to this device using the GDDM ('GSLSS'...). |

GDDM ('GSCHAR'...) Actually draws a character. It starts at the lower left corner using the current cursor X,Y location for that corner.

GDDM ('GSCHAP'...) Draws an entire string of characters from where the cursor is to the X,Y coordinate specified. You can specify, for font and size:

- GSCA Angle (default is horizontal): Angle of rotation, based on trig function specification, or X,Y.
- GSCD Direction (backward/forward/up/down).
- GSCH Shear or slant of individual characters within string, such as *italics*, using sine/cosine function.
- GSCB Slope of the character box, or delimiters.

This gives you some idea of the level of expertise you will need to use this product.

## 18.15. INTERROGATING YOUR GRAPHICS DEVICE

You can find out what is going on with your graphics device by using the following GDDM commands followed by these parameters in parenthesis:

- ('GSQCP'....)—Where is the cursor now?
- GSQCUR—Where was the operator cursor?
- GSQLW—What is the line width setting?
- GSQLT—What is the type of line setting?
- GSQNSS—How many fonts are already downloaded?
- GSQSS—Which fonts are downloaded?
- GSQCS—What are the attributes of loaded symbol sets?
- GSQCB—What size character box will be used?

- GSQTB—What size character string box will be used?
- GSQCEL—What is the hardware's character box size (if you are trying to match it)?
- GSQCA—What is the character slant or angle?
- GSQCB—What is the character direction (up, down, to, fro)?
- GSQCH—What is the character shear angle?

## 18.16. DRAWING YOUR OWN ICONS

You can create icons using actual finite screen pixels (pels), which can then be stored like characters for later reuse.

GSIMG is the GDDM command to use to draw an "image." Use bit strings of 0s and 1s in multiples of 8 (a byte). How many 0s and 1s you use in this command defines how wide and how tall your icon or symbol will be. The 1s will be converted to "on" pixels on the screen, while the 0s will leave the spot on the screen as it was before—no change. With the cursor's present position as the lower left-hand corner of your icon (and using the currently defined color), you use the GDDM command ('DIM'...) to write out the dots you have defined. You provide the 00011100 bit strings from hexadecimal constants defined in your HLL (COBOL, etc.). This DIM command operates very close to the device hardware; use it sparingly and use the GDDM manuals of instruction. Later, defining your own images, you can scale them up to larger sizes by using the GDDM command GSIMGS.

## 18.17. PRESENTATION EMPHASIS MARKERS

If you need to make presentations, there are ten markers you can draw to highlight a line of text on your slide. The most common is the small filled-in circle, but you can also draw small open circles, small open or closed squares or diamonds, plus signs, "x"s, and small 6- or 8-point stars.

To download a marker symbol set to your device, use the GDDM commands as follows:

| | |
|---|---|
| GDDM ('GSLSS'....) | Downloads the marker symbol set. |
| GDDM ('GSMSC'....) | Sets the scale of the next marker. |
| GDDM ('GSMS'....) | Selects the marker to use next. |

GDDM ('GSMARKS'...) Draws a whole set of markers, at locations specified in an array you supply with this command.

## 18.18. GRAPHICS CONTROL COMMANDS

When doing GDDM graphics you think of a hierarchy of space to work in, from the PAGE (the largest) to FIELDS within the page, to picture space within the field, to VIEWPORT within the picture space, to WINDOW within the viewport.

FSPCRT Creates a numbered page that will use all of your printer page or display screen, or only a portion of it. This is a frame inside of which you will build your graphics pictures. With GDDM control commands, you build the picture frame (the page) of a certain size, clear it of images (GSCLR), put something back into it, inquire about its attributes, and delete it.

GSFLD Within a page, defines a graphics field, which is a particular space to draw within. X,Y coordinates will apply to the field (0,0 will be the lower left corner). If you define the field within the page, you can then individually query it, clear it (the same GSCLR command as for the page, above), fill it with images, etc., with just one command.

GSPS Defines picture spaces within the field, which will delimit and define heights to widths for pictures you put into them, as well as where on the screen they will go.

GSVIEW An oblong or square that fits inside the picture space. It is the frame to which you will draw your primitive lines or symbols.

The window is a concept that is outside the physical bounds of space just described. You define a window as the limit to which you want to extend your X,Y coordinates when you are drawing a picture within a Viewport (GSVIEW). However, the window definitions are not tied to the hardware, as are the other definitions above. The window can be transported to other Viewports and change size. Though you define a window after you have defined the Viewport (this is a must), it is not tied to that Viewport. It is a logical definition, which allows you to disregard the hardware and even make the window larger than the hardware would otherwise allow.

## 18.19. OTHER THINGS YOU CAN DO TO YOUR SPACE DEFINITIONS

Clipping allows you to take a portion of a picture and scale it up or down in a window or in a different Viewport. This can be done successively, giving an explosion of a piece within a piece of your picture, on successive Viewports. In exploded maps or statistical pie charts, for instance, you could take out a section and repeat it in larger form in a different Viewport.

Segments are definitions of portions of pictures that control the separate portions. For instance, you could erase the upper right corner portion of a picture, or change its colors, without affecting the remainder of the picture.

### 18.19.1. Other Control Commands

There is a whole set of GDDM commands to query the status of these allocations of picture space, to select one of them, to erase them, to add to them, and so forth.

## 18.20. FILES OF GRAPHICS

Anything drawn within a graphic segment of your HLL program can be retained for later use in a special AS/400 file called a GDF file. If you want to retain the script that goes with the pictures, be sure to put it as well as the pictures into a segment of your program. (Don't expect script added to the screen by the Display File Definition's constant information to become part of the permanent graphics picture.)

When your pictures look right to you, save them in graphics

files, if for no other reason than performance. Because the drawing is already completely defined, the next usage is far faster. These GDF files, which are the binary bit strings that make up the commands and pixel bits to recreate the pictures, can also be sent to other computer systems (the AS/400, 370-type computers, or IBM System 36) to be used on their graphic devices.

There are commands to get the graphics data (GSGET) into your HLL program's work space, from which it can be written to a database file. There is also a command to take this file of data and put it back onto a graphics device as a picture (GSPUT). These are generally very long data strings, requiring large amounts of work space in main memory.

By this time it should be obvious to you that the GDDM graphics interface is not on the same ease-of-use level as the standard AS/400 user interfaces. This is because it was written to be compatible with the IBM mainframe software package of the same name and to work in the same way; it was then added after the fact to the AS/400, whose internal architecture bears no resemblance to the mainframes of the past. The internal architecture of the AS/400 takes the user interface level much, much higher than the older systems did. This package is a step backwards in that sense. So it gives the user all the old difficulties of having to understand how the hardware actually works and of having to program to the very low bit level, which opens up the possibility for countless programming errors, both logical and physical.

## 18.21. GRAPHS AND CHARTS

GDDM "Presentation" graphics provides the commands to write a program that will create charts. It contains both the formatting commands (the graph layout) and the drawing commands. It will create a running program on the AS/400, not an interactively defined one on your PC or terminal. This means that you must write and test the program before you know what the charts will look like. If you want to modify the chart, you rewrite, recompile, and retest the program on the AS/400 before you see the resulting changes. That being said, the command to draw linear charts is CHPLOT.

### 18.21.1. Steps to a Program

Here are the steps to the program you will write.

1. Use the FSINIT command as follows:

   CALL GDDM ('FSINIT') Pulls the GDDM routines into your HLL program and sets up graphics mode.

2. Follow FSINIT with DSUSE:

   CALL GDDM ('DSUSE') OPENs and uses a certain device (see GDDM manuals for detail).

3. Design the chart layout using the following commands:
   - CHAREA Specifies the area, size of the chart, and placement (where on the printer, plotter, or screen it will go).
   - CHCGRD Specifies the "box" size, the limits for the characters to be used for labels, headings, and notes. The default is the hardware's normal character size.
   - CHVMAR Defines vertical margins (the left and right edges of the graph).
   - CHHMAR Defines horizontal margins (bottom and top edges of graph).
   - CHSET Determines if you want a box frame around the chart with background shading. It makes a more effective presentation, but is a slow, CPU-bound process.

4. Design the headings and other labels and text for the chart, using the CALL GDDM ('.....') command plus:
   - CHHEAD Specifies up to 132 characters of heading text for the chart. To make a multiple line heading, put a semicolon (;) at the end of each line of text.
   - \+ CHSET Places a heading at the top or bottom or left or right on the chart space.
   - \+ CHHATT Assigns other attributes to the heading, like color, character mode (vector, image), font set,

and size expansion numbers for increasing the size of the characters.

- + CHNOTE Puts a text note across the chart at a particular place.

5. Define X and Y axes for the chart, plus their labels and any tick marks to be put on them, using the following commands:
   - CHXSET Defines the orientation of the chart: vertical or horizontal, where the X axis goes, and so forth.
   - CHYSET Defines the orientation of the Y axis as above and whether or not it should be log scale.
   - CHXINT Defines where the two axes should cross.
   - CHXTTL Defines the title for the X axis.
   - CHYTTL Defines the title for the Y axis.
   - CHXLAB Defines the labels for the X axis; you can have date labels generated for you, or you can define your own.
   - CHYLAB Defines the labels for the Y axis.
   - CHXSEL Defines secondary X axes.
   - CHYSEL Defines secondary Y axes.
   - CHAATT Sets the axes' attributes of color, fat or thin line, solid or other type of line.
   - CHXRNG Defines the range limits of data to be charted on the X axis.
   - CHYRNG (Same as above, for the Y axis).
   - CHXTIC Selects tick marks and intervals for the X axis.
   - CHYTIC (Same as above, for the Y axis).
   - CHXGATT Defines grid line attributes of color, width, and so forth (use CHYGATT for the Y axis).
6. Draw the chart using the CALL GDDM ('....') command with the following parameter inserts:
   - CHCOL Sets color.
   - CHLT Sets line type.
   - CHLW Sets line width.
   - CHMARK Selects a marker for text lines, if wanted.

- CHFINE   Gives line curve smoothing rules.
- CHPLOT   Draws a line graph or scatter plot—name the data to be used here.

7. Send to the device and end graphics mode in this program using the following commands:
   - CALL GDDM ('FSFRCE')   Puts the chart out to the device without asking for operator response (input).
   - CALL GDDM ('FSTERM')   Ends graphics mode and returns your program to COBOL or other HLL mode.

There are default values for most of the GDDM options; usually the default is to the device hardware norm for the device you are writing onto.

## 18.22. OTHER GRAPHIC FUNCTIONAL COMMANDS

In addition to line graphs, there are other commands to draw the following:

- Solid colored sectional (layered) charts.
- Surface charts (each set of data builds onto the one below).
- Bar charts.
- Sideways charts.
- Pie charts—as many as you need per page (most PC graphics packages limit you to four or fewer), placed wherever you like.
- Venn diagrams.
- Histograms.

There is one reason I might use these program routines instead of the interactive AS/400 BGU (Bar Graph Utility) or one of the many interactive PC tools for charting. It is that I may want to do *something very important that my available tools do not do*. Perhaps I only have to do it once or twice—say a company standardized form to be used worldwide or a standard graphical statistical report format to be used in exactly the same way throughout the company. Perhaps something has to be upside down, right to left, in Farsi, or have ten pie charts along the bottom of the page. Before I use these routines, however, I would try to use the locally resident PC interactive tool, if only to refine what it is I want prior to jumping on the AS/400 with this mip user.

## 18.23. HLL GRAPHICS PROGRAM SIZE COMPARISON

Although far from scientific, here is a language-by-language comparison of the number of instructions used in an actual trivial graphics program in the currently available high-level-language GDDM support. The program used four colors and drew boxes, filling one in with solid color and leaving the display terminal background color within the other areas. Most programs will be hundreds of times larger than this one, but the relationships of the languages are informative.

Number of instructions in HLL for the simplest graphics programs:

| | RPG | COBOL | PL/I | PASCAL | BASIC |
|---|---|---|---|---|---|
| Line chart | 44 | 49 | 14 | 21 | 16 |
| 3 charts:<br>1 bar<br>1 pie<br>1 histogram | 94 | 75<br>+<br>45 in<br>BASIC | 22 | 53 | 19 |
| Box and<br>3 lines of text,<br>3-color | 94 | 89 | 28 | 56 | 24 |

You can see that the older high level languages have a tough time accommodating this bit stream code.

### 18.23.1. Performance Hits

The really bad performance hits are curved lines, vector symbols (characters), filled-in areas, shading, and areas filled with patterns. Do everything else first, test it out, and then go back and add these features, hopefully just once.

## 18.24. GENERAL PERFORMANCE CONSIDERATIONS

GDDM takes up a lot of room in your memory pool; it locks itself in and pushes your other work out (causing paging). It also works with bits, not objects, the old-fashioned way—using many machine cycles. Most of what it does that consumes CPU cycles can be avoided by using a PC-based package to do the graphics work, after downloading the AS/400 data to the PC. This is especially true and easy if you have PS/2s with their built-in relational database, which is very compatible with the AS/400. (You can make it exactly compatible by using the SQL generator with a CASE tool to generate your data designs on both systems.) For simple office charts, you can also use the AS/400's own BGU package.

If you do want to use GDDM, ask your graphics programmers to use the machine during off-hours, when they can get dedicated performance, or, rather than building the graphs on the AS/400, have them do the design work on a 370-type system and then ship it as a GDF file down line to the AS/400, to be put away in the library for later use. It is your choice.

# PART 3

# High Level Languages

The AS/400 has compilers for COBOL, FORTRAN, PL/I, RPG, PASCAL, BASIC, C, SQL, and its own Command Language, CL, as well as a special data design language, DDS. CL is the language designed explicitly for the AS/400; with it you manage all the design of the system (for example, how many storage pools there should be and how many programs should be run concurrently). CL is also a compilable language with which you can write applications if you so choose. DDS is the AS/400's specific database design language. The others are high level languages, most of which were designed toward older architected machines. They had to be substantially updated in order to be used with the AS/400 because of the high data level of its design.

# 19

# AS/400 and the Older High Level Languages

## 19.1. INTRODUCTION

This chapter highlights some of the additions that have been made to the older high level languages to allow them to access data on the AS/400 in sets, or to use its data selection options, and to invoke the late binding of program to data and program to device that is inherent in the AS/400 ("externally described files").

All the HLLs on the AS/400 can now call subroutines that were compiled separately. They could have been compiled in any one of the languages, not just the calling language. For instance, RPG programs can call COBOL, CL, or other language subroutines, as can all the other languages. If a function is not available in one language, it may be in another (for instance, using COBOL with GDDM you have to invoke subroutines written in either BASIC or PL/I to do certain bit twiddling). The calling statement can attach to a subroutine that is active, with options to initialize the called routine's work areas or to leave them intact with their current data content.

In addition, these programs can reach an AS/400 area called a data-area, outside the program itself, which is reachable (and therefore sharable) by another program. You could have four concurrently running programs that handle seat reservations at a concert, all giving out unsold seat numbers. The next assignable numbers could be held in a data-area, reachable by all the programs (no matter what language they were written in), so that while one program is updating the next seat number to be used, it momentarily locks the data-area to protect against duplicate assignment. This lock is less than a microsecond because the program doesn't lock to the data. The single operation locks to the single data element in the data-area.

COBOL, RPG, and the rest of the HLLs have been extended to be able to use the full database and ease of user interface functions of the AS/400.

The HLL extensions fall into the following categories:

- Data function and control
- External data and device definitions
- "Set" data control logic in the program languages
- Screen formatting, including scrolling ability

We will look first at COBOL and then at RPG language extensions.

## 19.2. COBOL DATA FUNCTION

### 19.2.1. Externally Defined Data

Your program can use a name, instead of a Data Division, which at run time will link the program to a Logical View (File). You defined the Logical View to the system earlier using DDS via the data definition utility. For COBOL this means you do not have to code the Data Division in all your programs. DDS, coded for the system one time only, will suffice for all the COBOL programs that want to look at this particular data. Also, you can access all the data so defined, or just a sampling, by using the run-time CL override command OVRDBF to change the specifications of the data file.

Your COBOL or other HLL program picks up its data definition from the Logical File and benefits from all the flexibility of the Logical View concept. Some new functions you get from the Logical View (for COBOL and the other HLLs) are:

- Multiple format logical records (you can pull in masters pre-matched with their transactions)
- Duplicate key records
- Records in ascending or descending sequence
- Noncontiguous keys (without added user logic)
- Initial "file" positioning different from the norm

Here is an example of a COBOL program using externally defined data:

```
An AS/400 Library. Logical View DDS

     R Recordname
        Field1          5      description
        Field2         10      description
        ...
        Field10         3      description

The COBOL program

     01 Recordname COPY DD-Recordname OF Filename
```

*...which generates into my program:*

```
+   05 Recordname.
+      06 Field1    PIC  S(5)   COMP-3
+      06 Field2    PIC  X(10).
+      ...
+      06 Field10   PIC  S(3)   COMP-3.
```

In other words, your Data Division is picked up from the DDS in your library. This gives you all the selection criteria function that is inherent in the Logical View definition.

### 19.2.2. Dataset Selection

The SELECT function has been added to the HLLs to allow you to select a particular set of tested data as input from within your program.

Here is an example of code to do specific selection of data within your COBOL program:

Example of a COBOL SELECT clause:

```
SELECT MASTER-FILE
 ASSIGN TO filename (from which you will draw data)
 ORGANIZATION IS    (indexed, sequential, whatever)
 ACCESS IS          (random, sequential, whatever)
 RECORD KEY IS EXTERNALLY-DESCRIBED-KEY
 FILE STATUS IS MASTFILE-STATUS
```

You precede the run of this program with a CL override statement, OVRDBF, if you want to change where retrieval begins.

### 19.2.3. Commitment Control

Another important addition to the HLLs is the data journaling function of commitment control. This gives you the ability to back out a transaction (to the prior database status) if the transaction doesn't complete to your logical satisfaction. You control the timing of the backout from within your own program. Your COBOL program addition for commitment control looks like this:

```
I-O-CONTROL.
 COMMITMENT CONTROL FOR MASTER-FILE.
 ...
PROCEDURE DIVISION.
 ...
 WRITE Recordname...
 ...
 UPDATE Recordname...
 ...
 IF TRANSACTION-GOOD
   COMMIT
 ELSE
   ROLLBACK.
```

### 19.2.4. Display File External Definitions

Externally described display files let you control, outside the program:

- Where fields will go on the screen
- Display attributes per field (color, highlighting, etc.)
- Data validity checks
- Indicators in data to be associated with keyboard keys
- Condition indicators associated with fields and attributes
- When the screen is to be cleared
- Screen format sizes and placement

### 19.2.5. Subfiles

The AS/400 Data Manager can scroll records from a dataset (file) through the display, under display-operator key control (the ROLL keys), according to your specifications. The programmer fills a subfile work area as he writes out data. A special control record is used to specify when to clear the screen, how many records to show the user at one time, what headings to put above the data, and so forth. Here is how you program for a subfile using COBOL:

```
COBOL SUBFILE processing
READ SUBFILE Filename RECORD
WRITE SUBFILE Recordname
REWRITE SUBFILE Recordname
READ SUBFILE Filename NEXT MODIFIED
```

The last statement brings into the program's accessible work area only operator *modified* data records. The operator scrolls through the reams of data records, stopping to modify specific records and using the scrolling ROLL keys to continue. He only hits Enter when ready for the program to access a set of modified records.

### 19.2.6. SQL Support

The HLLs have preprocessors to find, parse, and compile embedded SQL statements, which you bound by placing an EXEC-SQL statement in front and an END-EXEC statement behind them. The SQL statements can be embedded anywhere in the COBOL Procedure Division and can be in more than one place. Why would you use SQL from within a COBOL program? To update entire sets of data with one statement and to be able to sift out just the one set you need to update on the basis of SQL data selection.

Here is a COBOL example of SQL embedded statements:

```
PROCEDURE DIVISION.
  ...
  EXEC-SQL
    SELECT Name, Dept, Jobtitle, Years
    INTO   :Report-Name, :Report-Dept, :Title,
                                       :Years-in-Co
    FROM   MASTER-FILE
    WHERE  SALARY  >  6000
  END-EXEC.
...more COBOL
```

## 19.3. RPG LANGUAGE EXTENSIONS

RPG contains extensions to do all the functions listed previously for COBOL, plus a few "set" oriented data control tasks (mainly loop control) that RPG wasn't originally designed for.

### 19.3.1. The CAS Test and Branch Command

RPG's CAS command does mathematic or logical checks to find out if a situation is true. If so, it branches to a different subroutine. You follow CAS... with a code that identifies the condition you want the system to check for. CASGE means "Test for the case that the named field is Greater than or Equal to . . . another field or a value named in the instruction."

Here is a CAS example:

```
AMTDUE     CASGE 125             SUBRTI
```

This means "If the Amount Due is Greater than or Equal to 125, branch immediately to Subroutine 1."

CAS... can be appended with:

GT—Greater Than
EQ—Equal to
LT—Less Than
GE—Greater than or Equal to
LE—Less than or Equal to
NE—Not Equal to

### 19.3.2. DO Loops

Mathematical control of looping in RPG can be done with DO loops, added to RPG for the AS/400. Plain DO does a loop a specified number of times. Fancier DOs are DOW: "Do While something is still true"; and DOU: "Do Until something becomes true." You append the GT, EQ, LT, GE, LE, and NE codes to the DOW.. or to the DOU... as above. You will then loop reiteratively through a block of your RPG instructions (delimited by an END statement) until the logical comparison you asked for fails (DOW) or succeeds (DOU). In the case of DOW the system tests for your truth test *before* the execution of the code sequence; in the case of DOU, the test is done *after*.

### 19.3.3. AND/OR

The DO loops can be complicated by adding AND/OR logic to the loops. With these statements you can make the test for truth a choice of multiples.

### 19.3.4. IF...ELSE Logic

RPG on the AS/400 now also has IF then ELSE logic. The IF statement, like those above, is appended with the six logic choices, GT, EQ, LT, GE, LE, NE. You code IFGT to mean "If the system check finds the field checked to be greater than the control field checked against, then continue with the next instruction. If the answer is no, jump down to the ELSE statement below." AND and/or OR can be added to further complicate the tests to be done.

Here is an example of an RPG IF statement:

```
AMTDUE    IFGT    1000    Says if the amount due is > 1000
CTLFLD    ANDLE   50      And the control field < 50
                          (print a listing of this name, etc.)
          ADD     1        CTLFLD
                          Increment control field by one till
                          it gets to 50
          ELSE            jumps here if AMTDUE < 1000
          END             and also as soon as CTLFLD
                          reaches 50
```

### 19.3.5. Data Occurrence Structures and Other Data Function

An RPG word, OCUR, lets you treat a data structure as an entire set of like records using just one statement. This is a SET update. Additionally, you can read, write, and update entire sets of like records using the Subfile concept described in Section 19.2.5. RPG also supports:

- Commitment control
- Resetting processing points in your data files
- Treating Indicators as data
- Data-areas, outside your program, reachable by you and by other programs, concurrently

One of the very first 4GL languages, RPG, a fill-in-the-blanks program definition language, is oddly apt as an interface to the AS/400. Its ease of use, together with the AS/400's high level of rich data function, combine to make it a very powerful data processing tool that is worth looking into again.

APPENDIX A

# System Object Types

| Generic Object Type | Function | Location or Rules |
|---|---|---|
| Access group | Physical grouping of different but related objects to optimize disk operation | Attached to data-views |
| Context | Rule set for addressing objects | Pointed to by object |
| Cursor | Placekeeper in open data space. Does data mapping and conversion into user's buffers | One or more per space object |
| Data Space | Machine protected space provided uniquely to every dataset | Assigned per user File specs |
| Data Space Index | Finds Logical View of data space entries. Does Select/ Omit and concurrent updates. Controls shared usage | Integral part of Logical Views. Can be more than one per View |
| Index | For data storage | |

| Generic Object Type | Function | Location or Rules |
|---|---|---|
| Device Description | Defines attributes of hardware input, output devices and controllers | Defined by user using CL |
| Network Description | Device Description for lines, protocols, etc. | Filled in by users using CL |
| Process Control Space | Job (related series of programs) run-space and environment parameters | Modified by user run-time CL |
| Program | Microcode, translated by system from compiled program statements | "Encapsulated"; user untouchable |
| Queue | Chain of pending work pointers | |
| Space | 16MB of assigned address space, hardware protected, expandable. | Separately assigned by system to each function as needed |
| Profile | House for parameters defining system usage: First program to run after sign-on, type of menu to start up with, security clearances, allowed data-views, etc. | System-supplied: for operator, programmer, Security officer, end user; modifiable |

## ABOUT OBJECTS

- Objects known as programs and pointers are manipulated by special machine hardware instructions dedicated to this purpose. Users can only *request* that the system manipulate such objects.
- Indirect pointers are always used to address objects.
- Operational space (also an object) is optionally associated with any object.

- Only space objects reveal the real internal structure of bytes.
- Objects are "encapsulated," brought down into the microcode, before they are actually worked on by the system.
- Objects can be any size. There can be 16 million space segments of 16MB each at any one time. Virtual addressing translation (VAT) is now actively supported by use of 48-bits of hardware's 64-bit capability. Both CPU and channels go through the Virtual Address Translator hardware. Microcode reduces 128-bit pointers to 48-bit addresses (presently, until the world needs more). Main memory is like a cache; the disk acts like main memory.

Some of the objects supplied with your system:

| Object Name | Function | Modifiable Parameters (some of) | CL Commands Used to Modify Object |
|---|---|---|---|
| QBATCH | Batch job control | Class, Timeslice, Wait, Purge option, Text, Log User, Routing, Storage Pools, Max # Jobs, Queues, Max Activity in a Pool, Sequence, Start program, Compare Value. | CRTCLS CRTJOBD CRTSBSD ADDJOBQUE ADDRTGE |
| QCTL | System control | As above, plus run-time priorities, terminals, program invocation data | CRTCLS CRTJOBD CRTSBSD ADD... |
| QFNC | Finance Subsystem control | Class, Priority, Wait, Timeslice, Text, User, JobQ, Routing, Log, Authority, JobQ, MaxJob Storage Pools, Data and Program to Invoke,Seq# | CRTCLS CRTJOBD CRTJOBQ CRTSBSD ADD... |

| Object Name | Function | Modifiable Parameters (some of) | CL Commands Used to Modify Object |
|---|---|---|---|
| QUINDUSR | Control of Indirect User | Class, Priority, Wait, Timeslice, Purge option | CRTCLS |
| QINTER | Interactive Subsystem job control | Class, Timeslice, Wait, Priority, Routing, Log, Text | CRTCLS CRTJOBD |
| QNFTP | Transaction Program | User, Job Queue, Transaction routing, Job and Log options | CRTJOBD |
| QDIA | Document Interchange | User, Job Description, JobQ, Routing, Log | CRTJOBD |
| QPGMR | Programmer Subsystem | Class, Priority, User, Timeslice, Wait, Log, Authority, Routing, Text, Terminal type, Pools, Invocation data and program | CRTCLS CRTJOBD CRTSBSD ADD... |
| QSPL(1,2,3) | Spool Subsystems | Class, Priority, Wait, Purge option | CRTCLS |
| QSPLDBR | Database Read Spool | User Job Q, Log, Routing, Messages | CRTJOBD |
| QSYSCLS | Backup system | Class, Priority, Timeslice, Wait | CRTCLS |
| QSTRUPJD | Startup job (Auto) | Job Description, Log, User, Authority, Text, Startup Data | CRTJOBD |

## MORE ON OBJECTS

There are three implicit functions all objects have. They are authorization, lock enforcement, and atomic operation (unique and singular, independent). The concept of "object" gives common attributes to a group of data structures, which allows approaching the group through a defined interface, providing the benefits of commonality and standardization throughout the system. This makes the machine instruction set easy and very high level.

Requests to use objects are made through templates that define the uniqueness of each request. System and users approach objects using the same interface.

"Encapsulation" of all objects means that the internal structure of an object is only available to the machine itself. Objects are encapsulated to maintain the integrity of the internal structure and to permit different implementations of the machine instruction interface without impacting users, including IBM code.

A space object, unencapsulated, can be associated with an object. It is a byte string area in virtual storage, of up to 16MB, in which to work or with which to define tables (attributes) or other control information.

APPENDIX B

# System Bind Times

At run time you can open a file in a different manner from your program's OPEN specification by preceding the program with a CL command. OVRDBF overrides file definition information; so does OPNDBF. The data will be handed to the program in the sequence specified in the file Logical View; the records fed to the user will be those specifically selected by the Logical View. The action allowed (read, update, add, delete records) is specified in the OPEN option parameter. You *can* specify this in your user program, as in older systems, but you lose the flexibility of the AS/400 binding if you do that.

Run-time parameters take precedence. Should your program try to update a file but you have used a run-time CL option of no update, the updates will not occur; an error message will be queued for the user program. At the OPNDBF command the system verifies that you have the authority specified in the OPTION of that command. The system decides at this OPEN time what locking of data is needed to maintain your program's and other programs' data integrity.

## USER CONTROL LEVELS

| | After User Program Compilation | | |
|---|---|---|---|
| **At System Design Time** | How to do It: | Needs recompile of program and DDS if you: | Program recompile not required if: |
| Data Flow: Define data layouts (files) and sequencing of input/output to program; with selection of only those records to be worked on, omitting those in file not to be seen or worked on in this program. | Use DDS via IDDU utility. | Reorder *physical* sequence of data fields for your program. | Additions to data type are at end of record and not used by this program. Only change SELECT/OMIT parameters if new field is not required by old programs. |
| Record (tuple) Access Path and data member (subset of file, superset of record type). | Keyword: ACCPTH on logical (or physical file) | But: can share older path from prior file. | |
| | or | | |
| You can change the sequence of physical file reads by DTAMBRS param. in CRTLF, if your program does not mind a different input sequence (sometimes a performance hit). | use: REFACCPTH to create a new file based on a prior one—picks up SELECT and and OMIT parameters. | | |

Note that there are three different methods to create data definitions and compile access paths. These are:

1. Use CL, the Command Language, outside your program.
2. Use SQL or Query interfaces to the system. They create their own access paths.
3. Use the interactive utility IDDU.

## DATA BIND OPTIONS

These are the available data Bind options by using CL (Command Language) statements before or during your program run:

| Function | CL Command | Command Parameter |
|---|---|---|
| File name (Logical View physical file) | CRTPF (Create phys. f.)<br>CRTLF (Create Log. F.)<br>CHGPF (Change phys. f.)<br>CHGLF (Change Log. F.)<br>OPNDBF ((Open date F.)<br>OPNQYRF (Open Query F.)<br>OVRDBF (Override f.) | FILE |
| Library name | As above | Library name |
| File Member name | As above, except CHGPF,LF | MBR |
| File Member processing options | OPNDBF, OPNQRYF | OPTION |
| Record Format Lock state | OVRDBF | RCDFMTLCK |
| Starting point in data-set file for processing | OVRDBF | POSITION |
| Program to do only sequential processing | OPNDBF, OPNQRYF, OVRDBF | SEQONLY |
| Program to ignore keyed Access Path | OPNDBF | ACCPTH |

| Function | CL Command | Command Parameter |
|---|---|---|
| Time to wait on file locks before giving user a message and moving on | CRTPF, CRTLF, CHGPF, CHGLF, OVRDBF | WAITFILE |
| Record Lock wait time | CRTPF, CRTLF, CHGPF, CHGLF, OVRDBF | WAITRCD |
| Prevent any/all overrides | OVRDBF | SECURE |
| Share OPEN data path with others | CRTPF, CRTLF, OVRDBF | SHARE |
| Select Record Format | CRTPF, CRTLF, (OVRDBF) | FMTSLR |
| Level-check Record Formats at OPEN time | ditto | LVLCHK |
| Inhibit actual writes to disk for this run | OVRDBF | INHWRT |
| Force Ratio (write update to disk per ratio) | CRTPF, CRTLF, CHGPF, CHGLF, OVRDBF | FRCRATIO |
| Number of records to be brought in from disk to main memory at one time | OVRDBF (I advise not to use this option) | NBRRCDS |
| Force your Access Path to be written to disk after *n* changes | CRTPF, CRTLF, CHGPF, CHGLF | FRCACCPTH |
| Duplicate key check | OPNDBF, OPNQRYF | DUPKEYCHK |
| Commitment control (system will not update actual physical disk records until *your* definition of the transaction is completed) | OPNDBF, OPNQRYF | COMMIT |

| Function | CL Command | Command Parameter |
|---|---|---|
| Change expiration date | CRTPF, CHGPF | EXPDATE |
| Change expiration date checking | OVRDBF | EXPCHK |
| End-of-file delay (to catch the straggler transactions and be sure they get onto disk, after CLOSE | OVRDBF (read and understand before using) | EOFDLY |

## HLL (HIGH LEVEL LANGUAGE) BIND TIME FLEXIBILITY

The high level languages RPG, COBOL, BASIC, PL/I, and PASCAL have been updated for the AS/400 with parameters in their data definition sections that make them flexible in the use of:

| All HLLs | BASIC, PL/I, PASCAL | RPG and COBOL |
|---|---|---|
| File names | Library names | Record Formats to be used this run (RPG, not COBOL) |
| Program Record length | File Member names | |
| File Member processing options | Change Record Format Lock state (not PASCAL) | Level-check Record Formats |
| Ignore all keyed Access Paths | Share open data paths with other programs (not BASIC) | Perform only sequential processing |
| | Commitment control (PL/I, not BASIC or PASCAL) | Duplicate key check (COBOL, not RPG) |

Other AS/400 binding options are being added to the HLLs as time goes on. Check your manuals.

COBOL and RPG have some restrictions that override the AS/400 capabilities in Name lengths for Data Fields, Records, and files, and for length of numeric fields. You can use AS/400 system rules for defining your data, then equate the AS/400 names to the HLL names through Logical Views, overrides, and the like.

## FILES

The format, name, and location (library) of a FILE, at least the parts your program uses, should be the same at execution time as at Create (compile) time. This does not mean that it must be the same file, only that it can be found and must fit. If "level-checking" is invoked at run time on the OPEN FILE, the file must also be at the same level as the program using it (created on the same version of the system).

# APPENDIX C

# Explicit System Limits

## DATA LIMITS

| | |
|---|---|
| Bytes in one record | 32,766 |
| Fields per record | 8,000 |
| Key fields in one record | 120 |
| Keysize in bytes | 256 |
| Records in one file | 16,777,215 |
| Bytes in one file | 2,147,483,648 |
| Database size | size of disk storage |
| Logical Files (Views) from one physical file | 3,686 |
| Physical files used in one Logical File (View) | 32 |
| Maximum files in a JOIN | 32 |
| Maximum field size in bytes | 32,766 |
| Maximum decimal number | 9,999,999,999,999,999,999,999,999,999,999 |

APPENDIX D

# Data-View and Display Screen Editing by the System

## I. SYSTEM ACTIONS ON DATA FIELDS

Listed below are things you can decide regarding what the system should do to a field of data before it is fed to you in your program or at your terminal:

- Whether or not to show you the field (See *Selection* and *Omission* in the table following).
- In what form to show you the field (for translations, editing and/or tests, see remaining DDS parameters in the table following).

| DDS keywords you put in your definitions for LOGICAL FILE, DISPLAY FILE, or PRINTER FILE: | The system will apply this function to the data field before it is included in your data-view: |
|---|---|
| ABSVAL | Treats number as absolute value. |
| SIGNED | Treats number as signed. |
| UNSIGNED | Treats number as unsigned. |
| ALIAS | Equates another name to field. |

| **DDS keywords you put in your definitions for LOGICAL FILE, DISPLAY FILE, or PRINTER FILE:** | **The system will apply this function to the data field before it is included in your data-view:** |
|---|---|
| ALTSEQ | Changes retrieval sequence algorithm to alternative one. |
| NOALTSEQ | Do NOT use the alternate sequencing. |
| DESCEND | Uses field for retrieval of record, in descending order. |
| UNIQUE | Ensures there are no duplicate keys in the View or dataset being gathered. |
| FCFO | If duplicate retrieval keys appear, the duplicate records are to be retrieved in a "first-changed, first-out" order. |
| FIFO | If duplicate keys, retrieve them in a "first-in, first-out" order. |
| LIFO | If duplicate keys, retrieve them in "last in, first-out" order. |
| CHECK | Verifies Input data for blanks, mandatory entry, Mod 10 or 11 arithmetic checks, names, etc. (see Display File specifications) |
| CHKMSGID | Generates a message to user if CHECK test is not passed. |
| COMP | Verifies input data for logical values: equal to, greater than, less than, GE, LE, not equal, NG, NE some value specified here.<br>*Selects* record for your data-view if this field passes this test. |
| RANGE | Verifies input data to be within specified range.<br>*Preselects* (or *omits)* this record from your Logical View if in this range. |
| VALUES | Verifies on input that this field matches one of up to 100 specified values you give here.<br>*Selects/omits* this record based on this field matching one of a list of values (up to 100 items in list). |

| **DDS keywords you put in your definitions for LOGICAL FILE, DISPLAY FILE, or PRINTER FILE:** | **The system will apply this function to the data field before it is included in your data-view:** |
|---|---|
| ALL | *Selects* ALL records not yet omitted, or *omits* all not yet selected for your data-view from the physical file(s) you are selecting from. |
| DYNSLT | *Selects/omits* this record live for your viewing if it meets criteria. |
| CONCAT | Pulls together two or more fields from physical data into one logical field for your data-view. |
| DFT | Initializes this field to this value. |
| DIGIT | Uses only lower order four bits of the bytes in this field (for key). |
| ZONE | Uses only high order four bits of the bytes in this field (for key). |
| SST | Picks up a character string from within a field as specified here. |
| EDTCDE | Specifies the monetary or credit symbol to be used when displaying or printing this field. |
| EDTWRD | Specifies the Edit format to be used when displaying or printing field. |
| REFSHIFT | Keyboard shift to be used on your displays. |
| TRNTBL | Translates this field based on a given translate table. |
| FLTPCN | Translates to single or double precision for floating point number. |

Here are some editing and selection parameters you can define for JOINED DATASETS:"

| | |
|---|---|
| JFILE | Names the physical datasets (files) to be used in the JOIN operation. |
| JOIN | Names JOINed files to be used. |

| | |
|---|---|
| JFLD | Names the fields to be matched in the JOIN. |
| JREF | Refers to a field reference file to use for naming fields, if two or more physical files being joined use the same names for different fields. |
| JDFTVAL | Default values to use for no-record-found in match attempts on JOIN. |
| JDUPSEQ | Alternate sequencing field to use if joined-to (secondary) data records produce duplicate fields in JOIN search. |

These attribute specifications for your Logical data View and for input or output editing can all be reproduced from a former set or from a master set in your library, then refined further for another use.

## II. SYSTEM-CONTROLLED DISPLAY SCREEN DATA EDITING

| DDS parameter you specify on your DISPLAY FILE definition: | System function performed on the DATA: |
|---|---|
| **A. System-Applied VALIDITY CHECKING Options on INPUT Data** | |
| CHECK + ab | Blank input is OK. |
| CHECK + me | Mandatory key-entry field. |
| CHECK + mf | Mandatory fill field. |
| CHECK + m10 | Number must pass IBM modulus 10 or 11 check. |
| CHECK + m11 | |
| CHECK +vn | Name must be on OK list. |
| CHECK + vne | Name must be on extended list. |
| COMP or CMP | Input field must match constant given here or be Equal, Less, Greater, NE, NL, NG, LE, or GE. |
| RANGE | Input field must be within range specified here. |
| VALUES | Input field must match one of the list of values specified here. |

| DDS parameter you specify on your DISPLAY FILE definition: | System function performed on the DATA: |
|---|---|
| CHKMSGID | Message will be issued if field cannot pass specified checks above. |
| CHANGE | Program is notified in a "response" area if this field on the screen is altered by operator. |

**B. DISPLAY CONTROL Parameters**

| | |
|---|---|
| CHECK + er | This field ends record. |
| CHECK + fe | Field exit check. |
| CHECK + lc | Lowercase OK. |
| CHECK + rb | Field right-justified—pad with blanks. |
| CHECK + rz | Field right-justified—pad with zeroes. |

**C. Display Control, Screen Highlighting, and Editing**

| | |
|---|---|
| ALARM | Display's alarm goes off when this record is displayed. |
| ALTHELP | Names any key of keyboard as Help key. |
| ALTPAGEDWN | Names any key as Page-Down key. |
| ALTPAGEUP | Names any key as Page-Up key. |
| CHECK + rl | Moves cursor right to left in this field, record, or file, instead of left to right. |
| CHECK +rltb | Advances cursor right to left and top to bottom among "input capable" fields. |

The following define display field attributes:

| | |
|---|---|
| CHGINPDFT + bl | Blinking field. |
| CHGINPDFT + cs | Column separator. |
| CHGINPDFT + hi | High-intensity field. |
| CHGINPDFT + ri | Reverse-image field. |
| CHGINPDFT + ul | Underline field. |
| CHGINPDFT + fe | Field exit. |
| CHGINPDFT + lc | Lowercase. |

| DDS parameter you specify on your DISPLAY FILE definition: | System function performed on the DATA: |
|---|---|
| CHGINPDFT + me | Mandatory key-entry field. |
| CHGINPDFT + mf | Mandatory fill-in field. |
| ALWGPH | Field of record can be used for graphic or alphanumeric data simultaneously. |
| ALWROL | Roll mode: allows program to scroll through a record area on the screen. |
| BLINK | Cursor will blink when this record is displayed. |
| BLKFOLD | System will fold over this field at a blank nearest end-of-line. |

# APPENDIX E

# Data File Security Options

## AUTHORITIES NEEDED TO MANAGE YOUR DATA FILES

| Data Management Function | Authorization Levels Needed | | | Data Usage Level Needed |
|---|---|---|---|---|
| | Operational | Existence | Managerial | |
| Create a Logical File | | | X | READ |
| OPEN a FILE | X | | | |
| Compile a program that refers to a FILE | X | | | |
| CL commands that display active file statistics | X | | | |
| DELETE a FILE | X | X | | |
| SAVE/RESTORE a FILE | | X | | |

| Data Management Function | Authorization Levels Needed | | | Data Usage Level Needed |
|---|---|---|---|---|
| | Operational | Existence | Managerial | |
| REMOVE MEMBERS from a FILE | X | X | | |
| ADD MEMBER to a FILE (both files) | X | | X | READ of "from" file |
| TRANSFER OWNERSHIP | X | X | | |
| GRANT or REVOKE AUTHORITY you have over FILE to others | X | | X | |
| CHANGE or MOVE MEMBER of a FILE in a LIBRARY | | | X | |
| RENAME FILE or MEMBER | | | X | |
| CLEAR a MEMBER of data | | | X | DELETE/ ADD |
| Initialize a FILE MEMBER | | | X | READ, UPDATE, DELETE ADD, READ, UPDATE, DELETE/ ADD |
| Reorganize a FILE MEMBER | | | X | |

Data locks the system uses for various data operations and the CL commands that can be used for the operation.

Lock types generated:

| | |
|---|---|
| EXC | Exclusive. The object is allocated to, and can be used by, this job only; no sharing. |
| EXC+R | Exclusive plus Read. The object is allocated to this job, but other users can read the object (not update it). |
| SHR+U | Shared plus Read or Update. The object is allocated to two or more jobs and can be shared with other users for reading and updating. |
| SHR+R | Shared plus Read Only. The object is allocated to both jobs, and can be shared with other jobs for reading but not updating. |
| SHR+L | Shared lock. The object can be shared with another job, only if the other job never requests exclusive use of it. |

| Operation | CL Command to Use | System Lock Type on: File | Data | Access Path |
|---|---|---|---|---|
| Add Physical File Member | ADDPFM | EXC+R | | EXC+R |
| Add Logical File Member | ADDLFM | EXC+R | | EXC+R |
| Change Physical File attributes | CHGPF | EXC | EXC+R | EXC+R |
| Change Logical File attributes | CHGLF | | | |

| Operation | CL Command to Use | System Lock Type on: | | |
|---|---|---|---|---|
| | | File | Data | Access Path |
| Clear Physical File Member of data | CLRPFM | SHR+R | EXC | |
| Initialize Physical File Member | INZPFM | SHR+L | EXC+R | |
| Create a File (Physical, Logical, or Source) | CRTPF, | EXC | | |
| | CRTLF | EXC | | |
| | CRTSRCPF | EXC | | |
| DELETE FILE | DLTF | EXC | | EXC+R |
| OPEN FILE | OPNDBF | SHR+L | SHR+L | EXC+R |
| Rebuild Access Path | automatic | SHR+L | SHR+L | EXC+R |
| Reorganize Physical File | RGZPFM | EXC | | |

APPENDIX F

# The System Values Table

These table values apply across the entire system. They can be modified by the CL commands RTVSYSVAL (Retrieve System Value) and CHGSYSVAL, issued from a program or interactively at any time. They can be called into programs as data variables and used, or brought onto your terminal screens by definitions in your Device Files or by program output. The SAVSYS command saves a copy of the table.

Some of the more pertinent table values are listed below.

- Date/time references:

  QDATE—System date

  QYEAR—Year portion of system date

  QMONTH—Month portion of system date

  QDAY—Day portion of system date

  QLEAPADJ—An adjustment used each leap year

  QDATFMT—European, American, etc., format of date

  QDATSEP—slash (/) or hyphen (-) or period (.) or comma (,) separators to use when you output date

  QTIME—Used to store clock times

  QMINUTE—Used to store clock times

QSECOND—Used to store clock times

- Security level control parameters:

  QSECURITY—Code representing overall level of system security to use: 10=physical; 20=password; 30=physical, password, and resource objects; 40=all of above plus interface.

  QPWDEXPITV—Duration of password viability.

  QSPSGNINF—0=NO, 1=YES: should sign-on be visible.

  QSTSMSG—Can suppress status messages.

  QPRTTXT—Print up to 30 characters of control information at bottom of each printed page.

  QLMTSECOFR—"1" limits "service info" on objects to be seen only by Security Officer profile user.

  QMAXSIGN—Limits sign-on attempts to some number.

- Library information:

  QSYSLIBL—System library list name—can be changed.

  QUSRLIBL—User library list name.

- Message and logging:

  QSTSMSG—Allows suppression of status messages.

- Amount of activity allowed in system:

  QTOTJOB—Total job secondary storage allotment. Lower it if disk storage is short.

  QADLTOTJ—Allows an adjustment to storage above, at run time, if needed.

  Q...POOL—See Chapter 9, on performance, for storage pools and for more job control.

- Starting and ending the system:

  QABNORMSW—Indicator for last system-ending status—0=normal, 1=abort situation.

  QPWRRSTIPL—System will auto-IPL after power is down and then restored.

  QIPLDATTIM—Day and time for auto-IPL.

  QIPLSTS—IPL status:
    0=Operator panel IPL is to be used

1=Auto-IPL when power is restored
2=Restart does IPL
3=Autostart at certain time of day
4=Remote control IPL

QRMTIPL—Means remote "Power on" and IPL.

QIPLTYPE—0=unattended IPL, 1=attended by operator.

QPWRDWNLMT—Maximum seconds before "IMMED" POWER DOWN will take place in spite of cleanup effort needed to save leftover data. Default is 600 seconds.

QAUTOCFG—1=system will auto-configure itself at IPL. Sets up any newly added devices or controllers, using system-standard names (e.g., DSP01 . . . for displays, PRT01 . . . for printers. You can change names later).

QAUTOVRT—Number of virtual devices to be auto-configured.

QINACTITV—Interactive job timeout interval. When no messages have been received job will terminate. 0 is default, can be up to 300 *minutes*.

QJOBMSGQS—Limit in Kbytes for job message queues. Keep small for better performance.

QLMTDEVSSN—Limit on concurrent sessions with interactive devices.

- For different hardware:

QKBDTYPE—Any of 52 different terminal keyboard types.

QCHRID—Graphics and code page used for displays.

QCMNRCVLMT—Communications terminal retry efforts and time limits before notifying an operator.

QIGC—means system works with one of the double-byte character sets (16 bits per character).

- Control of data and jobs:

QDSCJOBITV—How many minutes a job can be inactive before it is terminated. Use this item to control program loop problems.

QDEVRCVACN—What to do when device requesting work has an I/O error (message, disconnect, end job).

QSTRUPPGM—Name of startup program (usually a system supplied control program) for autostart to invoke, which program will start spoolers, readers, writers, etc. If *NONE, the system program QSYS, which calls QSPL, is invoked, plus the print spooler if QSTRPRTWTR=12.

QSTRPRTWTR—See entry immediately above.

QSRVDMP—Specifies which jobs to DUMP on abnormal termination, and where.

There are many more entries in the System Values Table, some more intricate but perhaps less interesting. There is one exactly right for you if you look hard enough.

# APPENDIX G

# Communications Protocols and Function Alphabet Soup

## THE AS/400 AS CENTRALIZED HOST

The AS/400, as the *central host* computer, supports connection via:

- Asynchronous (ASYNC) terminals and communications
- Binary Synchronous terminals and communications (BSC)
- Synchronous Data Link Control (SDLC) terminals and communications.
- X.21 networks
- X.25 networks, switched or leased lines
- ISDN Data Link Control (IDLC)
- EIA-232/v.24
- CCITT X.21/v.11
- V.35
- V.25 BIS Serial autodial
- V.25/RS-366 Parallel Auto Call
- IEEE 802.3, 802.3, 802.5 Ethernet and Token Ring

The AS/400, as host network manager, provides the following problem determination and management:

- SNA Generic Alert Support
- LPDA-2—Link Problem Determination Aid

- ECS—Electronic Customer Support
- Token Ring Management Support—AS/400 as LAN manager
- SAA SystemView System Manager/400 (Intermediate node cluster management)
- Configuration management—change, bypass hardware connection
- Change management using Object Distribution, and ECS, providing fixes from a remote site
- Operations management, including remote power on, automated system control, display station passthrough

There are IBM manuals to explain all these services.

## PEER-TO-PEER CONDUCTIVITY

The AS/400 can act as a *peer system* to other AS/400 systems and is fully supported as such. This means that a user on one system can transparently invoke any natural AS/400 function on a different AS/400 system without special effort or a detailed knowledge of communications protocol to get across to the other system.

Peer connectivity and linkage to 370-type systems is done through menu-driven protocol descriptions, prompted from an AS/400 terminal. This is much like the interactive utilities prompt for information, only in this case you are prompted to fill in the myriad of SNA and SDLC networking options that on 370-type systems are programmed into access methods. Needless to say, the menus are heavily defaulted. In general, CPU-to-CPU operations that may have taken days to write and test on other systems can be defined and tested this way in a couple of hours.

## THE AS/400 AS A DISTRIBUTED SYSTEM

The AS/400 can be the *distributed* system to a miniframe 370-type host system. It can be an RJE station or a distributed database. It can also be a secondary node in a network, controlling its own terminal array, a LAN net group, or other peer AS/400s.

## METHODS OF ATTACHMENT AND CONTROL

Terminal configuration on the AS/400 uses the system's device recognition and automatic configuration function. Peer networking among AS/400s and other IBM small systems uses AS/400's Distributed Data Manager, DDM.

Host control from the 370-type system, reaching out to the AS/400, uses facilities that the AS/400 participates in, as follows:

- DHCF—Distributed Host Command Facility
- HCF—Host Command Facility
- NetView
- NewView DM—Distribution Manager
- Distributed System Executive (VSE/SP host only)
- Display station passthrough
- AS/400 Automated Operations, including remote power on SNA Alert support on the AS/400
- 3270, 3745, 3725 AS/400 Passthrough support

A typical 370-type host would manage problem determination and control for distributed AS/400s as the following paragraphs describe.

The AS/400 sends alert messages to the host 370-type system when a network problem within its domain occurs. The 370 network operator, who needs more information, will connect (if not already connected) with the alerting node using the 370 NetView Terminal Access Facility and the S/370 Host Command Facility (HCF). The 370 operator can now access the AS/400's network management facilities, using DHCF (Distributed HCF), to examine the failure indicators in more detail. The 370 network operator, using NetView commands on the 370-type system, can invoke AS/400 diagnosis function and examine any error statistics collected by the AS/400 network management facilities. Using DHCF, corrective action can be taken on the AS/400.

If the alert message(s) came from farther downstream, the 370 host network operator will use the above path, plus the Display Station Passthrough support, which resides on the farther node. The AS/400 network manager will reach the farther nodal point (where the alerts originated), then disappear from the path (make itself invisible) while the 370 operator manages the remote problem from his control terminal. The alerts could be coming from another AS/400 or other IBM small systems. In this way the 370 network manager can reach and work on communications problems at any down-line node in the network that belongs to the CNM (Communications Network Management) club, be it other AS/400s, S/38s, S/36s, AS/Entry systems, 5363 systems, and Series 1s. (Check your IBM office for other add-ons)

## AS/400 FUNCTIONAL COMMUNICATIONS SUPPORT

The communication support function consists of most common support available today and is being added to continuously. Here are some of the products and their highlights:

1. SAA—Systems Application Architecture. SAA is an IBM standard whose goal is to get all IBM systems talking and exchanging all sorts of data using interfaces that look the same on each system. It is available on all the major IBM systems and is becoming available on other systems as well. The AS/400 SAA supports:
   - Distributed File Management (via AS/400 DDM)
   - Document Content Architecture (DCA)
   - SNA Distribution Services (SNADS—includes PROFS)
   - Document Interchange Architecture (DIA)
   - LU Type 6.2
   - Low-entry Networking (LEN) (via AS/400 APPN)
   - X.25
   - SDLC
   - IBM Token Ring Network Local Area Net (LAN)
   - APPN—Advanced Peer-to-Peer networking (system-to-system, non-370 IBM systems)
   - Common Programming Interface—Communications (CPI-C)
2. ODF—Object Distribution Facility. ODF allows AS/400 objects to be sent around the network to other AS/400s or to IBM S/36s and S/38s. Objects include:
   - Data files
   - Source code
   - Object code
   - Print spool files (can be printed on the remote site using Printer Passthrough)
   - Messages
   - Job streams

   - Any saved objects (in a SAVE file)
3. Document Interchange Facility. Using Office Vision, AS/400 users can communicate with remote systems as follows:
   - Send/receive mail
   - Send/receive messages
   - Send/receive documents (including PC "shared folders")
4. Display station passthrough. Terminals on the AS/400 can pass through their local system and sign on to a remote AS/400 or other IBM small system, and vice versa. I can execute a program on that other system, massage its data, or whatever, as if directly attached.
5. Ethernet and IBM Token Ring LAN (Local area high-speed ring communications nets) support. The AS/400 can be a LAN manager, or a participant on the ring, whereby PCs and others attached to the ring can access function and data on the AS/400, use its printers and other devices, and get data or programs from the AS/400 down to their locations. PS/2s have a built-in database that is also relational and can swap data back and forth with the AS/400. The SQL database interface on both systems is extremely compatible. Data design and SQL programs can be generated on the AS/400 (using CASE tools available from the KnowledgeWare company of Atlanta) for use on PS/2 systems.

There is more communications support on the AS/400, and it grows steadily because this is the coming growth area in computing. The above list shows the richness of the AS/400 support at three levels: host, peer, and down-line node. In addition, there is the ability to attach to PBXs; Unix systems (using PCP/IP and Telnet); the Retail Communications system; the Finance Communications Support as an FBSS controller or back-office machine; the IBM Point-of-Sale system; Group 3 facsimile support; direct attachment to ISDN, OSI application, message and file services—the list goes on.

If your communications needs are not listed here, ask your local user group or IBM about it. There is too much choice to summarize.

# APPENDIX H

# Simple Set Theory Review

## DEFINITIONS

**Set** A conglomeration of things (called *elements* or *members*), which we categorize together because we see some common attributes. It is easier to think about groupings of things than about millions of elements of all different kinds.

*Example:* I am a member of the *set* of (all) *human beings*.

*Language usage:* we say a member (element) *belongs to* a set or *does not belong to* a set. There are special math symbols for *belongs to* ($\in$) and *does not belong to* ($\notin$). A Lynx element *belongs to* the *set* Cats, while a Dachshund element *does not belong to* the *set* Cats.

**Subsets** If a *set* of intra-related elements (Cats) is wholly contained within another (different) *set* of intra-related elements (mammals), we say it is a *subset* of that other *set*.

*Language usage:* we say Cats (the *set*) *is a subset* of the *set* Mammals.

**Proper subset** The containing set has more kinds of elements than the contained *subset*.

*Example: Mammals* are more than just *Cats*. All Cats are contained with the *set* of Mammals, but there are more Mammals than that, there are also Dogs, Men, Otters, Whales, Bushbabies, and so forth.

*Language usage:* We say cats are a *proper subset* of the set called Mammals. The math symbol is $\subset$. Thus, Cats $\subset$ Mammals. Mathematicians use phrases like "If (there is) *an element* Lynx which *belongs to* the set Cats, then Lynx *belongs to* the set Mammals, but there also exists the element Fox, and Fox belongs to Mammals, such that Fox *does not belong to* Cats," then Cats is called a *proper subset* of the set called Mammals. A *proper subset* is like a slice in a pie chart. There have to be other slices, but this slice is an entity in and of itself.

You can see that this is just a very precise way of describing how our minds classify everything based on whatever attributes we choose to think about, and which we then consider to be the essence of that thing we are talking about. Recognize that the attributes with which we think about a thing (alive, walking, tall, blond, comprising all the parts of a mammal, speaking our language, and so forth) are just descriptions of the thing, and thus classify a thing in a different category. A certain person can be categorized as a student, as an employee, as a human being, as a mammal, as a biped, as a Serbian, or as an environmentalist, using as few or as many as we wish of the myriad of attributes that person has, depending on how we want to think about him. This is why set theory is a good structure for data storage, data retrieval, and data manipulation.

**Universe set** This is the PARENT SET, of which all sets of a particular kind are defined to be part (a superset of sets). Your database for a particular purpose is a universe set.

*Example 1:* "All personnel data" is a *universe set*, comprising the set of names and addresses, the set of departmental staffing, the set of payroll categories, the set of equipment assigned to people, and so on.

*Example 2:* The *universe set* "All Living Things" comprises the set Animals, the set Plants, the set Human Beings (if you classify them as nonanimals), the set Viruses, the set Bacteria, etc. The set called Vegetables is a PROPER SUBSET of the set called Plants, because there are other plants that are not vegetables. Vitamin-A-Rich Vegetables are a PROPER SUBSET of

Vegetables, because there are other sets of vegetables that are not rich in vitamin A. The set Carrots and the set Yellow/Orange Squashes are sets whose members (or elements) belong to the set Vegetables and whose sets are proper subsets of the set Vitamin-A-Rich-Vegetables as well.

## THE HIERARCHY OF SET RELATIONS APPLIED TO "ALL LIVING THINGS" SET

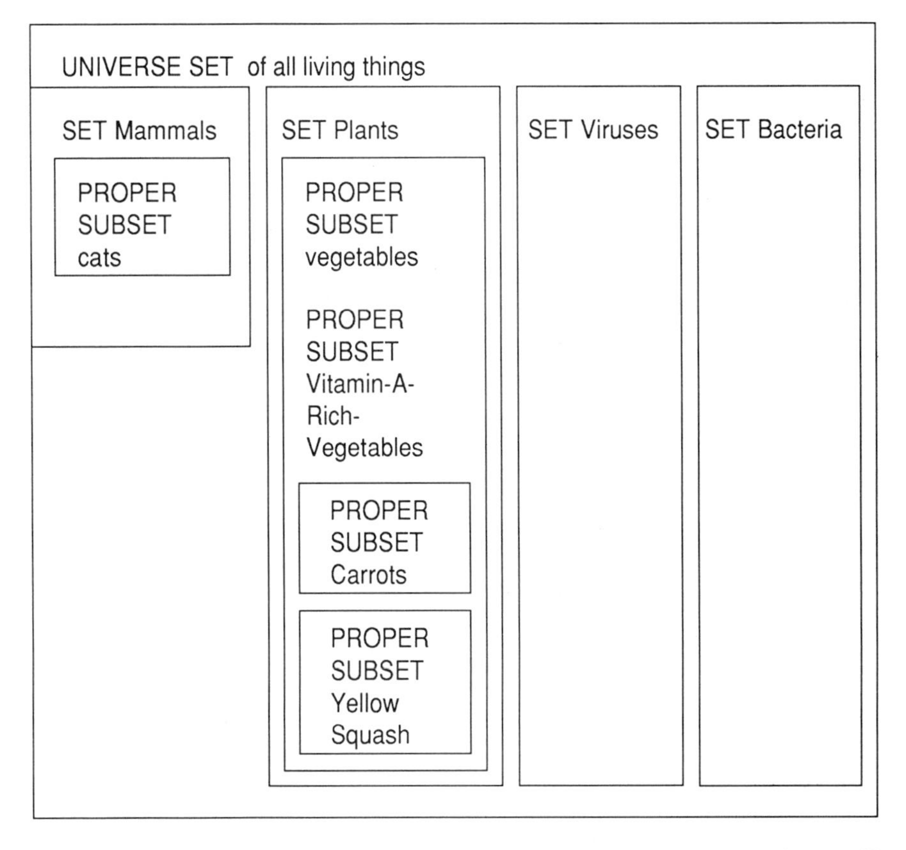


To make the math work, there are two special sets, the *null* set and the *infinity* set.

**Null or empty set** A set containing no elements or members.
*Example:* The set of all living animals that have a nose on the end of their tails.

*Language usage:* The set of no elements. The math symbol is the Greek letter phi ($\phi$).

**Infinite set** A set containing an uncountable number of elements. All the sets we have spoken of up to now have been *finite* sets.

*Example:* The set of all the designs you could ever think of is an infinite set. But all the stars in the sky make up a finite set because they actually could be counted, perhaps not now and not easily, but they are *countable*.

## SET RELATIONS

**Intersection of sets (and)** Those elements from two different sets that belong to both sets at once. The elements of the derived set, the *intersect* set, belong both to the set that has the attribute $x$ and to the set that has the attribute $y$. The two intersecting sets were defined with the attribute $z$ in common.

*Example:* The set Carrots is in both the set Vegetables-Rich-in-Vitamin-A as well as the set Root Vegetables.

*Language usage:* The symbol $\cap$ denotes INTERSECTION. Vegetables-Rich-in-Vitamin-A $\cap$ Root Vegetables has an intersection at Carrots.

**Union of sets (JOIN) (also Either/Or)** All the elements from two sets that overlap, including elements in only the one set or the other plus elements in both the sets at the same time (the intersecting part as well).

*Example:* Veggies-Rich-In-Vitamin-A joined to Root Vegetables gives a UNION comprising all the root vegetables as well as all other vegetables rich in Vitamin A, including the intersect set, Carrots.

**DIFFERENCE of SETS (OMIT)** When two sets intersect, the elements that are not common to both sets are the difference. The difference between the set of all Vegetables-Rich-in-Vitamin-A and all Root Vegetables is the set all Vegetables-Rich-in-Vitamin-A-Which-are-not-Root-Vegetables. This DIFFERENCE set does not include carrots or turnips, which appear in both sets. If you stated the set definition the other way around, as the DIFFERENCE set of all-Root Vegetables less the set all Vegetables-Rich-in-Vitamin-A, the resulting set would be all the-Root-Vegetables-Not-Rich-in Vitamin-A. See the difference? It is like arithmetic subtraction.

**COMPLEMENT (NOT)** If a set is contained within a UNIVERSE SET, as carrots are in the UNIVERSE SET called ALL-LIVING-THINGS, then the COMPLEMENT of the set called Carrots is: all the vegetables that are NOT carrots, plus all the animals and viruses and bacteria in the universe set that carrots are within.

*Language usage:* C(carrots) defines the complement of the set carrots, which is all the other living things that are not carrots. This is just a special case of the difference set (I=carrots).

Relational operations compared to arithmetic:

UNION (join)—Addition
INTERSECTION—Multiplication
DIFFERENCE—Subtraction difference

## RELATIONAL AND ARITHMETIC ATTRIBUTES

The rules that are attributable to arithmetic are also attributable to relational operations in the same ways. These are: commutation, association, distribution, complementarity, dualization, and involution.

### Commutation

Which item comes before which:

Set-A *union* Set-B = Set-B *union* Set-A

and

Set-A *intersect* Set-B = Set-B *intersect* Set-A

Similarly, in addition, you have:

A + B = B + A

and

$A \times B = B \times A$

### Association

Which items are in parenthesis and so done first:

Set-A *union* (Set-B *union* Set-C) = (Set-A *union* Set-B) *union* Set-C

and

A + (B + C) = (A + B) + C

Set-A *intersect* (Set-B *intersect* Set-C) = (Set-A *intersect* Set-B) *intersect* C

and

$A \times (B \times C) = (A \times B) \times C$

### Distribution

An operator outside the parentheses applies to each and all of the elements inside the parentheses, just as if it had been written separately with each of those elements. It doesn't matter whether you apply the outside operator to each item inside and then do the inside operations, or do the inside operations then apply the outside operator just once.

Set-A *intersect* (Set-B *union* Set-C) is exactly equal to
(Set-A *intersect* Set-B) *union* (Set-A *intercept* Set-C)

and

Set-A *union* (Set-B *intercept* Set-C) =
(Set-A *union* Set-B) *intercept* (Set-A *union* Set-C)

just as in arithmetic:

$$A \times (B + C) = (A \times B) + (A \times C)$$

and

$$A + (B \times C) = (A + B) \times (A + C)$$

## Complementarity

Set-A *intercept* Set-A' (A's complement — everything-else-but-A-within-this-universe set) = Null Set

and

Set-A *union* Set-A' = I
(Set-A *union* all-else-but-Set-A-within-the-universe-set-for-A, which is I = I {A's universe set})

just as in arithmetic:

$$A \times (1 - A) = 0 \text{ and } A + (1 - A) = 1$$

## Involution

The complement of Set-A's complement equals Set-A:

(Set-A')' = Set-A

just as in arithmetic:

$$1/1/5 = 5 \qquad \text{another way: } \frac{1}{\frac{1}{5}} = 5$$

## SET THEORY AND SQL OPERATIONS

### Comparison of Terms

| Set Theory | SQL | AS/400 |
|---|---|---|
| SET | Table | Physical record type (format) |
| Attributes of the MEMBERS | Columns, or attributes | Field types |
| SUBSET | View | Logical File |
| PROPER SUBSET | Subsetted View built from only one normalized table | Subsetted Logical File built from one single purpose physical file |
| UNIVERSE SET (I) | Database of related tables (Collection) | Library of related physical files |

A normalized table really should contain attributes of only one thing. For example, a table could contain all the attributes that apply to a department. The table is a set of records of a single type, in this case the record type used to describe departments of your organization. This is difficult to think about because we forget that the field names in a record are just descriptors, not data. They are just set-member attributes.

Example of a department table or record type:

| | |
|---|---|
| Name of Table (Record type): | Dept |
| Attributes (field types): | DeptNo, Dept_title, Address, Dept_head, Dept_Function, No_of_employees, Budget etc. etc. |

This "Department" table is a category that was classified based on the attributes listed. It (that is, the record type) could just as well have been described with attributes (fields) that did not include budget but did include project groupings, time of formation, whom it reports to, telephone number, and so forth.

The attributes you include in your physical record type (table) had better include all the things you will want to think about when querying about this item and cannot find elsewhere (they belong to this item and not to another). Usually this is the way you have classified data and records in your business all along, even when you did the work by hand, because the mind does more efficient work when it keeps things simple. The organizations that have a lot of trouble with so-called normalization of their data usually have been automated a long time, perverted their data descriptions to force-fit it into computers early on, and subsequently grew so large, adding more and more data types, that no one remembers what the data really meant in the first place.

All normalization should mean is precisely defining your data record formats to exactly match reality, in parcels as small as those you actually work with and think about, keeping fields together that belong more with the fields in this record than with any other and that are at the same conceptual level (level of complexity) *for your purposes*. Don't be bamboozled into months-long seminars in data analysis, especially for the AS/400, which allows you to redefine all or part of your underlying data definitions any time you want to without reformatting your entire database.

## COMPARISON OF SQL AND SET THEORY

The following SQL Commands:

```
SELECT DeptNo, No_of_employees, Dept_function
FROM Dept
WHERE Dept_head = Johnson
```

will give you back a record from the Dept record type (table). The record you get back will contain the data that is in the three fields DeptNo, No_of_employees, and Dept_function. You get only one instance of the data, from the record that had "Johnson" in the field called Dept_head.

Here is the set theory equivalent:

- From a *set* called Dept, find the *member* whose attribute "Dept head" contains the data "JOHNSON."

- Pull out the attributes DeptNo, No_of_employees, and Dept_ function from this *member* of the *set* “Dept.”
- Build a *subset member* for me from the contents of these three attributes (fields). (This could have resulted in an entire string of records.)

The complication here is that in SQL you are talking about descriptors (attributes) and data content in the record that the descriptor is defining, all at the same time. On the first line, DeptNo, No_of_employees, *and* Dept_function mean both the attributes (names of fields) and the contents of those fields. On the second line, Dept is just an attribute—no data content is referenced. On the third line, the term Dept_head really means “the data contents of the attribute Dept_head”, not the attribute itself. To get proper query responses you must be on your toes about these subtleties.

To create a *subset* called Function_List of the set called Dept, you use the SQL CREATE command as follows:

```
CREATE VIEW Function_List AS
SELECT DeptNo, No_of_employees, Dept_function
FROM Dept
```

You will have created a new subset of the set Dept. The new set will be called Function_List, and will contain just three attributes (fields), but as many record instances as there were in the set DeptNo. The three attributes (field types) are DeptNo, No_of_employees, and Dept_ function. You will be able to do all the set (SQL) operations on this new table, which means: finding out what the data contents of any and all instances of the three-field records are, searching for particular contents, matching against other table (record) types for merging or comparison of data, and so forth.

After your tables are set up, you can use SQL statements to do most of the operations you do in set theory math, such as:

| SET Theory Operation | SQL Operation |
|---|---|
| Union (Either/Or) | JOIN |

The JOIN operation adds a set of attributes (fields) to another set from a different table (record type) to form a new table (record type) that combines both sets of attributes. Logical Either/Or means that if any or all of the attributes are present, the record will pass the test and will be included in this record in the new set.

| *Intersect* | AND |
|---|---|

In SQL the logical operation AND (*intersect*) tests your data fields for intersection in that it asks the question "has the set (record type, table) got both this particular attribute AND that particular attribute? This time the word attribute refers to the data content of a field (column). Only the records that fulfill both of these comparisons will be culled out into the new "intersect" set.

| *Difference of Sets* | OMIT |
|---|---|

To derive a set that has all the attributes of Set-A minus the attributes of Set-B, use the SQL OMIT parameter in selecting your set from your table(s) at hand: Omit the attributes (Set-B) that do not meet your criteria. Again, we are talking about data content when we say attribute.

| Complement | NOT |
|---|---|

To get the complement of a set (where the set you want the complement of is an arbitrary collection of records based on your criteria of field content), you specify that you want to select those records that do not contain the attribute data you specify.

Note that the above comparisons *do not* represent how to use SQL; they are merely presented here to give you a glimpse of the *attempt* made to adhere somewhat to set theory.

# Index